MUSE

INSIDE THE MUSCLE MUSEUM BY BEN MYERS

Published in 2007 by
INDEPENDENT MUSIC PRESS
Independent Music Press is an imprint of I.M. P. Publishing Limited
This Work is Copyright © I. M. P. Publishing Ltd 2007

Muse – Inside the Muscle Museum
by Ben Myers

British Library Cataloguing-in-Publication Data.
A catalogue for this book is available from The British Library.

ISBN 0-9552822-5-X and 978-0-9552822-5-6

Cover Design by Fresh Lemon.
Edited by Martin Roach.

Printed in the UK.

Independent Music Press
P.O. Box 69,
Church Stretton, Shropshire
SY6 6WZ

Visit us on the web at: www.impbooks.com
and www.myspace.com/independentmusicpress

For a free catalogue, e-mail us at: info@impbooks.com
Fax: 01694 720049

MUSE

INSIDE THE MUSCLE MUSEUM

by Ben Myers

Independent Music Press

CONTENTS

Acknowledgements   6

Prelude   11

1. In The Beginning   13
2. God's Waiting Room   21
3. Devon & Hell   39
4. Coma City And California Dreaming   54
5. Inside The Muscle Museum   68
6. Numero Uno   85
7. There's No Biz Like Showbiz...   93
8. On The Road And Up The River   107
9. Like The New Born   127
10. Feeling Good   145
11. Hullaballo!   155
12. Sing for Absolution   168
13. Mass Hysteria   178
14. Return to Planet Muse   189
15. Black Holes & Revelations   199

Discography   216

Websites   230

Sources and References   232

ACKNOWLEDGEMENTS

Muse took over my life while writing this account of their rapid ascension. It was strange going to sleep every night and waking up each morning with the same peculiar sounds reverberating somewhere deep inside. Stranger still, I was happy to let it happen.

There are few bands I could listen to for more than twelve hours a day, seven days a week, for weeks on end, but Muse are one of them. As I delved further into their past, their albums commandeered my stereo for so long that my neighbours bought their own copies to drown out mine. Stack-'em-high studio flats just aren't designed for staging full-volume mercurial space-rock operas with lots of widdly bits.

On the rare occasions I managed to prise myself away from the keyboard and mouse for some fresh air, it was invariably either to talk to people about Muse or join the band themselves on tour. So thanks should first be extended to Matt Bellamy, Dominic Howard and Chris Wolstenholme for being more interesting than most. Thanks also for their encouragement in writing this book. Similarly, the band's biggest fan, Dennis Smith at Taste Media/Sawmills and fourth Muse member Tom Kirk were both happy to impart vital first-hand information and, in the case of Dennis, much vocal encouragement.

I'd also thank the following for making this work what it is: at *Kerrang!*, Dave Everley and Dom Lawson for the transcripts, Paul Brannigan for the shenanigans, Catherine Yates for the transcripts, videos and four-hour long Muse-ings, Laura Foster for the research assistance, Ronnie Kerswell at *Rock Sound* for her invaluable help and Kate Hoggett and Kate Lauren for the insight. Mel Brown at Impressive gave me free stuff and filled in all the gaps, Nik Moore at Work Hard shed light on some otherwise shady areas and vouched for me when he didn't need to, Martin James similarly put the word in, Julian Carrera at Hall Or Nothing took me on tour and Jeremy Hammett offered title suggestions. Martin and Kaye Roach at my publishers Independent Music Press showed faith and took a gamble – thanks. Many others indulged me in small but significant ways.

For their continued encouragement I'd also like to thank: Richard Myers, Lee Milmore and Justin Schlosberg at the Captains Of Industry collective (www.captainsof.com), my friend Kara L. Cooper, Kathryn and Stewart for the proof -reading, printing and potential loft usage and, as always, my parents Geoff and Dorothy, who were happy to get busy with the red pen.

Lovely people, all of them.

Dedicated to Joe Strummer who died a year ago today.

Ben Myers, December 22, 2003.

muse

~ *to be absent in mind; to be so occupied in study or contemplation as not to observe passing scenes or things present; to ponder; to be lost in thought.*

~ *to consider or say thoughtfully.*

~ *a guiding spirit, a source of inspiration.*

~ *a state of meditation.*

~ *a poet.*

PRELUDE

IT'S TRUE what they say: all roads eventually lead home. No matter how many miles you've journeyed, people you've met or places you've seen, no matter how far you've travelled – physically, mentally or spirituality – home is always there as a past reminder. Something that can never be changed no matter how much you've grown, a constant centrifugal force from which we all spin in dizzy circles into unknown futures.

First of all, that crowd is *loud*.

Secondly, this doesn't feel like a show; this shit is religious. Biblical. Solely watch the crowd for a moment and suddenly you're in the realms of evangelism. Close your eyes to shut out the sports arena and instead you're in a church – not one bogged down by guilty rituals and useless dogma, but a place of worship based on sound vibrations and a fuck-off light show. No words are spoken. This band rarely speak onstage. They have things to say – more than most – and they say them at full volume, but music is their medium, electricity the conduit. Tonight, for ninety minutes, everything else beyond the stage is superfluous, not worth wasting oxygen on. Compared to so many of their limelight-hogging contemporaries breathing hot halitosis air and fake sentimentalism down their microphone's each night, such silence is golden.

No. Something else is going on.

Something called rock 'n' roll and so much more.

December 7, 2003 and Exeter loves Muse. They love them because they made them. Few bands from these parts have ever become this big or have evoked such adoration in aeons and the Westpoint Arena is showing their appreciation with a homecoming that rivals any ticker-tape war parade. No band since Nirvana have fled their backwoods nests – those places writhing with resentment, seething frustration and offering nothing but dead-end roads if you're a bit different – and rocked so hard in so many countries they would otherwise never have reached. To return a mere half-decade later having conquered the world was Muse's crowning glory.

They came from back there – down the road in a town called Teignmouth. There's three of them, slight and unassuming in person (although each with a garrulous appetite for all that life has to offer) yet onstage they stand nothing less than twenty feet tall, with bodies of sinew, the voices of earthbound angels and the movements of pure rhythmic thrust. Their noise envelopes all within this vast arena's walls.

It was like this last night – and the night before that. In London, Manchester and Glasgow. Before that, Paris and Prague, Melbourne and Moscow, Reykjavik... and on and on, leaving nothing behind but a tangle of vapour trails and the lingering echo of something sacred.

In an era when at times it feels like the world is coming to an end, Muse's world tour is coming to an end – for the moment at least – in front of an enraptured crowd of fawning girls and macho mosh-pit boys, drooling drunks and drugged-up debutantes, proud parents and previous girlfriends, punk rockers, progheads and star-struck lovers, people of different ages, shapes, sizes, beliefs and persuasions.

A quarter of a million others like them have joined the swelling congregation for this trio's after-dark musical masses, a million more have thrown money into the collection tray and washed away their sins with Muse's third album *Absolution* in the last three months alone.

People are screaming, bouncing, laughing, fighting, puking, dancing, celebrating. I think some people are fucking too, but it's rude to stare.

It looks like hell but to some of us it's heaven.

Tomorrow we'll turn on the TVs and open our papers to wars and lies and death and corruption, but tonight we *rock*.

Muse have been around this world to return on a frosty black English winter night, back to where it all started, back to the womb that spawned them.

1. IN THE BEGINNING...

THE SHORT trip from Ireland to mainland Britain is a journey that has repeatedly been undertaken since man first figured out how to navigate the choppy waters across to Scotland and north-west England. From the first recognizable mass migration that followed the potato famine of the 1840s – widely acknowledged as the greatest humanitarian disaster of the nineteenth century – people had been crossing the Irish Sea in search of a better life. One million people left Ireland during that short but cataclysmic famine with another million following them over the next decade. All of them hoped to find a better life, searching for opportunity, for re-invention. A better way.

Opportunity was what a young Belfast-born red-headed girl called Marilyn was searching for when she left her Irish life behind to re-create herself in England. The 1970s was a time that saw 'The Troubles' at their most... well, troublesome. Certainly, in terms of frequency of attack and coverage afforded in the English media, IRA bombings were at their most high-profile, yet the core issues of contention that have caused much bloodshed down the centuries had become clouded. Governments, dissidents and religious separatists alike had come and gone, but the Ireland-for-the-Irish debate continued to open more wounds, to divide and to give rise to countless vendettas on varying scales. More recently, it had drawn in both support and opposition from countries all over the world, solidifying in a decade of particularly chaotic turmoil that achieved little other than widening the chasm between the Irish and their ruling masters, the British government in Whitehall.

Yet most who made the move east did so for personal and economic reasons rather than political ideology. The majority just wanted a job, a house, a partner, a change of scenery. Normal things that most of us strive for. A chance to see more than just the limited vista of our childhood and adolescence. In Marilyn's case, it was a chance to experience something out there – a pattern that would be echoed a quarter of a century later in the lifestyle choice of her second son.

The boat journey across the Irish Sea is more of a symbolic one than a particularly arduous passage. Naïve first-time travellers were perhaps surprised to find that England's Lancastrian coast looming up in a grey drizzle was much like Ireland's. All that fuss over *this* – a country not vastly dissimilar to the one they'd left behind. Yet somehow their new home *was* completely different. England, for better or for worse, offered the promise of a fresh start. On this point, Marilyn struck lucky. Upon stepping off the ferry at the country that had been responsible for dividing her own nation into three (pro-British government rule, anti-, and the quietly indifferent), she met the man who was to be her future husband, the father of her two sons, the man with whom she would set up her home.

*

George Bellamy was a musician who drove a cab for a living. Born on October 8, 1941 in the ship-building town of Sunderland, the aspiring guitarist gravitated towards London seeking work as a musician. The capital was in a period of post-war transition, one foot still in the world of rationing, colourless clothes and making-do, the other caught up in the influx of all things Americana – clothes, R&B records, diner-style café culture. For the first time, youth was tentatively being recognized as a commodity as both Britain and America witnessed a social and philosophical shift among its young. The younger generation was beginning to see that they didn't necessarily have to dress like their parents and that their was a middle ground between childhood and adulthood – and it looked like a lot more fun.

Having moved to the capital as a teenager with the express intention of making it in music, in 1961 George responded to an advert in the back pages of a music paper and was subsequently asked to play guitar for The Tornadoes, a band formed by producer Joe Meek, one of Britain's first and most influential pop impresarios, the Phil Spector of Tin Pan Alley. Meek was a colourful English eccentric, a tone-deaf musical maverick who would go on to be the first to produce a young Tom Jones and who once claimed to have contacted Buddy Holly during a séance.

Initially formed as a studio session backing band with a line-up of Bellamy, fellow guitarist Alan Caddy, organist Roger LaVern, bassist Heinz Burt and drummer Clem Cattini, the Tornadoes worked out of Meek's studio – a converted three-storey flat on the Holloway Road in north London. Intent on pioneering new sounds, Meek filled the studio with various devices which would have made Thomas Edison proud and developed techniques that pushed the boundaries of sound production: the close-miking of instruments; the introduction of distortion and his soon-to-be-trademark compressed sound; loud drums boosted by percussion from such instruments as pocket combs, milk bottles and even Meek himself stomping the floorboards. His idiosyncratic mad professor-style techniques paved the way for a new generation of pioneering producers – from Brian Wilson to Lee 'Scratch' Perry.

Working with such an innovator pushed The Tornadoes to develop their own career, rather than just assisting those of a long line of smooth-skinned passing pop dilettantes and proto-boy band stars like Billy Fury, Johnny Gentle and Marty Wilde who had emerged at the tail-end of the Fifties. However, the band's first two singles – the debut double-header of 'Love And Fury'/'Popeye Twist', released in the spring of 1962, and follow-up 'The Breeze And I' failed to set the charts alight. Fortunately, the beauty of pop music means of such failures are often soon forgotten once that elusive breakthrough comes. And it came.

Inspired by the first television pictures to cross the Atlantic on July 11, 1962, Meek penned what was to be his greatest work – a tribute to the Telstar satellite behind this technological feat. While the band's first two singles had pinned down The Tornadoes' distinctive keyboard-led sound but failed to capture the public's imagination, 'Telstar' backed with 'Jungle Fever' entered the charts in August 1962, a mere month after Meek had sat agape with pen in hand as the first flickering images bounced from America to Britain via a strange contraption drifting somewhere out there in the cosmos. The song was described at the time as "utilizing willful distortion, cheap tape echo, beeping satellite sound effects, a cheesy-sounding

Clavioline [a two-octave keyboard powered by a battery] and massive amounts of tube compression, the resulting production sounded like nothing else at the time, or since"[1], 'Telstar' stayed in the UK charts one week short of six months, four weeks of which were spent at the Number One spot. More significantly, the song was also a major international success and found massive favour Stateside, where it quickly became the first Number One single by a British group. The Tornadoes, it could be said, were bigger than The Beatles *before* The Beatles. Like a lone pack of explorers forging ahead on the first ascent of Everest, The Tornadoes at least showed Liverpool's finest that a three minute pop song could earn you the keys to the world. All this a mere four months after young George Bellamy first saw that advert.

The single went on to sell five million copies. Not to be confused with the West Coast band of the same name, The Tornadoes capitalised on their worldwide success with a clutch of further releases which achieved more modest success, albeit with a changing line-up.

Nevertheless, this initial flourish should have been enough to establish The Tornadoes as one of the biggest bands in the world and Meek – as writer, arranger and producer – a very rich man. But as so often happens in the fickle world of entertainment, the band were dealt a cruel roll of the dice when an obscure French copyright infringement lawsuit grounded them and tied up all royalties earned in a tangle of red tape and affidavits. When they should have been out turning smalltown American girls' hearts to ice cream, The Tornadoes were instead contractually obligated to stay in the UK as backing band to one of pop's earliest poster boys, Billy Fury.

The legal technicalities took six long hitless years to resolve – the equivalent of a full century in pop years. Without the hits to keep them in buying range of a burgeoning new demographic – the teenager – both band and producer Meek floundered and their careers slipped away, early casualties of an industry every bit as cut-throat and disposable then as it is in the modern era. The court finally ruled the lawsuit in favour of Meek, but by that time it was too late. Struggling to come to terms with his own homosexuality and riddled with debts, the thirty-seven-year-old pioneer of sound had blown his head off the previous year with a hunting rifle in his studio, having first brutally murdered his landlady.

The Tornadoes were well and truly over and with them ended George Bellamy's brief but insightful flirtation with rock 'n' roll. It had been a sharp learning curve. "Enjoy it while you're young and get laid" was the advice imparted to his son and future Muse frontman Matthew as he embarked on a career in music some thirty-odd years later.

"He was pretty cool about it," Matt remembered in 2001. "Because he had a number one four months after joining the band, he'd had things a lot easier than I did. It was good to be able to talk to someone in your own family to find out what it was like, and people were even more fanatical back then because rock 'n' roll was first coming out. He mainly suggested that I made sure we don't get fucked over and things like that, because I think he did get seriously fucked over."[2] To quote *The League Of Gentleman*'s failed Seventies wannabe Les McQueen – "It's a shit business."

Nonetheless, Bellamy Sr. wasn't totally burnt by the music business – as well as working as a plumber he still performs from time to time with a band called Rough Terrain.

*

George was still driving cabs in London when he met Marilyn on her first day on English soil. They hit it off straight away. As their relationship developed they moved from the capital to Cambridge, where they had their first son, Paul. A few years later, Matthew James Bellamy was born in that same University city on June 8, 1978. George was thirty-six at the time, Boney M's 'Rivers Of Babylon' / 'Brown Girl In The Ring' was at Number One and a disco reworking of John Williams' *Star Wars* music, *Star Wars & Other Galactic Funk* album, was confirmed platinum that same day.

Matt Bellamy's earliest memories were inextricably linked with music. In 1981, at the age of three he started playing piano, hitting the keys one at a time to the theme music of the then-hugely-popular soap opera, *Dallas*. Soon the older of the two

Bellamy siblings used to exploit the fact that his brother had a musical ear, indirectly encouraging his progress by giving him melodies to work out. Consequently, the young maestro graduated from humming TV theme tunes to the works of Ray Charles and, later, songs by popular Eighties leftfield bands like The Smiths, The Wedding Present and The Cure.

"For me, music was always associated with fun and pleasure," he revealed. "My parents originally gave my brother piano lessons but he wasn't very good. And because he hated it so much, they never gave me lessons."[3]

*

I See Dead People

The first ten years of Matt's life was like that of any young boy growing up in Britain during the Thatcher years, his time divided by school, home life and hi-jinks. At the age of six, Matt was in a supermarket when some older boys pulled down his trousers, forcing him run out of the shop in humiliation, naked from the waist down. At the same age he swallowed a key-ring – a little globe of the world – and the attached keys that belonged to his baby-sitter. Not surprisingly, he started choking. The alarmed babysitter turned Matt upside down and smacked him until he regurgitated the world and the contents of his stomach. At the age of ten he began to earn some much-needed pocket money, fetching and breaking the necks of wildfowl for 50p a time on posh pheasant shoots.

"It was for all these old fogeys who'd get the peasant kids from the town to help them out," Matt remembers. "We'd have to run into the woods and hit the trees to make them fly up, they'd get shot then we'd have to pick them up. Half of them would still be alive so we'd have to break their necks."

Life continued with a series of small but significant, character-forming incidents. Behind closed doors, things were changing in the Bellamy household as Marilyn began to involve her family in her spiritual pursuits. Matt stumbled across it by accident once late at night, when at the age of nine he wandered downstairs and discovered his parents and brother sitting round an Ouija board. Rather than send him straight back to his room,

Marilyn sat her curious son down and explained what it was they were doing – namely, contacting the dead.

An Ouija board is an age-old device purportedly used to contact spirits who have crossed over into the after-life or unseen paranormal forces that exist in this one. A standard board usually has the letters of the alphabet inscribed on it – although Scrabble letters work just as well – along with words such as 'yes', 'no', 'good-bye' and 'maybe'. A slideable three-legged device called a planchette or a pointer of some sort is then manipulated by those using the board. The users ask the board – and by extension, the spirits – a question and together they move the pointer or the board until letters are selected, gradually spelling out a response to a specific question.

Some users believe supernatural forces are at work in spelling out Ouija board answers, while sceptics believe that those using the board either consciously or unconsciously select what is spelled out themselves. Either way, coupled with a fertile imagination or a willingness to *believe*, the Ouija board is responsible for many a sleepless night the world over.

On that night in 1987, Marilyn Bellamy went on to carefully explain that what they were doing was nothing to be afraid of. Soon, Matt Bellamy was rushing to school with stories from the Ouija board to recount to a young and wide-eyed audience.

"It was exciting to go to school and to tell ten-year-old kids all about it, as they found it quite scary," he says. "I was quite impressed that I was doing something that was scary to other people but that wasn't to me. I did get quite into that."[4]

In later years, one story circulated that a nine-year-old Matt saw a ghost and physically shit himself with fear, but this was later denied by the frontman and put it down as a joke started by Chris and Dominic to enliven a particularly gruelling day's worth of interviews that "got out of hand"! Whatever insight was gleaned from those early dabblings with the Ouija board, the idea of other forces existing beyond the physical human form was something that was to interest Matt Bellamy for many years to come. Besides, everyone knows that rock 'n' roll is nothing if not an aural manifestation of the dark side. Much was later to be made of Matt's magical interests by a music press hungry for a tidbit of good old rock 'n' roll apocryphal to cling to, a story to take and run with and turn into something more suited to those darkest of rock 'n' roll dabblers Led Zeppelin.

"It was only when Mrs. Bellamy saw how dangerously obsessed her children were becoming with the psychic realm that she decided to pack it in," wrote John Mullen in *Select* in May 2000, "before they started speaking in tongues."[5]

Either way, a seed had been planted in the nine-year-old's imagination: there's more to life than meets the eye.

2. GOD'S WAITING ROOM

"I love your hills and I love your dales,
And I love your flocks a-bleating;
But oh, on the heather to lie together,
With both our hearts a-beating!"[1]

From 'Where Be Ye Going, You Devon Maid?' by John Keats
(1795-1821)

IN THE mid-Eighties, the Bellamys decided to leave Cambridge
to move back to George's native West Country, specifically to the
small north Devon town of Teignmouth where his gran (whom
Matt was later to live with) and extended family resided.

Like so many of Britain's coastal towns, Teignmouth suffers
from a mild schizophrenia brought on by nothing other than the
climate. In the summer it's one of many such desirable seaside
resorts for Devon day-trippers, families and urbanites seeking
temporary respite from far-flung cities, most typically the
sprawling grimness of the Midlands. Along the seafront, the
water calmly laps at the shore, seagulls swoop and soar and
couples douse their pink children in swathes of lotion. Daytime
drinkers sit alongside residents relaxing into their twilight years
and the ice-cream parlours and quaint gift shops do a roaring
trade. In surrounding areas carnivals, regattas and fetes hint at
an HE Bates-style sense of rural community.

The air is fresh and the scenery beautiful and if you sit at
Teignmouth's beach at night you could be a world away.
Benefiting from the sense of detachment that comes with being
situated deep in the West Country, Teignmouth is in many ways
– on a summer's day at least – an English idyll.

However, by October it's a different story. When the metal
shutters are drawn along the promenade and the sea turns
a gun-metal grey, things quieten down, settle in. As the
population draws back to its core of fifteen thousand residents
(Matt was later to sing "I fall down/And 15,000 people scream"
on 'Falling Down' from the group's debut album) it becomes
a tumbleweed town. For the thousand or so teenagers, life slows

to a deadening pace. The chatter of the promenade crowds disappears into the air, leaving a ghostly quiet as employment becomes non-existent. The sense of promise and abandonment of the long hot summer fades into winter and there's simply *nothing to do*. Like any small town, inertia creeps in. Claustrophobia takes hold. Apathy strikes. It's not a good place to be a restless teenager with a creative streak. Teignmouth in the winter is not so much a shit hole, as a black hole.

Poet John Keats made himself at home in the town. A plaque has since been placed at the address at 20 Northumberland Terrace – now called Keats' House – where he wrote some of his most famous work. Keats liked Devon, but described it in a letter as a "splashy, rainy, misty, snowy, foggy, haily, floody, muddy, slipshod county."[2]

Other 'famous' residents include Layla-Jade, who started out living in a care home, before going on to become the star of over 250 hardcore porn movies (first film: *Ben Dover's Butt Bangers Bonanza*) and still lives in the town now; Charles Babbage, inventor of the world's first calculator; and Donald Crowhurst, a local who set off from Teignmouth in the catamaran 'Teignmouth Electron' to sail the world single-handedly in a race but spent the whole trip ailing around in the Atlantic far away from normal shipping lanes sending fictitious radio reports as to his locations. Days before he was due to arrive back in Teignmouth, his boat was found sailing unmanned, complete with diary logs and film on board which revealed the sad and sorry truth [the mystery that surrounded this trip has been the subject of several TV documentaries]; and let's not forget George Bellamy, for a long time the town's most successful musician.

At the time of writing, after-hours attractions for teenagers and twenty-somethings in Teignmouth include night clubs Hot Bananas and Monty's, the latter described by appropriately-named and suitably sardonic local website www.knowhere.co.uk (perhaps written by a young disaffected resident) as having "dreadful music, bovine clientele, stale beers and simian door staff..." It also cuttingly identifies the best Teignmouth music venue as "somebody's car stereo, in the car-park."

"The whole conservatism of the area is the worst thing," notes the website. "The old don't understand the young and vice versa. If you're young you will be labelled a 'thug' or a 'hooligan' even if you've got a degree from Oxbridge. People just never take the time to find out about you. The local council take the biscuit, they rant on about skaters but never see them as just another group with legitimate concerns and needs. Unless you're retired you won't exist. Teignmouth is God's waiting room…"[3]

In short, Teignmouth is a great place to visit – and undoubtedly a great place to return to – but not the place to experience everything life has to offer. In showing their future life should they choose to stay in the town forever, some inspiration or motivation could at least be gleaned by the more aspirational of its younger residents.

"The only time the town came to life was during the summer when it turned into a vacation spot for visiting Londoners," explained Matt. "When the summer ended, they left and took all the life with them. I felt so trapped there. My friends were either getting into drugs or music, but I gravitated towards the latter and eventually learned how to play. That became my escape. If it weren't for the band, I probably would have turned to drugs myself.[4]

In terms of the ratio of population size to musical output, the United Kingdom is probably the most productive country on the world's stage. However, its success quota average is certainly lowered by certain areas whose contribution to pop culture is somewhat less significant. For every Lancashire that has spawned The Beatles, Buzzcocks, Joy Division and Oasis, there's an East Anglia (The Darkness anyone?), a Cornwall or a Devon to counter the balance. By the late Eighties, Devon's contribution to rock music was, at best, minimal. Negligible even. A simple internet search reveals no successful rock bands of interest from the past three decades.

"Being from a small town makes you look around and immediately see there's no opportunities," Matt explained in 2001. "If you grow up in a place like that [the city] you've got all these possibilities – you can become a rock star, you can become a journalist. In Teignmouth, you can become a sweet shop owner at best. You learn that from an early age. That gives you this attitude – I've got to do something, I've got to make something out of this place. We were out of touch and uncool compared to what was going on in places like London or Manchester, but that helped us develop something unique."[5]

He's right, of course, though to be fair, Britain's more rural towns are never going to compete with the well-connected, well-organised networks of clubs, bars, promoters and inspirational musical legacies of the bigger cities. Success breeds success and venues breed bands. The cities nurture bands like infestations of maggots sucking its lifeforce, feeding off their kinetic energy. Could the Sex Pistols have formed in Barnstaple?

Having said that, as Matt intimated above, such seclusion and detachment from any tangible scene has its benefits too. Nirvana came not from the coffee shop counter-culture of Seattle but the small backwoods logging town of Aberdeen – a place that makes Exeter's Guildhall shopping centre seem like the beating heart of Bohemia by comparison. Existing in a void can in itself be inspiring to a band. This way they develop at their own speed, looking not at the competition but inwards at themselves. If there are no venues to play and no bands to link up with, budding stars are forced to work twice as hard and scream twice as loud to be heard. Plus, becoming the best band in Teignmouth is an achievable short-term goal.

Soon a band called Muse was going to do just that. Soon Teignmouth would be part of modern rock's topography – soon Devon would be on the musical map.

*

The Outsiders
"If anything went wrong in my life, even getting told off by a teacher, I would just come home and play music. It would make me realise I'm okay with myself. There are various things that happen in your life, stuff with your family, when you're growing up, and music's always been my escape from that."[6]
Matt Bellamy, November 2003

Dominic James Howard was born in Stockport, Lancashire on

July 12, 1977. Memorably it was the summer of the Queen's Silver Jubilee and punk rock was in full swing. After half a decade of three day weeks, union dissent and Labour rule, the country was sliding towards the abyss of eighteen years of Conservative power. Yet that summer, any social and economic problems were swept aside as the nation was transformed into a mass of street parties in honour of a monarch recently reinvented with a safety pin through her nose by a bunch of anarchists in the capital. Over in the US, Elvis was about to enjoy his final bowel movement and pass to the great diner in the sky, his passing marking the end of rock's first era and heralding the start of another. Nastier, noisier more anarchic sounds were on the way. The times they were a-changing and rock 'n' roll was showing signs of wielding more power that ever previously imaginable.

The oldest member of Muse, Dom's discovery of music came even earlier than Matthew Bellamy's, when he first tinkered with his sister's keyboard at the age of five. Like any budding drummer, he soon progressed to working out rhythms on objects, work surfaces, indeed any object that resonated.

"But unlike Matt, my parents were not at all into music, or 'artists' in any way," Dom later explained. "I have an older sister who studied art, I guess this was somehow what got me in touch with this background. But it still had nothing to do with music. Honestly, when I was a kid, music was what I heard on TV. At least, until I got to high school. That's when I started to be interested in it – because there was a jazz band." As with the Bellamy's, Howard's family left the north-west for Devon in 1985 to return to the area of a parent's upbringing (in this case Dom's mother).

In the neighbouring – and historically-speaking – rival county of Yorkshire, Christopher Anthony Wolstenholme was born in Rotherham on December 2, 1978. His father was a Yorkshireman born and bred, his mother from Devon. The couple had moved north shortly after they'd married and, like his father before him, Chris was born there. He spent the first eleven years of his life in Rotherham forming ties and earning the nickname 'Cheers', until his parents decided to move back to Devon in 1989.

"I really like it up there and I do miss Rotherham and Sheffield," Chris commented in 2001. "I feel quite connected, I've got a lot of family up there. But I think it's good not to stay in one place all your life. You get a lot of people who are born into one place and live there all their life. I don't think I could ever do that."[7] He later joked that if he struck it rich one day, he'd like to buy Rotherham football team and give the club a new slogan: 'Fuck Off!'

Was it a coincidence that in a wider circle of friends the three Teignmouth immigrants were to form the closest of friendships – one that is at the very core of Muse today? Maybe. The 'new kid' status was certainly one more factor to strengthen the bond between three wannabe musicians far from enamoured with the idea of team sports or, worse, random violence as a viable pastime.

"There was a whole lot of nights when there was nothing to do and the only stuff that was fun to do was music," adds Matt. "So you ended up doing dodgy things for something to do. Most of the friends we have had have either gone to university or become drug dealers."[8]

"I think subconsciously not coming from Teignmouth helped us get together because out of all of our friends and all these people that I hung around with in bands, everyone was from Teignmouth," says Chris. "We were the only three people that were outsiders – there was always that sense of being disconnected from the people there, even though we went out with other people and got on really well with them. The one thing we had in common was that we were from totally different places, but had been through the same high school, together from the start."[9]

Well, almost the start. The school in question was Teign Secondary School in Kingsteignton near Newton Abbott, five miles from Teignmouth. [Unrelated note: Kingsteignton is also home to a number of sightings of an unusually large and unidentifiable cat-like beast]

As mentioned previously, life in Teignmouth was much like the experience of teenagers in any other tourist British town – or, indeed around the world. Regardless of geography, the teenage years instill a sense of alienation and elicit the first inclinations to break away from convention, to rebel against parental opinion. Which is why, when trapped by school and a small matter of the law, those pre-freedom years from thirteen to eighteen are particularly trying. And that's without taking into account the mysterious chemistry and hormonal rollercoaster of the teenage body...

School for Matthew, Dom and Chris was a typical cycle of GCSE studies, the formation of playground cliques (trendies/townies versus freaks/grebos/goths – insert appropriate terminology here, depending on your school) and living for those outside hours away from the stifling classrooms and endless recitation of never-to-be-needed French verbs. September to July, year in, year out. As with so many millions of kids of that age since the early Fifties – when the 'teenager' was first deemed a discernible sales demographic by corporate American companies – music provided the necessary outlet, the portal to another world.

Matt, Dominic and Chris gravitated toward one another in the early years of their comprehensive school days and friendships began to form. "School didn't really cater for people like us," Matt told *Flipside* magazine. "The system is there to make the country a stronger place, that 'make money, make money' mentality, and there's always going to be people who don't fit into that."[10]

*

1991 was when the Nineties really began.

In the year when the future members of Muse were first picking up their instruments, five Oxford-based students called Radiohead released their first EP on Parlophone. Although critically acclaimed from an early stage – as On A Friday they aroused interest in the down-page live sections of music weekly bibles *NME* and *Melody Maker* – their time was to come later, after their label had wisely allowed them time and space to develop into something more than just another dour under-achieving indie band from the provinces.

That same year, another well-read band harbouring ambitions

beyond a headline spot at the old Marquee club debuted: Manic Street Preachers. Their grandiose masterplan to sell sixteen million copies of their double-album debut before splitting, while totally flawed, did at least indicate that self-deprecation, apathy and lack of ambition hadn't completely suppressed British music. They built a fanatical following, seduced by their cheap glamour and provocative sound-bites.

Indeed, by 1991 the independent British music scene was awash with bands – some interesting, some utterly inspired – united by their inability to make an impact on the world's stage. That watered-down dance-rock acts Jesus Jones and EMF had been the only new British acts to impact upon the upper echelons of the US charts in recent years was not a good sign. The Madchester acid explosion had bridged the gap between dance music and rock nicely, but it was just that – an explosion that had far less of an impact on British music than its greatest champions would suggest, primarily because its two major exponents – the Stone Roses and Happy Mondays – were too disorganised, too shambolic. They were lifestylers, not world-beaters; ego-driven party boys. To an even lesser extent, the shoegazing scene of the turn of the decade – inconsequential, murmured, low-mix vocals atop swathes of FX-laden guitars, as played by studious young men and women with nothing to say – served only to highlight the torpor that had set in.

So, not for the first time it was left to the Americans to inject life – and, subsequently, tragically and inevitably, *death* – back into rock music. In 1991, it all came together in a perfect symbiosis of underground DIY work ethics and major label marketing budgets in the form of a once-in-a-generation band called Nirvana.

The trio's focus and major-selling point was on wiry, troubled frontman Kurt Cobain, a man whose songs seemed to embody something that few other rock stars are ever able to. Cobain was the voice of the detached underdog, the disenfranchised teenager, the mouthpiece of the lonely, the angry, the alienated. And in turn, he himself began to embody the songs, his contorted body throbbing in every sinew, his guitar nothing but a conduit for rage. This metal-punk-hardcore-pop hybrid that was centred around Seattle's modest Sub Pop label was jokingly referred to as 'grunge', a misleading term but one that stuck.

Of course, grunge was far more than just Nirvana – like punk rock before it, you could argue that it was over as soon as it infiltrated the pages of fashion mags and broadsheet editorials. Undeniably, however, it was this highly-charged trio from the wet north-west US state of Washington that had the most impact – and on so many culturally significant levels. Likewise, far from being the start of something new, Nirvana represented the zenith of a burgeoning underground scene that had fermented throughout the Eighties in detached pockets across America, direct descendents of the thankless work of seminal bands like Black Flag, Minor Threat, Husker Du, Sonic Youth and The Pixies. Nirvana signified the end of one movement (independently-released alternative music for the select few) and the beginning of another (mass market alternative-sounding music in the hands of the major labels). Nirvana heralded a seismic shift in rock music, the large labels realising that, whether they understood the music or not, like the Sixties counterculture or Seventies punk rock before it, the best generation-shaping rock 'n' roll comes from a place of genuine discontent – and in the case of the grunge, they wanted in. And so began the plundering of alternative culture, on a scale which had never previously been seen in rock music.

Aside from the crass and over-commercialised circus that grunge was to become, Nirvana lit fires through their *music*. Their cacophony was both fresh and ragged, strong and fragile. It was new and it struck a chord with anyone who felt what the understated Cobain felt. With the might of Geffen behind them, Nirvana took a sound inspired by the sludgy metal riffs of Black Sabbath, the physicality and devotion to volume of Black Flag and the pop melodies of The Beatles and dropped an album, *Nevermind*, that was to shape the recorded output of the decade that followed and beyond. If grunge was arguably finished the day Nirvana released *Nevermind*, then it was definitely over by the time Cobain took his own life in April 1994, a modern martyr to an unforgiving cause called rock 'n' roll. By then, the inspired and goofy Sub Pop sound circa 1987-90 (Mudhoney, Tad, Green River, Nirvana) was gone, in its place a formulaic hybrid of angsty rock as peddled by bandwagoneering chumps like Stone

Temple Pilots, Silverchair and Bush.

Yet before that, when Nirvana blew up, they blew *big*, sending shrapnel flying to the four corners of the globe, inspiring a new generation of insurgents to pick up guitars, to form bands, to attempt to express the inexpressible, regardless of social status, geography or hairstyles. Like the Beatles before them, Nirvana weren't a working class band that trumpeted some sort of class triumph, they simply *did it* and therefore led by example. In the years that followed *Nevermind* and floor-filling breakthrough single 'Smells Like Teen Spirit' ensured that for every lame shrink-wrapped grunge band clogging up the charts like a malignant tumour, there was a newer, fresher generation of firebrands waiting in the wings who wanted to be like Nirvana (raw, truthful, beautiful), without *being* them. 1991 was, as Sonic Youth put it in their film of the same name, *The Year Punk Broke*. Everything in rock had changed, irrevocably. For better and for worse. But it had changed nonetheless.

1991 was also the year in which something else broke. Back in Devon, George and Marilyn Bellamy's marriage was over and after nearly twenty years together they went their separate ways.

Matt and his brother Paul moved in with his cousins in Teignmouth, before moving to nearby Dawlish, a picturesque town on the south coast of Devon, just a few miles from Exeter. Matt was to live with his gran on and off throughout his teenage years. Rather than blow their lives apart, Matt and his older brother Paul were relatively accepting of their parent's decision to go their separate ways, even welcoming the extra freedom the divorce afforded them.

"The thing that shocked me the most about it was that I didn't feel anything – I couldn't even feel gutted," Matt recalls. "I tried to but I just couldn't and that was something I found slightly disturbing about myself. I felt guilty because I was happy to be living in Teignmouth with all my friends, but also because I could bring anyone around to the house whenever I wanted to, and could do whatever I wanted. I just never felt bad about it all, and that shocked me."[11]

The Bellamy boys didn't see their father for nearly a year until contact was made again and they began to see him every couple of months. Indeed, Matt became closer to his father after the split as they began to talk more openly about things. George Bellamy especially encouraged his son to pursue his interest in music. Matt got in scrapes on occasion, though nothing unusual for a mischievous teenager – "I shot a bull in the bollocks with an air-rifle," he told me. "I was hanging around with some farm boys – it's what they do, isn't it?"

"It sounds like a very American psycho-analytical thing to say, but looking back on it, music was probably one of the reasons I coped with the split so well," he said. "For me, music has always been intense so maybe it reflected stuff I couldn't really express in everyday life."[12]

Despite the marital split, the established Ouija sessions continued, Paul's girlfriend filling the seat vacated by his father while Matt was given the job of translating the letters as they were supposedly spelled out by dead family members. Matt later claimed the messages were intimate and personal enough to be authentic, with one subject predicting the Gulf War a full twelve months before the hostilities of the early Nineties began. Another time he asked the board if there was life after death, and he received the reply, "He who seeketh knowledge seeketh sorrow."

"Someone suggested to me that, after I stopped doing that stuff when I was thirteen or fourteen, I had this need to tap into something subconscious and quite dark," Matt reflected some years later. "I think there's truth in that; people who are searching for spirituality or religion are trying to tap into something. I'm tapping into something too, but it's not dead people. When you tap into those things the brain reacts creatively."[13]

The Bellamy's marriage wasn't the only thing that had broken. So too had Matt's voice and with it were revealed a whole new world of possibilities...

*

The very first seeds of Muse were sown when a thirteen-year-old Dominic played drums for the first time in a short-lived school band called The Magic Roundabout, whose hands-down greatest achievement was being the best group in Teign School. In Year 9. That week.

But Dom's band did have access to guitars, amps and whatever else was lying around in the music room store cupboard... and they were *playing*. Through amplifiers, with electricity – all that really mattered. It was enough to interest Matt who had by then acquired his first guitar. Helped largely by his natural ability to turn chords into cohesive melodies on the piano (thanks *Dallas*) and inspired by the blues of Ray Charles and Robert Johnson, Matt began to master the instrument at speed. "I really wanted to be a guitar player, so I spent hours playing," he succinctly explained.

When he was eleven, his parents bought him his first amp for Christmas. He plugged it in, played it and broke it within five minutes. It was the first of many pieces of musical equipment to suffer painful deaths at the hands of Matt Bellamy.

The ambitious six-stringer initially took Flamenco guitar lessons – a highly technical and masterful approach to playing – which only lasted a few months yet left enough of an impression to be heard in his music over a decade later. Mainly though, like all the best guitarists, he absorbed a plethora of conflicting styles and always played by ear.

"I couldn't get on with reading music," he recalls. "I had the ability but I always raced faster than the teacher was telling me I could do. I can do some things that are exceptionally complicated on guitar, but there are some simple things that I just can't do. I was running before I could walk really."

The thirteen-year-old's guitar playing initially only existed to complement his enjoyment of the piano. Despite the latterday success of Muse, as late as 2000 Matt was only just announcing he was finally at ease with the guitar.

"I've never really written stuff on guitar, it's only ever been on a piano, because you play multiple harmonies and assimilate a bass guitar," he says. "And I don't write anything down, not even the words. Never have."[14]

It was the ivories of the piano that Matt tinkled in his own short-lived school band, while his friend Chris, a budding guitarist who had switched to become a relatively accomplished drummer, was tub-thumping for another school band called Fixed Penalty, who were known to favour songs by the likes of the UK's premier transit-dwelling, the grossly under-rated punk-popsters Mega City Four.

"As for Dom, he was in the pre-eminently 'popular' band, the one in which everyone wanted to play," smiles Matt. "Somehow that's how I really started playing guitar, having in mind that I had to improve to be hired by a good band because the one I was in was crap. A little later I made friends with Dom and when they needed a new guitar player in his band I seized upon the opportunity."[15]

Around this time, Matt experienced his first 'proper' gig (ie. one concerning a band people outside of Exeter had heard of) – when the grebo kingpins Ned's Atomic Dustbin played in Exeter. Despite many high profile festival slots, countless music press front covers and an almost single-handed re-invention of the band T-shirt, Ned's sharply polarized opinions. Depending on your view, they were either a harmless and likeable enough band comprised of five kids with crimped hair and Stourbridge accents, or the apotheosis of all that was bad about indie music as the Nineties began in earnest – the great unwashed rehashing and watering-down melodic riffs half-inched from melodic Eighties American punk; a pop-lite version for snakebite-supping pre-Uni rebels. It all depended who you asked. Mind you, they did have two bassists and *at least they weren't The Levellers*. Ned's Atomic Dustbin (the name came from a Peter Sellers *Goon Show* sketch, incidentally) may have epitomised the bouncier end of British indie/alternative music of the time – celebrational, goofy, drunken, throwaway. The fickle dictates of the pop world ensured that for several years after their demise, Ned's were chided and described uncharitably in the music media. Yet it is easy to forget that at one time, they were *massive*. They were also a band that inspired many musicians of later years (for better or for worse) to pick up guitars – although only a brave few would openly admit it. Matthew Bellamy was certainly one of them.

The night of the Ned's gig also provided young Matt's first experience of that teenage *rites de passage*, the mosh-pit. "Dom fainted during the support band Kinky Machine," is Matt's succinct recollection of that important night. "And I remember getting my arse pummelled."

*

All arse-pummellings aside, in 1993 Bellamy felt confident enough on the guitar to start jamming Wedding Present songs with the more musically-respected Dominic and a series of other school friends in a band first called Carnal Mayhem, then Youngblood and then, on the suggestion of Dom's sister, Gothic Plague. For two years they jammed tunes and played on the school's boxing ring-cum-stage as band members came and went, most of them showing little commitment at taking things further than the rehearsal room (not an easy task on £5 a week pocket money and double Geography in the morning). In the end, only the energetic, nervy guitarist and the fresh-faced drummer who played far too hard for someone so slender remained in Gothic Plague ("The others might have left because of me actually," Matt later laughed).

Aside from emulating the most exciting bands of 1993/94 – Nirvana, Rage Against The Machine – on their weekend get-togethers, Matt was also taking tentative steps towards penning his first songs at this embryonic stage – more a collection of disparate riffs and vocal melodies that needed moulding into shape.

"But we needed a bass player," recalls Matt. "Obviously we knew Chris but, at this time, he was playing drums. I knew he was a scrupulous and serious guy, so we asked him if he wanted to play bass. And thankfully he did."

Although in the school year below Matt and Dom, Chris had been part of the same circle of friends for some time – indeed a couple of his former Fixed Penalty band mates are still making promising Squarepusher-style dance music (and may yet do a remix of Muse). Other friends in the close Teignmouth circle went on to work in everything from multi-media to banking.

Gothic Plague found themselves supporting the slightly younger Fixed Penalty one night, causing enough jealousy and inter-band rivalry for Matt and Dom to not only trash their gear while covering Nirvana's 'Lithium', but that of the other band as well.

"Obviously we'd known each for a long time and our bands played together, but [Gothic Plague] had split up," says Chris. "Matt and Dom were still mates but the other two guys hated them and there was all sorts of fights going on. I was rehearsing with Fixed Penalty next door to them, playing drums and doing backing vocals, and they asked me if I'd ever played bass. I said, 'No, never' and they said, 'Do you fancy giving it a go?' I was really pissed of with our band because we were doing lots of covers – Mega City Four, The Wonder Stuff, that sort of thing. There was a time when it was really cool but by then it had got to the point where those bands had split up, but we were still dragging it out. And the people I was playing with just weren't... music people. They were skaters or just wanted to be in a band because it was cool, rather than just enjoying playing music. So I said, 'Yes.'"

And two became three.

*

Context is everything.
In 1994, Kurt Cobain's death signalled the first rock star martyr of the decade. Depression, drug misuse (two weeks earlier in Rome he had OD'd on a combination of painkillers and champagne) and the growing disillusion with all notions of success contributed to the downfall of the finest songwriter, hell, the finest *singer*, American music had produced for years.

"I don't think that many bands feel that strongly about their music," said Matt. "It's sad but I think Nirvana was the last band who had that. Music should be an outlet for your emotions. If it wasn't for Muse I think I'd be a nasty, violent person. It's definitely a release and that's the way it should be."[16]

Cobain's death seemed to signal a shift in mood. Yes, grunge was nihilistic and destructive, but ultimately it was meant to save lives, not take them. Cobain's premature demise showed that the life of a star is not always fine and dandy; that sometimes people really do mean the things they're singing about. If one thing became apparent in the Nineties, it was that no matter how many people adore you or however many pounds you have in the bank, happiness can still be tantalisingly unobtainable.

1994 also saw the publication of Elizabeth Wurtzel's *Prozac Nation (Young And Depressed In America: A Memoir)*, a warts-and-all account of her spiralling depression and subsequent use of the then-emerging anti-depressant Prozac. The book became a best-seller and epoch-making tome – a kind of Sylvia Plath/ JD Salinger combination for an inward-looking age. In the same year, Radiohead were in the process of writing their breakthrough album, *The Bends*; in the US a young songwriter called Jeff Buckley had just released an elegiac and soulful album entitled *Grace*; and Manic Street Preachers recorded and released *The Holy Bible*, a malevolent-sounding thirteen-song set of poignant dark poetry that trawled the darker recesses of troubled lyricist Richey Edwards, tackling anorexia, the Holocaust and child prostitution along the way [it was easily their finest work to date]. The following year, after stints in hospital and The Priory clinic in Roehampton, Edwards disappeared without trace – either to sunnier, happier climes or, more likely, the bottom of the River Severn. Rock was robbed of another rare intelligent voice amongst a sea of empty showman. In the parallel insanity of Hollywood, actor River Phoenix suffered a similar fate to Cobain the previous year.

NME's choices for their 'Albums Of The Year' seemed to reflect this new-found sense of existentialism – Morrissey, Hole, Nirvana, Manic Street Preachers, Massive Attack and Johnny Cash all releasing vastly different yet ultimately hope-free (hope*less*?) records. Or rather, realist records. *Melody Maker* ran articles and organised debates to discuss this crassly-named 'culture of despair'. Even the face of good-time metal was changing with the release of the self-titled album by Californian five-piece Korn, a band whose entire oeuvre and the nu-metal scene they subsequently spawned were best encapsulated in their lyrical themes of alienation, abuse, catharsis etc.

The point is this – by the mid-Nineties, music was troubled and knew it, celebrated it, wore its heart on its sleeve, in a heart-shaped box. In Britain, mental health problems were at an all-time high – for example, self-harming was only just being recognised as something that affects way more people than previously believed. Whether revelling in its pain or suffering for it, rock music and its exponents were not ashamed to acknowledge that life can be hell.

And life *is* hell if you're trapped, frustrated, praying for change.

Context is, indeed, everything.

With their GCSEs approaching Matthew, Dominic and Chris were playing together regularly and discovering good new music on a weekly basis; bands that could change lives. Life was moving at a snail's pace and that sense of freedom – freedom from school, from parents, from rules – that the adult world promises was still tantalisingly out of reach. The trio spent what they later considered an almost unhealthy amount of time together and the songs that Matt was writing seemed to be taking a darker, harder edge, music which seemed to be following the general shift in alternative music towards what would later be termed, amongst others things, pre-Millennial angst. Gone were the bouncy, fraggle-rock songs of old, in their place a more serious sound that was more reflective of their world. Matt: "We just didn't have that 'normal guy' atmosphere most people have at that age."[17]

At the same time, his musical tastes were expanding to include people like South American composer Villa-Lobos' passionate orchestral arrangements, Spanish guitar master Andres Segovia and mighty Romantic heavyweight composers like Chopin, Berlioz and Rachmaninov. By drawing influence from all directions, even the nascent Muse's early songs displayed a depth lacking in most new bands.

"Berlioz made music so heavy and loud that, in a sense, nowadays you could achieve that volume with only three musicians," says Matt. "It's all about power and hitting people with large walls of sound."[18]

Dance culture wasn't totally overlooked either – Matt went to see leading lights like The Orb, Orbital and The Aphex Twin (twice) whenever they passed through Devon.

"I was really into all that stuff, but it didn't speak to me. It did something to me when I was off my face in a club or something, but it didn't really work at home."

This new incarnation, the first to feature the three future members of Muse playing together, was called Rocket Baby Dolls in honour of a Japanese porn film that Matt and Dom had seen on satellite TV one night.

"I think the first song we did was 'Small Minded', when we were fifteen-years-old, and it was about the attitudes of people in our town," explained Matt in 2000. "We didn't approve of this. Was there any other reason for forming? Lack of Christianity in the Western world, or the fact that we're the first computer generation and we've got no emotions whatsoever, soulless beings looking for some way to feel connected to other people. Maybe it was that, but I think it was more because we were just bored."

"We were sick of drinking cider and being beaten up," added Dom, in true drummer fashion.

3. DEVON & HELL

THIRTY MILES away in the relatively more cosmopolitan climes of Exeter, things were starting to stir.

In 1989, three punk fans Dave Goodchild, Patrick Cunningham and a friend called Russell were at the centre of a loose collective operating under the name Hometown Atrocities, who began to promote hardcore shows around town. The hardcore scene is traditionally often strongest in smaller or more detached towns which lack established venues. Arguably, this is because unlike more mainstream-sounding rock bands, extreme hardcore by its very nature has never been a form of music out to make money and therefore is not reliant on large crowds, door take etc. In addition, alcohol plays a less significant part in hardcore than most rock music sub-genres – largely because so-called 'straight-edge' hardcore is founded on a purist belief system of total abstinence of drink and drugs – therefore budding promoters don't have to worry about the effect of stringent licensing laws (the very reason that straight-edge first came about in Washington DC circa 1981) and thus can draw in crowds of all ages. Indeed, hardcore often provides many mid-teens with their ground level entry into the shadowy hinterlands of the music scene.

The Hometown Atrocities collective initially utilised Exeter pubs, putting on shows by US punk giants such as Fugazi and Quicksand until the pub owners got wise to all the trashing of their back rooms by sweaty young men and women letting off steam.

In 1990, once such pub The Hop & Grape went bankrupt and Dave Goodchild acquired ownership, reopening the pub as The Cavern Club. For many, it was Exeter's first decent venue and remains a favourite stop for many a touring band to this day, hardcore or otherwise.

Ronnie Kerswell, an early supporter of Muse and now a music journalist for *Rock Sound*, helped run The Cavern Club for a number of years. "The Cavern became the focus for this whole scene down in Exeter," she says. "A lot of people from the local college would come down to hang out – Dom would be there and their friend Tom [Kirk], who still works for them now. And Matt would be down there a lot, in his usual corner down by the mixing desk. He was a bit shy, quiet, talking very fast, giggling like a little child – exactly as he is now. In fact, the only major difference was that back then they all had long hair, in chin-length bobs. And I'm *sure* Matt used to wear a Radiohead T-shirt..."

The Cavern also provided the boys with their first underage pints. Despite being the youngest, as the biggest and hairiest member of their social circle Chris was sent up to the bar "with wobbling legs" to buy their drinks.

Rocket Baby Dolls were up and running and writing yet more songs. Some good, lots bad, but either way just enough to constitute a short set to perform in public. At this juncture, the songs were of the highly-charged, trashy punk bent that's so often the chosen sound of a young band mastering the rudiments of playing while hoping to offend everyone around them. The feedback-drenched squalls of Sonic Youth were a big influence.

After only a few weeks with their new line-up, their first gig was booked at Broadmeadow Sports Centre in Teignmouth in February 1994 as part of a 'Battle Of The Bands' contest. Any groups wishing to take part paid a £10 entrance fee to play a maximum of six songs (which was just as well, as that was as many completed songs as the Dolls had). To mark their public debut and pre-empt any possible ridicule, Rocket Baby Dolls piled on excessive amounts of badly-applied make-up and cranked it up.

"We went in there and took the piss out of all these guys in their mid-thirties with really expensive instruments and basses up to here," laughs Chris doing an impression of Level 42 bassist Mark King's famously lame guitar-at-chin-level posture. "Typically competent, funk musicians with no edge about them whatsoever – everything we had always hated."

The short, sharp set climaxed with a stage invasion from the thirty or forty of the Teignmouth faithful as the organisers desperately ran around trying to throw people off the stage, including Matt who was dragged away while still playing.

It wasn't to be the last time.

"The belief was always there, the confidence, the ability and the desire to get to the level they are today," says childhood friend Tom Kirk, who as the band's multi-media man now films them on tour (he made the *Hullabaloo* DVD), is in charge of artwork and runs the official Muse website. "Every day on tour now, looking around at the size of the venues is a bit of surprise, but not that much because we always knew they could do it, right from that first show."

One week after the 'Battle Of The Bands', Rocket Baby Dolls decided to change their name to the infinitely more refined Muse (Tom Kirk: "I think they realised that they might actually get somewhere and Rocket Baby Dolls wasn't exactly the coolest name to stick with"). The exact explanation for the band's name differs, depending on who you ask or how many interviews the band have done that day – and Muse are a band who have done *a lot* of interviews invariably including the no-brainer 'how did you get your name?'

"I remember a medium talking about muses," Matt later explained. "How you could summon up muses when you were at a very spiritual point in your life. And...well, I suppose I summoned up this band."

Matt also admitted to *Select* in May 2000 that at the time the band were starting to become a serious proposition, he had few friends – primarily his two bandmates, and three girls who referred to themselves as witches and sang to themselves in eerie, high-pitched voices – his muses.

"We did a lot of strange stuff that I don't really want to remember," he added, cryptically. "We've gone our separate ways since then."

This explanation may allude to the true origin of the word – a muse being the word first used in Greek mythology to describe any of the nine daughters of Mnemosyne and Zeus, each of whom presided over different kinds of poetry (as well as the arts and science) and became known as the source of an artist's inspiration; while the 'strange stuff' may well have coincided with the three teenager's discovery of alcohol, recreational drugs and sex, and various related recreational pursuits that bored teenagers with inactive imaginations have indulged in since time immemorial.

"I have always been stimulated by the idea of making a lot of money, in some easy and fast way," is another one of Matt's explanations. For this reason, there was a lot of ferment. Every day a new song came out. There was even a weird legend that said that all energy had come like a 'muse', descended from the sky; that's where we got our name from."[1]

Chris's recollection is somewhat more prosaic.

"Matt and Dom did art at school and they were talking about art with the teacher and she just started talking about muses and inspiration and things like that," he says. "Matt and Dom went away and looked up in the dictionary what it meant and we just sort of just thought, yeah, it sounds like a cool name and it's nice and short, and it looks big when you put it on posters as well. To fill up the space it has to be big, so everyone can always see it."[2]

*

In June 1994, Dom and Matt left Teign Secondary school with a mixture of As, Bs and Cs (all GCSE pass level) and the odd D, with Matt picking up an A* (highest possible grade) for Drama, Dominic the same for Art. Their overall results were slightly above average – the type of grades intelligent young men with things *other* than just the prospect of an academic career on their mind would achieve. Enough to suggest natural intelligence, but not good enough to suggest a complete dedication to the text book. However, the subjects in which they excelled hinted at their possible future careers – theatrics, artistry and musical accomplishment all soon became words used to describe their band. The young Matt took part in school residential drama courses where attendees were encouraged to "improvise weirdness and run around being berserk and having a laugh." Chris, meanwhile, still had another year to go.

"Dom was always the artistic one, Matt was into art and maths and Chris was the one on the music scene," remembers Tom Kirk. "We all did pretty good actually. On the arts front, the school was really good. The facilities at Teignmouth High weren't brilliant but one teacher called Miss Bird was particularly keen to encourage the band and really pushed Matt on the piano because she wanted to see more of that side of him. From the age of thirteen/fourteen, music always took priority over everything else."

When later asked in an interview to discuss the notion that school days are the best of your life, the responses of the band were suitably varied and give a brief insight into the differences between the three members.

Matt: "No, it bored me... it's all bad sex, cheap drinks and terrible teaching methods." (The 'bad sex' at school may have been an exaggeration – Matt later laughed that he had lied to friends about losing his virginity at fifteen, when really it hadn't worked out quite as planned!)

Dominic: "Actually, yes I reckon they are the best days of your life because you don't have the stresses of money, career etc."

Chris: "No. It was fucking shit."

Having done only one show that summer at the Pavilions in nearby Totnes, in September Matt, Dom and Tom Kirk enrolled at Exeter College to do three A-levels each. They quickly made new friends with other students and began to build a following.

"Muse were the biggest band in the college, although there were only a couple of others," says Tom. "We had some other mates who they used to play with, including some guys from Ashburton [in south Devon] who were in a band called something like Dripping Womb..."

For those who choose to attend, the two years spent studying A-levels at a sixth form college often provide certain first new experiences – sex, drinking, smoking, working, music. Of course, everyone experiences these things at some point, but Exeter College was typical of such higher education in drawing together working-class/middle-class students on the cusp of adulthood from a wider catchment area, most with a vague notion of continuing their studies – or at least killing time before facing the real world. Suddenly, Friday nights were a lot more interesting.

Beyond their half-hearted studies, the band set about getting gigs – not an easy task when you live in Teignmouth – and recorded tentative demos to flaunt their wares. The Cavern Club was top of the list of venues to hit up for gigs.

"I still have a TDK tape of that early demo they sent to The Cavern to get a gig," laughs Ronnie Kerswell. "What was it like? Interesting! It's not quite like they are today, put it that way. But when the first album came out five years later, you could see where some of the songs had come from. The ideas were in place pretty early on."

Fortunately, these rudimentary recordings proved good enough to get them a slot at their favourite local haunt. "There were a few bands coming through The Cavern," says Tom Kirk. "Local bands would get bigger in Teignmouth, Torquay and Exeter, which was great, but nothing much would happen beyond that. There were some great shows at The Cavern, we had a lot of really good nights."

In October 1994, The Cavern provided the trio with their first real taste of performing in a decently-run venue with proper facilities and a steady stream of passing bands to be inspired by or react against. They would play the venue a handful of times over the next year or so, including taking part in a further 'Battle Of The Bands' contest.

"At the time, the Cavern Club had bands such as Menswear, Gene, These Animal Men, S*M*A*S*H and Supergrass playing and everyone thought that entering the competition would give Muse a chance to get noticed, and the possibility of a support slot with bands like these," explains Ronnie Kerswell, then promoter and sometime performer. "There were no old blokes playing pub rock, it was all entered by young bands throughout the south-west – as far afield as Cornwall."

Much has been made of Muse's early triumph in local band competitions, but the truth is they didn't always win. After working their way through the heats, Muse found themselves in the final and were indeed firm favourites to emerge victorious.

"Everybody said we were going to win the grand final, so in the heats they placed us second each time, in order to get us through to the final but not enough to win all the heat prizes, which was deliberate because that grand prize was ours."

After a semi-final performance at The Cavern, disaster struck. On the way home, Tom Kirk was having trouble replacing the bike seat he had stashed behind a seat at Exeter train station when Dom offered assistance – by punching the solid saddle.

Result: one broken hand, no gigs for three months. Conclusion: don't pick on bicycles. Instead, the band lost out to The Cavern's own Ronnie Kerswell, performing with her friend Lucy in the not-entirely-serious vocal duo Kindergarten Sluts ("a bit like Shampoo, only darker"). They also missed out on the top prize of a guitar, plus strings, drumsticks and so forth. They certainly could have used it – right from that first performance, Muse have always viewed their equipment with a certain sense of... disposability.

"We just entered it for a joke," says Ronnie. "Everything was on DAT including some of the vocals. But still, technically we beat Muse. They came down to see us play in the final, including Dom with his broken arm. We were so gutted and because we thought they should have won we gave our prizes to them. What were we going to do with guitar strings – we didn't even have guitars! But Muse were serious and won a lot of respect and we had them support a lot of the bands coming through town a lot more after that."

Muse built a following throughout their two years doing A-levels, progressing in ability with each show. By 1995 the band were soaking up or disgarding the music of their time, picking up on Rage Against The Machine, Jeff Buckley, Pavement, Helmet, Primus and Smashing Pumpkins' *Siamese Dream* – which didn't leave Matt's stereo throughout his GCSEs – all bands whose influence is obvious in their stage show today.

At the time Britpop had not yet become a national concern and was still confined to the pages of the indie music press. Bands like Oasis were releasing their first singles, the energetic likes of aforementioned punk/new wave revisionists like These Animal Men and S*M*A*S*H were revitalising the live scene while Suede and Blur were attempting to wrestle the nation's attention away from America's grunge hegemony, the latter by affecting Mockney accents and celebrating such British institutions as fried breakfasts, geezers and nights at the dog track. Blur's Kinks-ian ditties were central to the emergence of Britpop, a renaissance which enlivened the music, arts and fashion scenes although tellingly meant little outside of this nation and appears to have had little lasting cultural impact. (Interestingly, in 1997 with Britpop's star fading, frontman

Damon Albarn began to namedrop distinctly American college rock bands like the aforementioned Pavement, whose sound Blur tried to emulate in something of a musical *volte-face*.)

"Something happened when Nirvana died," Matt later commented. "The whole grunge thing died and England reinvented itself with the Britpop scene... but it became too quirky and English. It became too Union Jack, too insular. It became quirky jokey London Cockney, you know what I mean? It just became a joke. It didn't become about making music, it became about fashion."

Or to paraphrase Ian Brown, it's not where you're from, it's where you're *at*.

*

When Muse made the natural progression to playing their first London show in 1995, Britpop had no yet made it onto *The Six O' Clock News* – that came with the Blur versus Oasis debacle in August of that year. Noel Gallagher had also yet to visit Downing Street as part of Tony Blair's Cool Britannia public relations exercise. But nevertheless, the small venues of north London were awash with indie bands, most of them either rehashing macho American grunge riffs, punking things up *a la* the New Wave Of New Wave or simply pretending to be Suede/Oasis/whoever-was-on-this-week's *NME* cover.

For that first foray into the capital's web of gigs, Muse bagged themselves a slot at The Bull & Gate, a venue that has long been a regular first port of call for rising bands. It is an intrinsic part of the London toilet venue circuit, a short walk up from Camden Town and next door to the much bigger Kentish Town Forum. Like so many venues that pride themselves on supporting new talent, The Bull & Gate is a shit-hole.

So while many make the long schlep into the city expecting to find a venue packed with music businessmen, journalists and A&R men eager to see every young band from the provinces, the cold reality of a pub back-room on a Monday night, leaking toilets, a bag of greasy chips and total indifference can be jarring – at best, educational.

The trio made the two hundred-odd mile journey up to

London, taking with them as many school friends, girlfriends and family members as they could persuade to make the trip. They played to rapturous applause (from their friends) and…well, that was it. No big fanfares, no red carpet, no streets paved of gold. Just a smoky back room, some warm beer and little enthusiasm beyond the Teignmouth inner circle.

*

I have played in every toilet…
Over the months that followed, Muse were to play other places besides Teignmouth and London – The New Railway Inn and The Piazza in Torquay and The Ark Royal in Plymouth to name but three – occasionally finding themselves having to perform to an aged audience insistent that they play hits from the Sixties – "stuff off of *Heartbeat* son, that type of thing."

While these gigs offered the trio a chance to refine their live set and learn how to *perform*, little else made them worthwhile. Unless an A&R man down from London happened to wander in for a quiet pint or a chicken-in-a-basket meal, they were never going to be 'spotted' playing dead-end places to people who view music as an unwanted distraction from the jukebox. Building a following by playing non-venues – pubs which might have a PA system but no clue about promotion, advertising or, indeed, any insight as to how rock bands and fans act at shows – is virtually impossible too. All of which is fine if you're content with being the second best band at Camborne's Berkeley Centre on any given night (for some reason there always seems to be a funk-rock band who'll be more technically proficient); not so great if your ambitions reach higher.

For a while they were being managed by a Teignmouth fan called Phil Korthals who, being in his twenties was only a few years older than the band. He helped them get gigs and began making tentative steps towards getting the band any coverage they could. "There were a few local magazines where we're from and they occasionally did a review of us," Chris remembers. "The first was probably at The Cavern, and it was weird because we were all dead chuffed that our name was printed in a magazine, even though it had a circulation of about twenty."[3]

47

Korthals certainly helped establish the band on a local level and therefore undoubtedly contributed to their later success, but the working relationship was believed to have ended acrimoniously. Indeed, it's said that one song written about him would later make it on to Muse's debut album…

Next up was a local show with Sarah Records' twee indie types Boyracer in June: "Nice times in Teignmouth playing crazy golf in the sun," says an entry on their website. "Highlights included a dog plus three people in the audience in Plymouth. Muse owe a lot to the mentorship of the Racer…" Muse then took part in their first overseas venture when a contact booked them to play The Charleston, a pub in Cherbourg, France. The town of Cherbourg is about as close to England as you can get without getting your feet wet, and indeed the first port of call for British campers and holiday-makers – *but* it was as unlikely a place to kickstart a career in foreign climes as, say, a French band heading to Dover. However, to Muse not only was it outside of Devon (and not, thankfully, London) it was *abroad*.

"It was actually like some sort of gay sailor's bar," laughs Matt. "A real dock-side bar with a couple of loose sailors off work and some skinheads. There were only twenty people there and none of them gave a shit about us. I seem to remember one sailor guy getting into it – either that or he was losing it. We just thought 'What are we doing here?' It was a joke."

There was a reason other than the pursuit of international recognition for travelling across the Channel: the contact who had booked Muse's show was ostensibly using the band as a handy cover for a smuggling venture. With their assistance, he was able to stash 200,000 Regal King Size cigarettes, packets of tobacco and many cases of red wine, beer and spirits to stock the bar he was running back home. Result.

"He was a dodgy geezer," said Chris. "Seemingly that's what he did for a living – taking advantage of young bands for the purposes of smuggling." The band played the gig then squeezed themselves into the twelve inch gap on top of the pile of cigarettes that their friend had generously left for them to travel in and took the next available ferry home. Three hungover young men rather more than returning conquerors. For their troubles they were paid £50.

Muse didn't play further gigs until June in a pub called The Beer Engine in the small Devon town of Crediton, followed shortly by their second show at Totnes' Pavillions.

"We also once played this working men's club on a Sunday afternoon," remembers Chris. The 'audience' was made up of families having their Sunday dinners. There was one two-year old girl who was dancing and falling over, and these scary blokes coming up to us shouting *'Too fucking loud!'* We didn't even have a PA..."[4]

More encouragingly, the Cavern Club were impressed enough by Muse's efforts to ask the trio to round off their, ahem, two-month, four-date tour with a slot at Dodgy's 'Big Top' gig in Exeter in August. Dodgy were three cheery reconstructed hippies who'd tasted moderate chart success with summery, spliffed-up Britpop songs like 'Good Enough' and their previous year's hit, 'Staying Out For The Summer'. True earth brothers that they were, the London trio had set about travelling around the UK that summer playing shows in a circus big top tent under the banner 'The Big Top Trip', backed by up and coming bands and local acts (Dodgy themselves had been signed to A&M after running their own night The Dodgy Club in London and releasing records on their Bostin label).

While Dodgy and a not-yet-famous Catatonia headlined the main stage, promoters of the show, Hometown Atrocities (aka The Cavern club crew) offered Muse a headline spot on the smaller, unsigned bands stage.

"By then, they were achieving that sort of status locally," recalled Ronnie Kerswell in late 2003. "Enough to justify headlining above the other Devon bands. A lot of people were coming down to The Cavern to see them, including Dennis Smith from Sawmills who used to come down for a drink and gradually became a kind of mentor to them."

Their next show wouldn't take place for another seven months, back at The Cavern once again. In the meantime, all education dispensed with, Matt went travelling around Europe for six weeks.

In September 1996, as Teignmouth's shutters came down for the slow autumnal crawl towards a long winter by the sea, Muse lost their one true asset outside of their music – their fanbase. With their following so far predominantly comprised of fellow Exeter college students and Cavern-dwellers (more or less one and the same), come the start of the academic year many of their contemporaries moved away to attend various universities.

"Obviously we were all friends of the band, but we were also into all the same music," remembers Tom Kirk, who left Teignmouth at that time to pursue higher education. "Muse's sound was a cross between all of our favourite bands so we were bound to like them more than any other Devon bands. They were playing what we had grown up listening to together."

"Being at college was the only real time that the band was really buzzing, up until we got signed anyway," says Chris. "We made loads of new friends, we'd hang out together, pile into The Cavern and then… everybody left. All the people who we thought were fans of Muse were really just our mates so when they left Exeter, so did our following. We then spent the next two years desperately trying to get gigs and playing to no-one."

Matt, for one, gave little thought to such higher education. "Everyone says that's what you've got to do to get by nowadays, which is absolute bollocks."

With no record contract or management and little in the way of gigs on the horizon, it was enough of a blow to remind Muse that after two years playing together they were still barely on the bottom rung of the ladder; they were faced with an uncertain future.

So they wrote some more songs. Lots of them.

*

Jobs For The Boys

Exeter has two porn shops. Matt Bellamy chose to live above the one on Forth Street in the slightly seedier, stale-piss-and-kebab-shops end of town, opposite a music shop. He was living with a friend who sold drugs for cash and playing in a band with a lot of potential but few prospects. The flat had been up for demolition when an estate agent told Matt and his friend it was theirs if they were prepared to make it habitable.

"It was in the only area that was slightly dodgy or cutting edge in Exeter," says Matt. "All sorts of people were coming around the house because the guy I lived with was a full-on drug user and after a while it turned into a scene from *Trainspotting*, white powders and mirrors everywhere, although I never really took part in it. I just saw people moving from one drug to the next – the harder ones. I don't touch the cocaine or the heroin – I've seen what it does to people. For me, I've only been into hallucinogenics and hash."[5] (Anyone who has met Matt in person would acknowledge there's little need for artificial stimulants such as amphetamine or coke…)

While his flat mate was drug dealing (later imprisoned) Matt was working – elbow-deep cleaning shit out of the toilets at a local camp-site, erecting scaffolding and doing decorating and demolition jobs. He was once employed to demolish an entire shopping centre. Chris meanwhile was being paid £90 a week to help out in a guitar shop and Dom did various things, including dressing students for graduation ceremonies. "Helping ladies to dress?" he says. "There are worse jobs."

"No offence to the noble art of painting and decorating of which I was once a less-than-able practitioner," said Matt, "but [being in a band] knocks the socks off having a normal job. And I've done all the dodgy jobs, me. To be honest, that's why all three of us have stuck at this game and persevered and worked so hard: we were horrified at the prospect of a proper job."[6]

Muse may have been dedicated to the art, using all their money on equipment and going to The Cavern at a weekend, but they weren't entirely honest grafters.

"I got in with a group of dodgy friends for a while and we'd steal shit cars and sell them," he later confided. "We got this Escort from a scrap-yard run by the hardest guy in town and he found out we'd sold it to someone for a few hundred quid. He came round to my house and said he'd burn it down when my family was in it if I didn't give him £500. So I had to give this bloke the tour bus we had at the time."

Another time, Matt and some friends had sneaked into an outdoor swimming pool in Teignmouth one night for a spot of skinny-dipping, only for a police helicopter to appear overhead. Two policemen arrived to drag them out and give them an official warning while they stood shivering, their nakedness illuminated in the helicopter's probing searchlight.

The band were gigging infrequently but in June ventured east to play The Bull & Gate again. And once again they spent the day driving up from Devon – this time without an entourage – loaded in, set up, soundchecked, ate, hung around, played their hearts out, thanked the audience of one, then left. If they could just double their attendance with each show, in ten gigs time they'd have a crowd of over five hundred. As they say, one step at a time...

Muse hit the M-way back to the sticks. They wouldn't play another proper paying gig in the capital for eighteen months – and by then the circumstances would be very different.

*

Dinosaurs and denim: an unrelated aside

In the year that Chris met girlfriend and future mother of his children Kelly, an early taste of success of sorts did come about for him. A strange turn of events led him to one of rock's longest standing, most conservative bands – and particular Wolstenholme favourite, Status Quo. In 1997, the denim-clad two-chord wonders were working their way around the British venue circuit, creaking their way through a set of rock standards when their real-life David St. Hubbins, guitarist Rick Parfitt, took ill in Plymouth. It was the band's first tour since Parfitt's triple heart by-pass operation and fellow frontman Francis Rossi's hair transplant.

A friend of Chris's had moved to Plymouth to attend university there a couple of months earlier and happened to be living in the halls of residence with the son of Status Quo's keyboard player. So when Rossi asked if any of the students could stand in on guitar during the soundcheck – Parfitt was resting back at the hotel – they all pointed to Chris and yelled, "He can!" The band got the bassist on stage and they ran through 'Don't Waste My Time', much to the amusement of the lingering Plymouth students. Playing with 'The Quo' was an irony not lost on Chris, although what his former Fixed Penalty charges thought of his new jamming buddies is anyone's guess.

The first thing he did afterwards was call his mother – a massive fan – who nearly burst into tears with excitement. Little did Rossi, Parfitt and Co. realise that a budding star had just had his first taste of playing through a massive PA system – and he liked it...

He liked it, he liked it, he li-li-li-liked it, li-li-li-liked it...

4. COMA CITY AND CALIFORNIA DREAMING

EVERY MAESTRO needs a mentor, and Muse's came in the form of Dennis Smith, the man who would gently guide the band through the pitfalls of the music industry and negotiate some very favourable deals along the way.

A likeable man of boundless, infectious enthusiasm who can out-talk even Matt Bellamy, Dennis is the owner of Sawmills, one of the country's most in-demand residential recording studios. Situated in an old water mill, whose history stretches back to the eleventh century, beside an unspoilt tidal creek on the western banks of the River Fowey in Cornwall, Sawmills is one of the most beautiful and secluded locations of any residential studio in the world. Accessible by boat – a perilous journey for many a drunken gang of young urbanites – high profile clients have included Oasis, The Verve, Stone Roses, Robert Plant and Supergrass. Dennis had already proven himself as a spotter of talent when in 1992/93 he signed a new Oxford-based trio formerly known as The Jennifers to a production deal. Having developed the band he then licensed them to EMI, they changed their name to Supergrass and the rest is history…

Dennis first heard about Matt in 1991 when his local mechanic approached him enthusing about a performance he had just seen. "He said, 'Here Dennis, you're in the music business aren't you?'" Dennis explained to me in December 2003. "When I said I was, he said, 'Listen, I was up at my daughter's prize-giving evening at her school and I saw this young lad and he's the most amazing keyboard player…' He told me this and I thought, well, he might be a piano genius but it's obscene to be going talent-scouting a thirteen-year old kid, so I left it alone. I was intrigued but that was as far as it went." [Home video footage of Matt playing a prize-winning boogie-woogie piece was later used for a Channel 4 documentary about the band in 2003] It wasn't until three years after the mechanic's tip-off that Dennis and Matt's paths finally crossed.

"I got this phonecall from a young lad from Teignmouth,

aware that Sawmills was the only professional studio involved in making hit records in the area," continues Dennis. "He basically called for advice and to see if there was any interest. It was only a few days later after I'd given it some thought that I realised he might be the lad from the school, and we both giggled at the strange coincidence. Looking back on it now, we see it as being, I don't know... good karma? I didn't bother the kid at thirteen, but he eventually came to me anyway. I've always been a believer in doing right by people."

"Matt really hasn't changed since that first day I met him," continues Dennis. "He's still definitely a thinker, and quite a deep thinker at that. I can see why people sometimes level this charge of arrogance – the music does have a certain swagger to it – but Matt is not like that as a person at all. And when people say that he is [arrogant], they've got it wrong. Matthew has an incredible range of thoughts, he's got such a restless and imaginative and creative mind. An older head on much younger shoulders is how I've always seen him."[1]

When Dennis first became aware of Muse, they were still being managed by local friend and passionate music fan Phil Korthals. "I don't think the boys were sure of Phil's agenda – you'd have to ask them about that... but credit is due to him because he was the first person to recognise the boys' talent and offer to help them – before even me."

Dennis first saw the band perform on October 11, 1995, at The Berkeley Centre in Camborne after another tip-off – this time from a local journalist who had written a piece on Sawmills. Three months after interviewing Dennis, she called to say she'd heard this band who were making a bit of noise and came from his area.

"So I went to see them," said Dennis. "They played a lot of their own material and there was very little being said between songs – typical early Muse really. The performance was spirited but rough around the edges. They had songs, but they weren't yet in a decent shape. I did manage to score points with the boys by recognising a Primus cover that they played. Being twenty-five years older than them, they wouldn't have expected me to know a band like Primus, but fortunately my son had just come back from America with their album. I think that impressed them."

Convinced by the maturity and the potential already emanating from the band at such an early stage, Dennis offered first his encouragement, then his experience... and later his studio.

Along with Safta Jaffery of SJP Productions, Dennis had recently formed a production/publishing company, Taste Media, to help develop and sell new bands.

With a background as an A&R man, since 1985 Safta had been managing a stable of some of the country's leading producers, many of whom worked out of Sawmills, including Ron Saint-Germain (Bad Brains, Sonic Youth), John Cornfield (Supergrass, Catatonia) and Radiohead/Stone Roses producer John Leckie.

"The inspiration behind setting up Taste Media comes from two sources: first, from a general frustration coming from SJP producers, who were typically frustrated by not being allowed the artistic freedom with the artists they're commissioned to work with," says Jaffrey of the company's intent. "There's often a lot of interference from A&R departments who are looking to mould the artists and make them sound all the same. The second comes from the sad reality that there is very rarely any real artist development being implemented within record labels today. If the first two or three singles (if you're lucky) taken from an album do not receive substantial airplay or receive Top 30 chart placings, the artist is normally dropped."[2]

Taste Media also decided upon a policy to license their artists' recordings territory by territory around the world, a move that would later be the making of Muse. But first, they took care of the band. Throughout the subsequent months and years, Dennis was in frequent contact with Matt's mother and grandmother, who Matt was particularly close to and had lived with at various times since George and Marilyn's split, enthusing over Matt and the band's natural talent, assuring them the band were in good hands and convincing them that Muse may very well make it.

Things moved slowly. Eighteen months passed before Dennis and the band were officially working together. Instead, they stayed in touch, calling Dennis for advice and alerting him to their sporadic live outings throughout the area in 1996-1997.

"I'd get these messages every couple of weeks," remembers Dennis. "It's Matt from Muse'. It was always 'Matt from Muse' and never Phil, their manager. So I'd keep going to see them until it got to the point where I was dangling a carrot in front of them. I said, 'Look, you can come into the hallowed portals of Sawmills, but only when I see that magic show.'"

"That show was in June or July 1997 at The Cavern, nineteen months after I'd first seen them. Afterwards I said to them, 'That was the one, let's go into the studio.' This was after two years in which I had said, 'Don't go running off to America, don't even go to London, stay here and build a buzz from the ground up. Do your growing up in private and then when you're ready, we'll hit the ground running.' At that point they had done one showcase for Parlaphone in London, who at the time were having a lot of success with Radiohead. It was possibly because of this that they didn't take it any further with Muse. To be fair though, it was obvious the band still had a lot of growing up to do."

Pledging to allow the band to use his studio for free on the proviso they could pay him back if they got signed, Dennis pushed the band to nail down some ideas. Ordinarily he would have offered such a new band project to producer John Cornfield, but he was booked for months working on Supergrass's second album. Instead, Dennis called a young engineer called Paul Reeve, whose own singing voice as a Sawmills recording artist had reminded Dennis of Matt's. Reeve had previously played in Bodmin-based band The Change, Blueskin and London-based Wayland (who had signed to BMG), before moving to the other side of the control panel.

Reeve saw the band at a show at the Plymouth Cooperage and was convinced straight away. Preferring not to have the studio standing empty, he let the band and engineer record in downtime between bigger artists' sessions.

"I was very pleased with my decision of getting Paul and the band together," says Dennis. "I suggested which songs they should record and left them to it for five days while I went away, on the agreement that they'd pay me back – the same production deal I had had with Supergrass. When I got back I listened to it and made some comment that the boys laughed at at the time, something like, 'Wow, people are going to go mental for this, you're doing something really special here...' Sonically and performance-wise it wasn't spot on, but it was powerful and it was serious. I said, 'Look boys, we've got to put this out...'"

Four songs made it onto the band's debut release, the simply-titled 'Muse EP'. 'Coma' was a goosebumps song – Muse at their hectic, howling libidinous best – and one of the strongest of their live set so far. With a hip-swinging, swooning chorus that recalled Suede's Brett Anderson at his camp peak, 'Overdue' showed the less dark (you could never call it light) side of Muse. 'Cave' was another live favourite with a Nirvana-inspired intro and scorching chorus that again showcased Matt's vocal talents.

"The idea for 'Cave' came from that rubbish American book, *Men Are From Mars, Women Are From Venus*," Matt explains. "There's this bit about how men go into a cave when they get stressed and I think that's probably true, although, personally, I tend to let it out..."

Finally, 'Escape' (originally titled 'You're Meaningless') was nothing short of elegiac, a Jeff Buckley-inspired velvet-draped torch song with a chorus that could have been lifted from that particular Matt favourite, *Siamese Dream* – this time it's the Smashing Pumpkins to whom 'Escape' is most clearly indebted.

The EP was to be released on Dennis's dormant label, Dangerous Records. "I wasn't interesting in making money selling records," says Dennis. "That release was a pure statement of intent to the music industry, a way of raising their profile." The cover for the 'Muse EP' carried a relatively straight-forward image of Dom's photo-copied face, divided in three and coloured red, blue and orange. Beside it, the introduction of a logo that would launch a hundred thousand T-shirts: the word MUSE sandwiched between two heavy lines. No messing. The release was limited and individually numbered to 999 copies, although an additional 251 promos were pressed for the media. As a introduction to Museworld, surely the EP was about to set the planet alight like a fireball from the hands of Satan himself.

Not quite. It was released in May 1998 to...well, relative indifference.

Nonetheless, with Dennis and Safta behind them, Muse had some clear goals for the first time. Between them the pair had a lot of valuable experience within the music industry and a fair share of contacts to assist them on the collective mission of making Muse a worldwide concern. They carried a certain amount of *weight*. Above all, Dennis in particular was an enthusiastic fan as much as an (unofficial) manager/mentor, and it was his early encouragement that convinced many that Muse were more than just the best band in Devon. Furthermore, the music was already at a developed stage – the sporadic-gigging and lack of industry involvement in the wilderness years had helped nurture a creative streak such that the band had stock-piled enough ideas for *eighty* songs. With such an archive on tap, the plan was simple enough: get Muse in the studio, get them signed, get them out there.

They worked backwards. First, they gigged sporadically nationally – including a trip to Matt's old home turf of Cambridge to support another mid-table band, svelte indie-crooners Gene; then they concentrated on building their local following with a second appearance at the Soundwaves festival in Plymouth in order to try out new ideas which would lead them to... step three: getting signed.

"At the time, all their peers were going off to university," says Dennis. "It was clear that these three lads were bright enough to have gone too, and perhaps should have gone to college as some sort of back-up plan if it all went pear-shaped. But they fully and consciously ignored that and stuck with the band one hundred per cent."

Muse's new benefactors also stuck to their promise of backing the band whole-heartedly. Dennis began to call their parents from time to time, particularly speaking to Matt's mother and gran.

"They're lovely people," laughs Dennis. "Matt's Nan is particularly amazing for a lady of her age – she was eighty even then. The band would be rehearsing down in the cellar and they didn't seem to mind at all. She loved it. I spoke to all their families because, as a father myself, I wanted them to know that I was responsible, honest and decent and wasn't some weirdo hanging round them for... well, alternative reasons. There's a lot of it about and I wanted to reassure them. I also wanted them to know that I thought the band had a special talent which should be encouraged. Fortunately they agreed."

While there was little in the way of column inches – try millimetres – devoted to Muse's debut (signed copies of which would later change hands for upwards of £350), there was enough interest to get them a spot at 'In The City'.

First started in 1992 by Phil Saxe and Factory/Hacienda label impresario Tony Wilson, 'In The City' is an annual, week-long music conference, with so-called 'ITC Unsigned' gigs aimed squarely at the record industry in showcasing new talent. The geographical choice of Manchester may have been an admirable and much-needed attempt to place the onus on a city other than London while exercising a bit of northern civic pride, but 'In The City' is nevertheless a piranha-like feeding-frenzy in which the A&R men, MDs, publicists, journalists and lawyers descend *en masse* from London to over thirty venues to see the brightest unsigned bands battle it out in a bid to make themselves heard and, hopefully, rank as one of the best three bands of the conference.

Before and after the shows, insiders tend to meet to discuss the methods and mechanics of the music business. This is either in formal discussion panels or, more realistically, late at night in various hotels and bars over a nice mound of expense-account marching powder and a steady flow of drinks. To cynical outsiders, 'In The City' might carry the air of something of an odious old boy's club, sustained and perpetuated by established industry insiders for their own means – all of which would be true – but its record for unearthing new talent is unquestionable. By 1998's conference, the likes of Oasis, Placebo, Kula Shaker, Idlewild, Stereophonics, Catatonia and Kenickie were just a handful of bands who had been selected, spotted, signed and sent on their way to greatness or something approximating it after an appearance at 'In The City'.

So just getting selected for an 'In The City: Live Unsigned' slot is potentially a big deal for a new band, enough to offer hope that they will at least be seen by a few people with the ability, experience and resources to make a band's career. With big plans in mind, Safta and Dennis fortuitously submitted the 'Muse EP' to the conference selection panel and the band were duly offered a headline spot on September 13 at one of the many showcase nights.

The venue was a converted Methodist church youth hall called Colliers situated just off Oldham Street, a venue that none of the industry visitors particularly liked as both smoking and drinking was prohibited. Muse drove up from Devon and following performances from Lifestyle Of The Rich & Famous ("What you might expect if Dave Grohl had written 'The Girl From Ipanema', according to the 'In The City' A&R Guide) and Grimace ("a mixture of infectious ska and song-fuelled rock *a la* No Doubt") played what would be termed in sporting parlance, a blinder.

Journalist, publicist and all-round industry talent-spotter Nik Moore was in the audience that night. "They weren't a big 'buzz band' at that point – or at least not before 'In The City'," explained Moore. "They hadn't toured or spoken to the press and there was nothing established, so 'In The City' was a perfect springboard for their career. Some band's gigs were rammed to the rafters, if only because the venues were so small but when Muse played, it wasn't full although there was sufficient interest. Mind you, at 'In The City' a band can play to six people and two days later *everyone* will be talking about them."

That year was arguably 'In The City's most successful to date – at least in terms of launching new bands. The likes of studious, sensitive types Coldplay, cantankerous art-rockers Cay, Muse and ironic popsters (and overall winners) Younger Younger 28s all went on to score record deals. While two of the bands have sunk without trace, two have gone on to achieve massive success, not least Coldplay who have inherited Radiohead's multi-platinum-selling crown.

Although for all the pomp and promise of 'In The City', the response to Muse was relatively muted. Nik Moore loved them and having tracked down Dennis and the boys at the Crown Plaza hotel "where the lobby was a maelstrom of two hundred people, all off their trees", reached a gentleman's agreement that he would help publicise the band for free on the premise that if things started happening, they'd stick with him.

"Of the fifty-odd unsigned bands, Muse absolutely stood out from the pack because they were so original and had such great songs," says Moore. "It was just one of those wonderful things. They were very young and very quiet – neither overtly arrogant nor overtly confident. But very genial." Yet beyond that, UK labels themselves weren't immediately forthcoming. In fact, at that point, not one British label wanted to sign the band.

So, once again, even after performing to some of the key figures in the industry, outside of their immediate circle Muse had come away with someone offering to push their initial releases in *NME* and *Melody Maker* on the hope of getting a small review, but little else.

"They're like sheep, labels," says future Muse publicist Mel Brown of Impressive PR. "That's just the way it happens – many other big bands around today were initially overlooked before suddenly all the labels were interested. So when things did start to happen for Muse, I think it was a big shock to them. Bear in mind that until then they'd pretty much spent all their time in either Teignmouth or Exeter dreaming about this."

Encouragingly, however, the UK's indifference was not matched by the Americans – interest was such that a couple of companies from the US got in touch with Muse. It was enough to justify a trip to New York where the band had been selected to perform at the annual CMJ (College Music Journal) conference after Safta had touted the 'Muse EP' around some of his high-ranking industry contacts during a business trip. "Safta came back from the States, his eyes wide with dollar signs!" Dennis remembers. "The Americans got it where people in Britain hadn't."

Along with the more alternatively-minded South-By-South West conference held in Austin, Texas earlier in the year, CMJ is a major event in the music industry's diary, the US equivalent of 'In The City', although arguably even more significant in terms of the exposure gained amongst all the 'right' people. Publishing company Zomba had seen Muse in Manchester and offered to pay for the band's flights out there. Their motives weren't entirely benevolent though – they knew that the ownership of

Muse's future output would be worth something.

"It was really strange to go from a [guitar] shop in Torquay to finding ourselves in New York," remembers Chris. "People back at work just didn't get it. And the other people, the people out there, didn't quite realise where we had come from."

While Hurricane Floyd (why don't they ever give them real American names like Hurricane Bubba or Hurricane Otis-Lee Junior?) bothered America outdoors, Muse whipped up their own storm inside the Mercury Lounge in downtown Manhattan. Alongside Dennis and Safta, joining them in the stuffy club were John Leckie and the band's future publicist Mel Brown, then in the process of launching her own company Impressive PR.

"The place was packed, full of record label people," she recalls. " It was obvious at that point that Matt was a great guitar player, had a unique voice and the music really shone, but what you see [in later years] had not yet emerged. Matt didn't *perform* like he does now."

Despite its glittering moniker, the Mercury Lounge is just another small showcase club, similar to the London dives the band had grown accustomed to. Playing on a bill with fellow British rockers Feeder, an unphased Muse overcame a few technical glitches with the unfamiliar equipment that they'd had to hire, stepped up to the occasion and played a set that showcased their much of their first EP and what would become their second EP and forthcoming debut album.

"It was the first time I'd seen them and the show was absolutely incredible," says Mel Brown. Dennis endorses her enthusiasm. "Some people would come along at these early shows and say, 'Where's the backing track?' They would refuse to believe that a three-piece could make such a racket live as they did. I'd get very uppity with these people – I was protective of my boys! I knew they were doing it all with just guitar, bass, drums and vocals, and wanted people to realise the same."

*

The recording business is an industry that thrives on rumours, Chinese whispers, gossip and hyperbole, a place where well-kept secrets only remain that way for the briefest of moments.

The downside of this is pointless hype lavished on pointless people. The upside, however, is that if you're a genuine musical talent, it could be argued that in the contemporary climate you have far more chance of being discovered – so long as you don't mind prostituting yourself. As I said, secrets only remain that way for a moment. Muse's time was coming.

It's often common for many rising bands to spark interest amongst the five major record companies (since reduced to four following a merger in October 2003) and their many subsidiaries, not because they're a cutting edge new force in rock 'n' roll or because they're sexy young men in tight trousers, but because a rival company is interested. Labels don't necessarily always sign bands because they *like* them, rather they just don't want their rivals to have them. Band X could bombard Label A with demo tapes for five years but might only get to be heard if the grapevine suggests Label B are interested, which is when Label A would enter the fray and happy but stupid Band X would have a bidding war on their hands, and suddenly think they're the bee's knees. In a trend-driven marketplace, the idea of a label not even being in discussions with a hot new band is the type of oversight that has young A&R men clearing their desks after six months.

This is exactly what happened to Muse, only without the bee's knees part. And it happened in Los Angeles, the city that best epitomizes both the cut-throat nature of the American rock industry and its generosity with a cheque book.

Following their triumphant CMJ performance, Muse were invited to fly out to LA around Thanksgiving 1998 at the expense of Columbia to showcase their wares for the label at a gig on Santa Monica pier. A forty minute drive (if you're lucky) from both the well-heeled music and movie industry haunts of Beverley Hills and West Hollywood and the more heavily starched business district of downtown LA, with its golden sands, eccentric street life and faded boardwalk glamour, Santa Monica feels like the end of America – the epitome of the promised land of California that drew so many settlers across the dustbowl in the mass migration of the twentieth century's formative years. The pier meanwhile goes one further. Symbolically speaking, it is a perfect launching pad for a career.

Worlds apart from the bustling, boxed-in and sub-zero streets of New York – although no less alluring – Santa Monica in December is a wonderful, rejuvenating place to be, particularly if you're used to ground-frost, ash-coloured sunsets at 4pm and the slow, weighted drag of a British winter in a seaside town.

Looking out at the shimmering sea with America behind them, a tangle of rollercoasters over to the right and nothing but space before them, Matt, Dom and Chris knew their time had come.

The intimate showcase went well, despite half-hearted attempts to black out the bright California sunshine with some makeshift drapes. Dennis Smith recalled one of the Columbia executives being moved to tears by the vocal performance. True to form, word spread quickly in LA.

"It looked as though we were about to sign to Columbia," remembered Matt. "We were packed and the taxi was waiting outside to take us to the airport. And then the other half of Maverick [ie. not Madonna] turned up. He had been to the showcase to see another band and thought we were already signed in the UK. When he found out we weren't and had no deal in America he came over to see us."

"Guy Oseary, the head of A&R and a partner in Maverick, rolled into our hotel and said, 'You guys ain't leaving town until you've showcased for us,'" recalls Dennis Smith. "We said, 'Fine', but they'd have to pick up the tab for us if we were staying on in LA [they did]. In the meantime, we were taken out to dinner by Rick Rubin and [producer] George Drakoulias, who were representing the whole Sony-Universal-Def Jam thing. That was fun. Rick Rubin picked us up at 2am in his Bentley straight from the studio where he was mixing the new Tom Petty album, and we all went wanging up to Sunset Boulevard for some late night food and some beers."

The following day, the band booked a rehearsal room and performed five or six songs to Guy Oseary, Dennis and Safta, the band's new LA attorney and a tanned, muscular man who accompanied Oseary but to whom they were never actually introduced – he later turned out to be British ex-pat and former Sex Pistol Steve Jones ("Chewing gum and looking most disinterested," recalls Dennis. "But he gradually warmed to us.") "After the second song I stopped them and said, 'You don't need to play any more,'" Oseary told *Billboard*. "It was extremely powerful and beautiful."[3]

Owned by Madonna and run as part of the vast Warners empire, Maverick was quick in establishing itself as a strong label with a growing stable of new acts, but pitched towards the mainstream, including the equine-sounding Alanis Morrissette and a particular favourite of Muse, stylish Sacramento metal five-piece the Deftones. They were also The Prodigy's US label and therefore central to that Essex band becoming only the seventh UK act [at that time] to enter the *Billboard* album charts at Number One, with their generation-defining album, *The Fat Of The Land*.

Talks with Maverick moved quickly, the band suitably impressed that, unlike the other labels currently courting them with lobster dinners and expensive wines, they were talking to the people who actually made the decisions. The LA big-wigs had no qualms about signing a band to whom the UK was ambivalent. "That's the least of my concerns," Oseary told *Billboard*. "I didn't know that and I don't care about it."

Seemingly the mythology of music moguls signing bands after hearing them for a mere five minutes are true. After playing 'Cave' and 'Muscle Museum' for Oseary, Muse had to persuade him to at least hear some of their other songs. He asked them to play 'Cave' and 'Muscle Museum' again, then told them he could do business with them.

Being thrust into the black heart of the LA industry in such a way was certainly enlightening for the three wide-eyed young men. "When we first signed to Maverick, our management didn't tell us what was going on," remembers Chris. "We thought we were going to play an acoustic session at the radio station so we went in there with our guitars. They had all this food laid out and the people from the radio station didn't say anything to us, they were just eating all the food. We were going, 'When are we going to play?' and they went, 'Ah, you're not playing', then some guy came over to say thanks for buying the pizzas. Maverick had rigged it up as if we had gone in there buying everyone their food! The problem is the industry is so tightly controlled you can't go in there unless you play the game; they need you to bow down and if you do that, then they'll let you [in]."[4]

Muse were 'let in' on December 23, 1998 when they received the greatest present they could have wished for – a recording contract with a label owned by the world's biggest pop star and funded by one of the largest music and film companies. The deal was for the US only.

"The great thing about Maverick is they've only got about fifteen acts and they've taken us as a priority," said Matt somewhat fortuitously the following year in *NME*. "They're not the sort of label who'd drop a band if their first album doesn't sell well. But we're not corporate at all. We're still independent."

Ironically, the relationship with Maverick was to prove an awkward one – but those headaches were yet to come. While Dennis stayed out on the west coast to take care of the business details, for the moment Muse flew back to the UK somewhat wealthier than when they set off. Next stop: mainland Europe. Then: the world.

5. INSIDE THE MUSCLE MUSEUM

FIVE FULL years after their first ever gig, things were finally happening. No false starts, no false promises, no fucking about – it was happening, it was real.

The sudden surge of interest within the industry spread to the local Devon press, aware at last that Muse were true contenders – not to win a local band competition or secure a support slot with a known band passing through the south-west, but to make it on a *grand* scale. The fact that Madonna's name was now associated with the band certainly helped, even though the band had never met the Queen of Pop (nor had she necessarily even heard them, but then no-one needed to know that...).

Reviewing a show at The Cavern, *The South Devon Herald Express* told of Muse's new record deal that signalled the beginning of a glittering career. "Matt's wearing a shiny top, which appropriately shines like gold," they wrote under the heading, 'Some star spangled Muse-ic', alongside a live shot by The Cavern's Dave Goodchild. "This boy has been a choirboy in the past, as he puts pre-ball-drop Aled Jones firmly in the shade with a vocal display that shatters drinkers' glasses at twenty paces. Muse know it's happening for them and so does everyone in The Cavern... This is the sound of a band waving goodbye. Muse are going places. Places far away. Let's hope they remember us."[1]

The 'Muscle Museum EP' was that next step on the journey. Released on January 11, 1999, in the final death throes of the second Millennium, it contained six tracks taken from the same Paul Reeve sessions that had spawned *Muse EP*, but was a stronger and more revealing collection of songs than their debut.

An exotic and aromatic haze of a song, 'Muscle Museum' was conceived by Matt during a month-long post-college sojourn on an Aegean island, the indigenous music filtering into the song by way of a haunting guitar riff that sounds Yiddish polka, Spanish flamenco and traditional Greek wedding *all at the same time*. Yet the song, with his big clunking power chord crescendos and dramatic wailing finale, was resolutely rock 'n' roll.

"I think that a lot of that traditional European music is really passionate," Matt later explained. "It has so much feel and flair to it, I've spent important times of my life in Spain and Greece, and various deep things have happened there – falling in love, stuff like that. So maybe that rubbed off somewhere."

"It's about the conflict between the body and the soul or mind. It's how sometimes one element of your being will not allow something to happen. For example, say your body wants to have sex with a girl but your mind reminds you that you have a girlfriend. It's about the conflict of not knowing what it is you want. Not just relationship-wise, it could relate to the band as well, about how there are still people who will knock you down even though you are down already."[2]

The making of 'Muscle Museum' also unveiled a new guitar technique, discovered accidentally. "I wanted to do this big epic guitar solo at the end of the chorus and as soon as I started doing the solo I missed a chord," explained Matt. "So I suddenly found myself singing the guitar solo instead. I ended up singing it into a Marshall amp and it sounded exactly like a guitar."[3]

The Banshee-like effect of Matt's distorted voice was used on a number of other songs and achieved during live performances through two microphones, one clean and one filthy-sounding. The song's intriguing title was lifted from the Oxford English Dictionary one day when Matt looked up the word 'muse' and noticed the two words either side made for a powerful and haunting image.

Second track 'Sober' was quite different, though no less gripping than the lead track. Capturing Bellamy at his enraptured harmonising best over a strident up-beat, it appears to be a song about whisky – or at least the metaphorical healing qualities of the drink after the betrayal of a loved one, name-dropping brands Wild Turkey, Abourler and Jameson along the way.

From its clunking, growling bass intro and evil cocktail lounge lizard *Pulp Fiction*-style swing, 'Uno' captured Muse at their most vitriolic. Symbolically, it certainly seemed to represent Muse moving away from their past and not lingering to see who wants to come along for the ride. They'd seen plenty of lost opportunities – this wasn't going to be another one.

Appropriately, 'Uno' would shortly be the band's major label debut.

As poignant and endearing as anything off Jeff Buckley's *Grace*, the angelic, candle-lit tones of 'Unintended' were written in the studio after Matt had a phone conversation with a girl he was involved with. "We called it 'Unintended' because it came out of nowhere, and I didn't mean it to happen," he said. "All of these feelings for this girl..." on the website *www.inmuseworld.net*.

The final two tracks were 'Instant Messenger', a song about the emerging phenomena of internet relationships, courtship down the wires of the world [later re-titled 'Pink Ego Box' for a B-side – although this first version didn't feature the *"You've got post..."* line at the beginning]; and a slightly different mix of the title-track, 'Muscle Museum #2' that had on it the added sound of rain and Matt's vocals sounding as if they were recorded from a distance.

If the first EP pushed Muse's name into the public domain, 'Muscle Museum' showed to anyone sussed enough to notice that this strangely enigmatic three-piece had the songs... *in abundance.*

Rave reviews weren't long coming. "Kicks off with what sounds like a bouzouki and winds itself up into a six-string strangler that has much in common with Radiohead's most recent output, despite the band's hackneyed 'we don't compare ourselves to anyone' stance," slavered fanzine *Robots And Electric Brains* of the title song in what may well be one of their very first ever reviews [for more on dreaded comparisons, see below]. The review also printed the band's old e-mail and PO Box address in Teignmouth.

The 'Muscle Museum EP' went straight in at Number Three in the *NME* Indie singles chart, behind Mercury Rev and Fatboy Slim – not bad for an unknown band on Dennis' label, who had yet to tour.

Nonetheless, reviews of the release had been relatively few and far between and the EP's success had been down to word-of-mouth more than anything. That changed when *NME* jumped on board in February with an 'On' new band piece by Mark Beaumont, who would go on to conduct a number of interviews with the band.

"We really got started on January 11," says Dennis. "We hired a van for them, got a tour manager, some local crew and the band got out on their first tour as a signed band. We also got an agent on board, who consequently booked them loads more dates and is still with the band today. I have a photograph somewhere of the band jumping into a white van outside the flat Dom and Matt were renting in the centre of Exeter, on the very first day of their first tour."

Don't mention the R word....
Alternative guitar music in 1999 was a game of two halves. In the red corner, a clutch of Korn/Slayer-inspired nu-metal bands each as subtle as a sledgehammer wake-up call, ranging from the good (Deftones, System Of A Down), the bad (Limp Bizkit) and the ugly (all of them, including the good ones, but especially Slipknot).

In the blue corner, a new generation of earnest songwriters, inspired by Radiohead, but most of whom were less interesting. While bands like Chester's Mansun went from Northern scallies to indie-glam boys to up-their-own-arse neo-prog rockers (complete with suitably ridiculous artwork) and back to obscurity in the space of three years, Travis were the first to emerge 'post-Radiohead', quickly watering down their sound for mass appeal to become a kind of woolly Wet Wet Wet. Old Muse muckers Coldplay suffered the indignity of being branded a 'post-Travis' band, but nevertheless were already on the cusp of greater levels of success than their Scots counterparts, and would soon supercede them – going on to Grammy-winning US-breaking mightiness.

Then the floodgates opened for a whole wave of sappy cardie-wearing nice boys like Starsailor and Turin Brakes to find favour. Somehow they were still being mentioned in the same sentence as those innovators Radiohead, yet in practice were nothing more than cosy, unchallenging sounds akin to early Seventies songwriters like James Taylor or Jackson Browne.

And in the middle of it all – actually, far away on another planet – were Muse, increasingly dismissed by many critics as a baby Radiohead, yet capable as rocking as hard as anyone.

Capable of rocking like *muthas* (note appropriate spelling). In fact, if forced to choose, Muse – who had grown up on Nirvana, Jimi Hendrix, Rage Against The Machine – would more than likely pledge their allegiance to their noisy American cousins.

Somewhat understandably though, the subject of Radiohead was hammered home in one particular *NME* interview: "If there was a 'National Sounding Like Radiohead Championship' they'd be on the expert judging panel alongside Radiohead and another band who sound exactly like Radiohead."

To deny the early comparison between the two bands – or more specifically between Matt Bellamy and Thom Yorke – would be foolish. Through constant musical evolution, by the late Nineties Radiohead were by far the biggest British guitar band in the world (under the age of forty, anyway); the one interesting act to whom a massive US following could be ascribed (aside from The Prodigy). Muse had grown up listening to them, worn their T-shirts, seen them play and Matt had taken obvious vocal inspiration from Yorke (as he did, equally, from Jeff Buckley); it wasn't as if they were being compared to Anal Cunt. Out-right denial in the future was going to be difficult. Setting a pattern in interviews that still continues to this day, Matt answered these obvious comparisons with both acknowledgement, resignation and vague dismissal. "We take our influence from a lot of American bands like Nirvana and, yeah, Radiohead at the time of *The Bends* were doing new things with guitar music that it's hard *not* to be influenced by," he contested. "If that's your opinion, fair enough. I just don't care." Chris told a local magazine shortly afterwards, "NME don't support little bands. They're too clever and sarcastic; we never know if a review is good or bad." Only a month later, they were getting more defensive when the R-word reared its head. "We're really not in the business of just peddling some lame pastiche," Matt spat in *Melody Maker*. "We're Muse, not Radiohead de-caf."[4]

*

Muse was now officially signed to Maverick – the thirty-odd page contracts had been hastily drawn up, looked at and signed within a mere three weeks of the Santa Monica show. Over the course of early 1999, Taste Media embarked upon securing a number of shrewd record deals, opting not to put all of the band's eggs in one basket (ie. one worldwide deal with one record label), but instead signing different deals in different countries. While the band and the team around them were hardly taking a DIY, anti-corporate stance (quite the opposite, in fact), they set it up in such a way that they retained creative control.

Many bands rely on one benevolent paymaster for all financial support and as a result are little more than subservient hooker to an uncaring pimp, who'll undoubtedly turn them out on the street when younger, cleaner, fresher meat comes along. And when the purse strings are pulled tight, it's the bands who often suffer most, finding themselves without that promised funding, or worse, a deal. This is the reality of the music business and if an eager young band and a wise old label have entered into an agreement, then no-one is to blame but the band themselves when it all goes pear-shaped; grand plans, goodwill and newly-forged working relationships can count for nothing when a label is haemorrhaging money.

Years of experience between them managing studio producers and working closely with bands on a day-to-basis had given Dennis Smith and Safta Jaffery countless valuable insights into the inner workings of the worldwide music business. Most importantly, they knew what *not* to do. Outside the US, Taste Media retained the rights and struck several separate licensing deals for the release of the band's forthcoming debut album. In France they signed with Naïve, in Germany, Switzerland, Austria and the Eastern European regions they signed with Motor/Universal. And for the UK, Ireland and Australasia they signed to Mushroom, a label who had been tracking the band's movements for some time. Remarkably, along with all the other big labels in the UK, Mushroom had already passed up on signing Muse once before.

Founded by former A&R man Korda Marshall in 1993 with $8000 of his own money, Mushroom had grown into a massive company in a short space of time with subsidiary labels including Perfecto, Ultimate, Infectious and Dilemma encompassing artist such as Garbage, Ash and future Muse remixer Paul Oakenfold. Coincidentally, Marshall had grown up in Cornwall and had known Dennis Smith before either had been involved in music. As a youth he used to get off the train at the station near Sawmills.

By the late Nineties, Mushroom was already turning over millions per year. In June 2003, Marshall was to sell Mushroom and all its artists – including Muse – on to major label East West for a deal worth a reported £15 million, with Marshall staying on as Managing Director of East West where his first signing was hair metal revisionists The Darkness.

For the band's part, this recent barrage of record biz interest was not about to erode their grasp on reality. "You have to realise what work there is involved," Matt explained of the band's initial struggle to get signed during an interview. "The people that really want to do this sort of thing, go ahead and do it. There's some that say they want it but don't really, they just want all the rewards, which is like wanting to win the lottery. The people that make it and do well are the people that realise what work there is involved. There's so much more to it than what it looks like. The reward for me, was that when I was 16, 17, I just wanted one day to play in front of 300 people who would just go mental and love it. That's all I wanted. And already we've achieved more than that…"[5]

"It was when they signed to Mushroom that things really escalated – deals everywhere around the world," remembers Mel Brown. "And it was a big deal for them because it was a while coming. You've got to remember they'd had years of complete disinterest, but when it happened, it happened *quickly*…"

Be careful what you wish for and all that…

*

Behind the scenes further plans were being hatched. As one of the very first to pick up on the Muse's potential, Work Hard's Nik Moore had, as agreed at 'In The City', been handling the band's publicity circa the 'Muscle Museum EP'.

"The first time I was involved was a show they did at the LA2 [latterly The Mean Fiddler]. They were on early, about 7pm," Nik remembers. "It was a case of them performing, out of the blue, a support to whoever happened to be on. There was about ten of us there. I remember getting a number of people interested in coming, including *Time Out*."

"Some bands need to tighten up but Muse had *songs*. 'Unintended' – the 'slow' one – was a massive favourite of mine, but they wouldn't play it live. When I asked them why, Matt said it was because they needed a keyboardist for it, but couldn't afford one. They were so tight live, as opposed to Coldplay who also had the songs but were shambolic live. Muse were the finished thing, a dream. They couldn't fail."

Moore worked with the band for a few months and did a sterling job, considering he was working with three anonymous unknowns from the back-of-beyond, whose major selling point was that he felt they were the finished deal, the most musically accomplished new band around.

And to most people, so were Radiohead. Convincing a media that needs a selling point, a story or an angle to distinguish a band from the scores of other future burger-flippers releasing records each week was not going to be an easy task – and the Radiohead problem was distracting. Since 'In The City', Nik had been working the band for free out of his Work Hard office in south London, but they wanted more.

"Dennis called me and said the band were playing in Tunbridge Wells that night and that I might want to come down and see them," he recalls. I said. 'Why would I want to do that?' It transpired that they wanted someone who could solely devote themselves to Muse. At the time I had Cay, another young band out of the same left-field stable, who I had got a lot of press for, whereas Muse hadn't had much. There was a rivalry between the bands and everyone was concerned, so I was told another press company was going to be at the gig."

Moore watched the show and went backstage afterwards where he told Matt, Dom and Chris that whoever they decided to go with, he loved their band and thought they had a big future and wished them the best of luck all the same. "And that was it," he says now. "I made the effort but they took it elsewhere. I was pretty put out."

Despite the best efforts of Nik Moore and Mel Brown, the band and management decided to go with Anton Brookes at respected independent company Bad Moon, primarily because he had handled publicity for Nirvana and was a close-friend and confidante of Kurt Cobain. Muse's connection, however tenuous, to one of their biggest influences was just too good to pass up on. Brookes was likeable, humble, had good relationships with the music press and a fan's appreciation of underground rock music; perfectly qualified then to spread the good word of Muse. Unfortunately, the working relationship was to be short-lived. Impatient to get more coverage as soon a possible, the band switched to Mel Brown at Impressive, their third publicist in six months. This is perhaps indicative of the band and entourage's impatience to climb to the top rather than any one person's shortcoming – they'd waited five years already, why wait longer?

*

Public Image
"You never listen to a word that I said," sang John Lydon on 'Public Image', his seething attack on pop culture's all surface/no substance obsession, written while freshly emancipated from those walking, talking, puking mannequins, the Sex Pistols. "You only seen me for the clothes that I wear/Or did the interest go so much deeper/It must have been the colour of my hair...."

These words could have been written for Muse, a band undergoing something of a non-identity crisis. Not within themselves, but from other people. If five years had been spent developing Muse's sound, five minutes had been spent on presentation. Like it or not, the image portrayed by the band – or rather their lack of an identifiable sense of style – was surely holding them back.

Even a non-image like Nirvana's deadbeat thrift-store threads – bought for convenience, cheapness and, well, because ratty jeans and flannel work shirts were what people wore where they came from – becomes an image when it's put in the context of the time. Muse didn't even have that going for them.

"Not long after I first met them, I saw them at a gig in London supporting Rialto and I remember thinking that they really needed to change their look," laughs Mel Brown. "I just thought they needed to up the ante with their clothes. They had everything else, but they didn't look good. And as much as I tried to suggest changes on that front, they wouldn't listen to anything I had to say as far as outfits went."

Early press shots saw Muse looking like a band struggling to find the best way to present themselves – they looked as if they'd been given £25 each to spend on any clothes they liked, so long as they were ill-fitting and bought from either Mr Byrite or Dorothy Perkins. The most used early promo picture shows the trio standing rigidly, wearing what appear to be colourful – well – *blouses*. They're squeezed tightly into the shot, arms by their sides, save for Matt who has one hand resting on the opposite arm as if he's just been told to look lively. At this point it was about the best rock star poses they could muster. The frontman also sports a short-lived wispy goatee and all are heavily made-up, looking more like the brickies-in-lippy in the more lumpen Seventies glam rock bands than the tense pre-millennial Bobby Dazzlers they were fast becoming. Not good.

If Muse were aiming for sexual ambiguity, then it clearly wasn't happening. In encapsulating the schizoid explosiveness of their live show, the picture undersold the band – not the fault of any photographer, after all they only had so much to work with. Bands who say it's only ever about the music generally look like shit. Rock 'n' roll is meant to be about flash and swagger, not looking like you've dressed to blend in with the high street masses. Muse's seemingly indifferent approach to style also did little to divert attention away from comparisons to that other band from Oxford.

"Getting press was difficult because the perception of the band was that they were just more Radiohead copycats," says Mel Brown. "We just had to ride it out. Muse are nowhere near as downbeat as Radiohead, they're a very loud, very *up* band. I think the main problem with [their early records was they] didn't reflect the power of them live. Right away it was obvious to me that they were an amazing live band, so my pitch to the section editors at the magazines was to just get as many people to see the band play, because I *knew* that all the live reviews would be brilliant."

It seemed to be working. *NME* followed up their new band piece in July 1999 with a live review of a Muse show at Exeter, reporting on the hysterical local following, a "classic Small Body Big Head singer with tubercular Tom Cruise looks", concluding Muse to be the sort of band "that both mainstream rock fans and tormented romantics will obsess over: ballroom-dancing punk poets with fire in their eyes and grit in their veins."

Influential French magazine *Les Inrockuptibles* also first noticed Muse in March 1999: "We have seen Muse and cannot decently keep a such secret – a violent and possessed trio, gifted with a superior singer."

Buoyed by the press interest, however tentative, the band nevertheless braced themselves for the constant accusation that they were nothing but a doppelganger of a certain five-piece band who had seized the late Nineties *zeitgeist*. (Dennis called such on-going comparisons "lazy journalism.")

"Seeing them [live] was when it clicked with everybody and then everything fell into place," says Mel Brown. "But it took a lot of leg-work to get there – calling all the freelancers to make sure they'd heard them, seen them, *anything* to convince them Muse weren't just a Radiohead rip-off."

*

Rocketman
Flushed with the advance money from Maverick for recording the debut album, Matt treated himself to a gift. Having previously spent spare money on guitars and equipment, this gift was something he had always dreamt of buying, but could never previously afford on a painter and decorator's wage: a Paramotor.

Propelled by a jet engine shaped like a large fan and steadied by a small parachute, when attached to your back a Paramotor allows you to fly through the air like some sort of lost extra from a Fifties sci-fi B-movie. It's the only device which allows you to fly from the ground upwards without the use of an actual vehicle or wind assistance. A snip at $6000.

"It's basically one of the best things I've ever experienced," Matt enthused to anyone who would listen. "It spins around, you take off, you fly and you feel like you're the next step up on the evolutionary ladder. I've been up to 3,000 feet in it but after that, things begin to go a bit blurry. You can go up to 10,000 feet if you've got enough oxygen."

A young man soaring up in space to gain a new perspective on mankind below? Make your own connections. At least the press finally had something else to ask about other than Radiohead and/or Teignmouth – only a madman or a great English eccentric thinks he can fly.

That Matt Bellamy. He must be proper mental.

*

Before anything else, there was an album to record. For Muse, nothing less would do than an album to announce their rival as the most exciting rock 'n' roll debutantes. With a set of sophisticated songs already so developed they'd shame many more established acts, half the work was already done. They were lucky. They were smart.

They were a bit of both.

The band decamped to London for a three-week period spent recording in the live room at RAK Studios in London, where the bulk of the songs were recorded with John Leckie. Leckie had heard of the band through Safta and had quickly become a fan, seeing them play in Devon and at that first New York show.

One of the most successful and respected producers in contemporary music, Leckie's career at the controls began in 1970 when he wrote a paper on electronic music which he gave to Abbey Road studios as an alternative CV. He was subsequently hired and worked as in-house engineer on the likes of solo records for each of The Beatles, Pink Floyd, Mott The Hoople and Badfinger until 1977. Then, in the Jubilee year, he left to work as a freelance producer, gaining invaluable experience working with the likes of Phil Spector and Mickie Most. His resume of early production work reads like a list of great innovative British bands of their time – XTC, Magazine, The Fall, Human League – but it was his work in 1988 on the self-titled debut album by a Manchester band called Stone Roses (released the following year) that he's still most famous for today. Though that may change in time if three young men from Devon have anything to do with it...

Following his work with the Roses, demand for Leckie in the Nineties has consistently been high – he went on to produce a stream of defining/influential records by The Verve, Ride, Elastica and, yes, in 1994, Radiohead's *The Bends*. He won a *Music Week* award for Best Producer in 1995, a *Q* Award for Best Producer in 1996 and a Brit Award in 1997 for Kula Shaker's *K*. In short, just the type of person any young band would like as a fan.

"We get on with John really well," said Matt. "He's a great guy who started coming to our gigs because he was a fan and he really liked the music we were playing. When it got to the point where it looked like we were going to get a record deal, he started saying that he'd like to do the album with us. There's no one I'd rather work with on a first record. He thinks... well, he said that we're the best guitar group he's ever worked with."

After the initial recordings in London, band and producer then moved back to Sawmills, which had recently updated their facilities with lots of new digital equipment, although Leckie preferred to work with traditional analogue tapes. With a clear idea of how the songs should be arranged and recorded in the studio, the band were given a co-production credit. Few brand new major label bands are trusted with such a hands-on approach in the making of that crucial first release – least of all with an experienced producer like Leckie. It's testament to the band and producer's vision that any ego conflicts were avoided; they worked quickly, economically and effectively. Of the nine songs released on Muse's first two EPs, seven were to make it on to their debut album in various versions. Some, like 'Muscle Museum', merely required the drums to be re-recorded, while the original Paul Reeve recording of 'Uno' remained untouched.

"When you're doing a track and it's not quite right and you keep doing it, the worse it gets," Chris told a college newspaper in 1999, explaining the band's own fastidiousness. "It's a bit like, *fuck it*. It can be quite draining. Sometimes it's best to leave it and come back later and try again. We're quite fussy like that.

We'll record a track then listen to it and if we don't say, 'Yeah this is it!' the first time, then you end up doing it again. One of us might go, 'Oh, I'm not sure about that bit' and the other two might think it's all alright, then listen to it the next day and all agree, 'Oh, it's shit.'

*

Support Band Syndrome
Aside from initially applying the final brushstrokes to their debut album – to be called *Showbiz* – the bulk of 1999 was to be spent on tour spreading the good gospel of Muse. They began first in the smoky bars and nowhere holes of Britain in early January and embarked on a touring schedule that, unbeknown to them, would stretch out over eighteen months of living out of a suitcase and never quite knowing what tomorrow would bring. The year hadn't started out with quite such a hectic string of dates, but as the band played more gigs to increasingly swelling crowds and anticipation of their debut album grew, events unfolded before them. Sometimes it's best not know where you're going to be every single day for the next twelve months.

They started the year's opening UK tour at the Princess Charlotte in Leicester and ended it with a show at London's University Of London Union (ULU) with emotive Swedish band Kent and passionate Scots rockers Annie Christian (a bill booked by a drama student perhaps?).

In March, Muse went back to the US to play the KCRW radio festival where they also recorded a seven-track acoustic set that would later show up in various bootlegged forms; while in April they recorded a day-time performance at The Astoria in London to an audience numbering a few record company people and a few fans who'd managed to get in for the live broadcast on a Japanese music TV show. Aside from Matt once spotting his face on telly during an Exeter-Arsenal football match, it was their first proper TV appearance.

If TV exposure had so far been non-existent, radio coverage for Muse had been scant to say the least – until Steve Lamacq, the DM'd doyen of the indie rock airwaves, had taken up their cause. If the 'Muse EP' piqued his interest, 'Muscle Museum' turned him into a fan and he began to air various tracks from it on his Radio 1 show *The Evening Session*.

"I didn't think they sounded much like Radiohead," says Lamacq. "They have their fragility, and obviously Matt has that same Thom Yorke thing of being an anti-star who still ultimately wants to be a pop star. What's really good about them is that they can really play. They're not one of these groups that are going to be held back just because they can't find that extra chord."[7]

Lamacq was so certain Muse had a future, he offered them the opening spot on his *Evening Session* Tour in May, opening for ass-kicking Californian punk quartet The Donnas and black-clad Brit punks 3 Colours Red. The tour was a five-date whistle stop dash round the country taking in Birmingham, Manchester, Sheffield and Portsmouth, and beginning in Cardiff on May 11.

Which is when I first encountered Muse.

Dispatched to review all three bands for *Kerrang!*, I travelled to Cardiff to see the opening night of the tour. 3 Colours Red's new single 'Beautiful Day' had recently entered the UK singles chart at Number 11, a triumph for that anthemic and photogenic punk-metal four-piece; The Donnas had garnered more press than record sales, but were getting better with each album – a band on the up. With plenty of plugs on Radio 1, the show was well intended. A solid four hundred or so handed their money over and turned up on the night.

But it was Muse who were the most interesting and the most complex band on the bill. Stripped of preconceptions, I was confronted by a band whose singer's furrowed brow seemed to cast a perpetual shadow across his face, as a lion's voice roared from a tiny, shaking frame. Sporting a quiff and over-sized maroon bowling shirts I remember thinking he looked a little like Michael J. Fox. A bit anonymous, but somehow still captivating. Christ, that voice. Angelic and satanic all at once. They were a band capable of exuding a general air of confidence from the stage outwards, of killing time until the world caught up with them so they could get on with the real business of being stars. The rhythm section was just plain brutal, without being heavy metal.

It was true. They *did* sound like a certain other band, but Thom Yorke never threw cocked-hip poses like *that*. I needed little convincing. *NME's* reviewer, also along on the same mini-press junket, was not sure, writing "Muse's moody, sleazy glower feels disappointingly anaemic when sandwiched between the stupid brilliance of The Donnas and the confrontational crunch of 3 Colours Red."

"That was our first proper tour in terms of supporting other bands – certainly the first tour that we had a bus," remembers Matt. "Up until that point, it had been transit vans. We'd only done those smaller tours around the release of the first EP, going to places like Hastings or Tunbridge Wells, but that felt like the first real tour."

More dates followed as Muse supported slightly bigger bands for albeit small but curious crowds. If they thought their career so far had been about paying their dues, the trio had seen nothing yet. This time though there was a sense of purpose to playing to such paltry audience numbers [even if they went down like a lead balloon – a rarity – it was at least in front of a crowd of paying music fans instead of the disinterested domino players in the pubs of the hinterlands of Devon]. Every night they got to play to the equivalent of The Cavern crowd and every night at least one or two people would leave a believer. True, they were still on the toilet circuit but it was to preface a far speedier ascension to bigger and better places than most bands could ever imagine.

"When a band first get known, it's by people who read magazines, people who are more interested in finding out stuff for themselves," Matt was to later tell me. "And they're often of the same age group as you. But when you start to play bigger venues to bigger audiences and you've been on television and in the living rooms of the nation, things start to broaden out and become more mainstream. Small, three hundred or so capacity clubs and bars – that's where the good times are. At big gigs you have a better sound and a different feeling onstage, but at the smaller places you can hang out more and have less responsibility than you would when you're playing an arena."

For now, such talk of arenas was all for the future. The good times continued to roll on through April and into May, where

Muse toured the UK with Britrock trio Feeder and Straw, just as their debut album was being prepared for release. If the live performance is the real reason for a band's existence, then singles and albums are what sustain them. To tour far and wide – to stay in hotels, to eat decent food – for prolonged periods, a band needs to sell records.

So, it was time to release some. This time, however, there would be more than 999 copies available.

6. NUMERO UNO

NOT UNWISELY, Muse chose to release 'Uno' as their first ever single, a song of crunching, juddering majesty and arguably the most effective and instant moment on their forthcoming debut album. The artwork was relatively straightforward – the band's name emblazoned over a blue-tinted photo of a crowd of anonymous upturned faces. Initial promo copies were sent out backed by 'Jimmy Kane', 'Forced In' and 'Agitated', although the latter only made it on to the two-track seven-inch single release (the band's first vinyl outing).

On its June 1999 release, 'Uno' garnered Muse their first real national coverage for an actual record release, including a small introductory piece by their new fan at *Kerrang!*, where I mentioned the band's stockpile of over eighty songs before enthusing, "Uno' burns with the raw rage of youth and is a tasty hors d'ouevre of meatier things to come." In the same magazine a couple of issues later, guest single reviewers Wayne Static and Johnny Santos from nu-metal bands Static-X and Spineshank (a genre of musicians in which Muse would later find a fair amount of favour) were impressed enough to give it a 4/5 score and debated whether to make it their favourite single of the week, Santos remarked that it reminded him of twang-tastic surf guitarist Dick Dale; Static added, "It's a very dynamic song... it's very Radiohead, but also reminds me of Violent Femmes, there's a lot of things going on there."

In the end, Muse narrowly missed out on 'Single Of The Week' to Red Hot Chili Peppers with their return-to-form comeback single 'Scar Tissue'. Unbeknown to Muse, the two bands would very soon be sharing stages.

For the release of 'Uno', *Melody Maker* interviewed the band for the first time, heralding them as a much-needed alternative to the redundant Britpop acts who Muse were often sharing stages with. "For us, the only two groups to have really meant anything in the Nineties have been Radiohead and Nirvana," explained Matt. "Radiohead around about when *The Bends* came out, though. There was a genuine vulnerability and sense of innovation about those two bands that set them apart. You got the impression that they were genuinely exploring themselves, rather than just their big brother's record collection. Britpop was just an exercise in imitation. 'Tonight, Matthew we are going to be The Small Faces!' Utterly pointless."[1]

The band promoted the debut single with a string of dates alongside raucous Dutch-English quartet Cay (aka Cool As You), another edgy guitar then band tipped for greatness. After one album for East West Records and a change in the band ranks, Cay would unfortunately split.

Q magazine was the first of the monthly music publications to recognise the brilliance of Muse, picking up on the smalltown frustration and bitterness that 'Uno' oozed from every stinking pore: "At last the West Country has produced something more convincing that Reef. Chronic overuse of the word 'nothing', plus crashing guitars and a pleasing Thom Yorke whine equals three 'look at what you could have won…' songs to shout at your ex. In a seaside town. In winter. In the rain."

On June 21, with virtually no daytime airplay, 'Uno' still managed to give Muse their first chart hit and for the first time suggested there was an audience out there for them.

Matt had sang, *"Could have been number one…"*

Was actually number 73.

*

Sarcasm aside, the chart placing of 'Uno', however brief, was nevertheless a genuine morale-booster, proof positive that hard work does pay off, that the men at the big record label were doing exactly as they said they would some nine months earlier when they'd proselytized while wining and dining the Devon trio.

This relative success of the debut single merely showed that many of the new fans garnered during the months on the road had reacted to what they already had seen and heard. Agreed, single sales might be in a seemingly terminal decline with little required to push a release into the charts, but even so…

Galvanised by the interest, Dennis Smith and Safta Jaffery set to work pushing the band even further. With financial support from their (many) labels, a booking agent on a mission and growing support in the music press, things finally began to fall into place. Part of that momentum came with the aforementioned switch from Bad Moon PR to Mel Brown's Impressive. "We sat for about forty-five minutes and got to know each other," recalls Mel. "And that was it. My first job for them was taking a journalist down to see them at Glastonbury."

*

The band were booked to perform at the grandaddy of the world's music festivals on the New Bands stage at 1pm on Friday, June 25, the first day of the festival, opening for the likes of David Gray, Built To Spill and short-lived press darlings Gay Dad.

Despite such an unholy daytime slot, it was becoming apparent that the groundwork of the first half of the year was beginning to pay off. Festivals are an ideal time to play to people who might otherwise not go and see a particular band. A good time to steal yourself a fanbase. As the most significant event in the south-west of England and almost as famous of Stonehenge itself, playing Glastonbury was a big deal to Muse, another significant step up the ladder.

"After a skin-tight fifty-minute set, the words 'storm' and 'went down a' sprang to mind," observed Q of the band's first major festival appearance. "It was twenty degrees inside the tent, it was 1.39pm in the afternoon, but people were still slam-dancing and crowd-surfing in a Brownian commotion. Yes, they do owe a debt to Thom Yorke but they've got enough of their own distinct energy and charisma to keep the plagiarism police at bay. 'They were reet good,' said one of our friends from the North. And for once, I am in complete agreement."

Exactly one month later, following more shows with Cay and an early slot at the well-liquored T In The Park festival, Muse were booked to play that other legendary festival, one that even their grandparents had heard of – Woodstock. Like Glastonbury, Woodstock was a cultural event, although things had changed drastically, irrevocably since the heavily-attended original weekend of peace, love and dodgy brown acid in 1969. Along with the moon landing and the assassination of JFK, Woodstock was one of the most significant events of the Sixties – culturally, musically, socially – representing as it did the tide turning in favour of counter-culture. When the idea was resurrected twenty-five years later and billed as an anniversary event, one glaring difference was immediately apparent: corporate America had bought into it.

Critics bemoaned the major label nature of the bands on the bill, the inflated food and drink prices ($12 a pizza, $4 a small bottle of water) and the appearance of cash machines on site – the sight of which in a muddy field is guaranteed to spoil any acid tripper's high. Even an appearance by master of ceremonies, Wavy Gravy, merely served to remind everyone that the cherished hippy ideal of the first Woodstock was a distant relic of the past. Cynics pointed out what they saw as a crass and commercialist approach and argued that to stage Woodstock *again* in 1999 seemed a totally redundant idea.

Yet the bill did offer a sufficiently varied line-up to cater for the sonic needs of those 225,000 people setting up camp to watch turns from the likes Aerosmith, Korn, Fatboy Slim, Counting Crowes, Rage Against The Machine and Willie Nelson. Another band low down on the bill was Muse.

Unfortunately, snipes about expensive pizzas were quickly superceded by far more sinister events. What started out as bit of supposedly harmless corporate revisionism developed into an incendiary expression of discontentment, as rock gave itself over to the jocks – that low-brow section of society who equate a gig with an anything-goes wrestling bout. This was the short attention span, consumer-age offspring bouncing back to bite the hand that fed, clothed and Pepsi Max-ed them out. The Ritalin generation rattling to the strains of lame rap-rock. The tension had been bubbling under on the opening day but things turned ugly on day two when Limp Bizkit took to the stage in front of a highly-charged Saturday crowd awaiting performances from Rage Against The Machine and Metallica.

As Fred Durst's set progressed, bottles began to be thrown and garbage set alight. Then, as *MTV* reported: "Some of the fans set their sights on temporary structures on the field in front of the east stage. Fans first climbed and then tore apart an already inoperable misting tent [for cooling/calming down punters] throwing its metal framework into the air. Next, fans went after a production tower in the middle of the field, tearing apart the plywood wall that surrounded its base. Fans then hurled the slabs of wood throughout the crowd, with one eventually making its way to the stage, where Limp Bizkit frontman Fred Durst mounted it like a surfboard and rode it out over the audience..."

MTV crews were evacuated from the site amid fears for their safety (retribution for foisting Paula Abdul and MC Hammer on the world, perhaps) as small factions of the crowd went on the rampage. The discord did not subside once Limp Bizkit left the stage, although by the time Rage played the crowd had cooled, but the damage had been done.

In the aftermath, a number of disturbing assault and rape cases emerged. Peace and love? More like hate and war. Where once the youth of America took Woodstock as an opportunity to dance naked, get off their heads and get political, now it seemed they wanted to grope girls and break shit. The entire weekend was little more than a jock rock gathering – another significant cultural event, but for all the wrong reasons. The mindless nihilism seemed to have even overshadowed the accusations of excessive corporate exploitation.

By the close of the weekend there had been one death, three weddings (like wow, man!), thirty-eight arrests (with more to follow), *three thousand* injuries, five trailers destroyed in arson attacks and a lot of exposed breasts, at a total cost of $38 million. Welcome to rock 'n' roll, the Nineties way.

"It was badly laid out in my opinion, the stages were two miles apart and there was just no atmosphere like you get at Glastonbury," said Matt the following week. "I think the riots started because people were getting treated like cattle. We played much earlier than Limp Bizkit but trouble was already brewing while we were onstage. People were chanting, banging drums and stuff and it looked like a protest of some kind. We thought: what is this? From a distance it looked like some sort of party, then maybe a football crowd. Then we saw the whole riot going off. But then people *were* being charged $5 for a can of coke..."

By the time the riot was in full swing, Muse had vacated the site.

Three days later, the band travelled south to play their first proper headline show in New York, at Brownies, a small club on Avenue A. Although it was the first time paying customers could see the band in Manhattan, the club was packed full with industry people, including an entire table reserved for MTV staff seduced by the Radiohead comparisons surrounding this new British band. The guest list ran for pages...

Armed with a guitar pedal set-up that looked more like a plane's cockpit, Muse played a very loud forty-minute, encore-free set that highlighted the greatest strengths of the forthcoming debut album – 'Uno', 'Cave', 'Muscle Museum' – to a front row comprising of older, balding men who nodded along approvingly and two fans from home clutching a banner that said 'Teignmouth' (prompting one American to enquire as to whether that was a country). Despite the industry hype, the crowd was nevertheless a sparse one. More US dates followed on the west coast – Rich's in San Francisco, The Roxy in LA, a Warners convention, then, the following day, a festival in Germany. Muse were beginning to accrue enough collective airmiles to get them to Mars.

Back in London four days later at a show at The Borderline Muse were introduced to a band called... Muse. They were from the USA and owned the rights to the band name. Somewhat ironically they had been described in a Stateside review as "sounding like Brett Anderson, fey and nasally and, of course, very British – the sad thing is, these guys are from Miami..." Luckily for the Teignmouth trio, their American counterparts were on the verge of splitting and therefore were able to free up the name for them to buy up the worldwide performance rights.

After more live dates at the end of the month, Muse was back in London to attend the annual *Kerrang!* awards as a guest of publicist Mel Brown and Mushroom Records. The *Kerrang!* Awards has a reputation for being the most – the only? – hedonistic, unhinged and truly destructive music ceremony. It was a chance to catch up with their two touring mates to date Cay and 3 Colours Red (both of whom won awards that night), but mainly an excuse to drink shameless amounts of free alcohol, mingle with and/or fight other bands and/or journalists and schmooze legends of metal such as Iron Maiden, Judas Priest, Motorhead and Marilyn Manson.

I still have a tape of an aborted attempt at an interview with a worse-for-wear Matt at the post-Awards show party. "It's a very rock 'n' roll night," said Matt puffing on a free cigar and drunk on beer and vodka. "Good fun."

"Who's the most famous person you've met tonight?", I enquired.

"That guy over there," said Matt, nodding towards Roy Wood, frontman with Seventies glam band Wizzard. "I dunno who he is though..."

The conversation disintegrated soon afterwards.

A few days later, Muse arrived at the August Bank Holiday Reading festival by way of Cologne, Germany, where they played three shows including a televised street party. Their debut at rock's favourite festival was marred slightly when Chris arrived late for their slot on the Carling Premier stage. "Blame British rail!" Matt bellowed from the stage, at the start of a hastily-shortened set that saw them go straight for the pumping jugular of the indie heartland. The band had first been to the festival as paying punters in 1995, so appreciated the significance of playing a festival that had staged all their favourite bands in front of thousands of young music fans, all potentially ripe for conversion.

Muse's lives were becoming increasingly absurd. One week they were playing such salubrious towns as Hanley, Newport and Middlesborough, the next they were back in New York for a one-off show. One day a crappy, cramped tour bus, the next sipping complimentary wine 30,000 feet above the Atlantic. Other such lifestyle adjustments were occurring. Matt and Dom were enjoying the first taste of success by embracing it all head-on, torn between their girlfriends back home and the many new-found temptations that were trying to seduce them. All three band members may have still been occupying their same abodes back in Exeter and Teignmouth, but metaphorically speaking as time went on two-thirds of the band were showing signs of shaking off their past with increased ease.

In September, Chris became a father when girlfriend Kelly gave birth to a son, Alfie. "The name was my girlfriend's idea," he told *Select* magazine, deep into an arduous Japanese promotional tour seven months later. " I never wanted him to become Alfie. It sounded like the name of a dealer in school – 'Oi, Alfie, can you score mate? But as soon as his head popped out it was like, 'He's definitely an Alfie!' When you see something like that, you realise you don't have to constantly question everything in life all the time. Matt would disagree with me though…"

The lascivious, sneering 'Cave' was the next single to be released, a pure slab of sonic groove-rock. It was backed by an alternative remix of 'Cave' and 'Twin', one of the first songs they had ever written and notably their first ever release when it had originally appeared as 'Balloonatic' on a 1997 metal/hardcore compilation on Lockjaw Records called *Helping You Back To Work Volume 1*.

The second CD of the two-part release featured 'Host', complete with trademark distorted vocals. It was more typical teen angst, another Teignmouth escape song, the irony being, at twenty-one years old, Muse were far from wasting their youth. Finally there was 'Coma', taken from the 'Muse EP'.

Promotional copies were sent out in stark, clear-cut Perspex and plastic packaging. *Tres chic*. Guest-reviewing the singles that week in *Kerrang!* was another brawny American, Pete Steele, sardonic frontman with Brooklyn doom-meisters Type O Negative, who made 'Cave' Single Of The Week: "That chick has a great voice," he boomed. "It's a guy? Whoah, there goes my erection. I apologise to the singer – I guess I'll not be asking him out on a date now but he sounds real good. When I listen to his voice I feel like someone is tickling my penis with a feather."

The penis-tickling tune entered at number 53 in the national singles chart.

7. THERE'S NO BIZ LIKE SHOWBIZ...

"Showbiz' is nothing to do with me saying I'm going to break down the walls of the record industry. I just love showbiz. I love that glitz and glamour and Broadway cool. It can be sad as well, but it's always there, just untouchable..."[1]
Matt Bellamy

TRULY GREAT albums need a strong opener. 'Sunburn' was that song. With its dream-like fluttering piano-and-drum introduction, the listener is lulled into a false sense of security before being jolted awake with a surge of electricity. The song had more or less been written entirely in the studio with John Leckie.

"I remember Matt playing around with a line on the piano and then on the guitar," explained Dom. "Then the rest of us joined in. It's a song we still love playing live and always will. It's about moving into a new world, mentally or physically, realising it's not what you thought it was going to be. It was written at a time of change for us – we'd gone from painting and decorating and signing on, to flying first class to LA!"

"I was listening to a DJ Shadow track which had this really edgy keyboard, and I really liked it," added Matt. "I wanted to create something a bit like that. I used this old microphone which the army used in tanks. If you strap it around your neck it picks up the vibrations from the throat. It's pretty scary – it sounds a bit like *The Exorcist*."

Lyrically the song could be seen as a reaction to the record label indifference shown towards Muse between 1994 and 1998 and their early financial struggles in an industry that happily burns cash on excessive expense accounts so long as appearances are maintained.

"It's just a funny thing to sing when you're doings those things," said Matt of the many corporate showcases the band had found themselves playing in the run-up to getting signed. "It's just a joke."

The second album track we already knew about, 'Muscle Museum'. Arguably the band's best known work to date, when placed back to back with 'Sunburn' it made for a compelling double-whammy opener. Five years on since its initial release and the song still seems to offer something new with each repeat listening. 'Fillip' was a say hello, wave goodbye-type song, an account of a period of transition, the end of a relationship, a life in flux. Rather than being a pun and/or foreign spelling on the boy's name, in this instance 'Fillip' meant something that adds stimulation or enjoyment.

Next up was a bluesy lullaby torch song, 'Falling Down' clearly heavily influenced by Jeff Buckley's 'Grace'. This provided the album with its first poignant, downbeat moment – the merest suggestion that Matt Bellamy could easily croon as effectively as he could howl like a polecat on heat; that Nina Simone was as powerful as Nirvana, that slow and sombre doesn't necessarily equate to slushy and sentimental. Dripping with emotion and tinged with bitterness, Matt recalled a place where when he sang, no-one listened. No prizes for guessing where he was singing about.

The chart-molesting 'Cave' had turned many a new head towards Muse, while the album's title track 'Showbiz' was in turn moody, malevolent, malignant, and ultimately beautiful. ("A song is about how we all have an inside personality that we sort of hide from the outside," explained Matt.)

Building up from a restrained and atmospheric introduction, 'Showbiz' grew first into a mid-tempo song, then into a display of vocal histrionics over an urgent and electrifying musical display. Matt's lyrics were at their blackest, telling of unseen forces pushing us into self-destruction. At over five minutes long, it felt like something approaching an epic. The following velvet-lined spurned lover's lament of 'Unintended' provided a stark contrast, and was an emotive mid-point intermission in the album before the serrated nuclear tango of 'Uno' kicked in, its force ten Richter Scale bass line threatening to split the earth in two. Again, 'Sober' – the whisky song – had already seen the light of day, but only to the select few who had picked up the Dangerous Records release of the 'Muscle Museum EP' back in January of that year. Both 'Escape' and 'Overdue' meanwhile – arguably two of the weaker tracks – were lifted from the obscurity of 'EP1' and sent out into the world.

Sardonically-named album closer 'Hate This And I'll Love You' – a title that pre-empted the love-hate reaction that Muse always seem to provoke – perpetuated the accomplished neo-classical feel with which *Showbiz* began, adding just enough aggression in the closing stages to remind us that we've just witnessed the birth of a very fine rock band. It also brings us full circle, offering, for want of a better word, closure.

Just short of fifty minutes after beginning, *Showbiz* had run the musical gamut from roaring grunge to atmospheric baroque, from space-age ballads to rare Eastern rhythms. And all the while it guided the listener through an emotional minefield which, despite pitfalls and traumas, left a sense of satisfaction gained through the survival of such a terse reminder that life is a series of high and lows, neither of which ever last.

It's hard to see how Muse could have made a better debut.

Sample CDs containing 'Cave', 'Muscle Museum', 'Unintended', 'Showbiz' and 'Falling Down' were sent out *en masse* to the press, followed shortly afterwards by promotional copies of the whole album. In the deluge of freebies that fall through the letterboxes of those lucky enough to get sent them, the *Showbiz* promo certainly stood out. Encased between two opaque pieces of perspex and held together by a simple plastic nut and bolt through the middle (some copies even came with a free spanner! Muse fans on e-Bay will pay about £50 for it), the presentation of the album was sparse, enigmatic, serious, expensive and futuristic. Indeed, for a while Muse may well have been known as "that band with the fancy packaging."

The actual finished artwork for the album was just plain strange. Ill-advised. Tacky, even. If first impressions are everything and an album's packaging is designed to sell the sounds inside, then the cover woefully undersold *Showbiz*. A painting of a faceless woman in a white cocktail dress walking barefoot on the scorched earth of a faraway planet, the blue-black colouring neatly suggested a sense of detachment and foreboding. Yet to these eyes, it also recalled the sort of artwork that Eighties prog-rock revivalists like Marillion used or, worse still, the doodlings of a sci-fi-obsessed A-level art student, rather the work of an exciting, new, distinctly *modern* band. Coupled with the title *Showbiz*, it seemed misleading. Matt was directly involved with the cover, so it certainly wasn't the case of an uninformed marketing man rustling up an image in five minutes. More a rare Muse moment of questionable taste...

The final three months of 1999 was the same as the first three – an ever-increasing blur of activity in the build-up to the album's release. Unusually, Muse's debut was first released in France on September 7, followed by Germany a week later, the US on September 28 and finally the UK and Australasia on October 4 – almost five years to the day since the band's first show at The Cavern Club in Exeter. Other albums released on the same day in the UK included S Club 7's self-titled debut, Pet Shop Boys' *Night Life*, Gay Dad's *Leisurenoise* and the Alice In Chains box-set, *Music Bank*; in the same week, Black Sabbath were inducted into the Rock 'n' Roll Hall Of Fame. This staggered release schedule shows Muse's distinctly pan-international plan of action. It's perhaps no surprise that the country treated to the record first – France – is still the biggest supporter of Muse to this day – UK included.

Reviews for *Showbiz* were mixed, varying from scathing to the indifferent to the gushing (and the just plain lazy – contrary to some opinion, Muse were not the new Nirvana). Overall though the reaction was a positive one.

"*Showbiz* is no maverick masterstroke, but it is passionate and loud and also unexpectedly gentle," concluded *Rolling Stone*. "A great first shot from three guys barely old enough to drink on their U.S. tour," said early supporters *CMJ*. "It's hard not to become thoroughly intoxicated by its dusky beauty."

In a somewhat undecided appraisal, the now-defunct *Melody Maker* opted for sarcasm while clumsily missing the irony of the title, declaring "Muse know nothing at all about showbusiness – a more honest title might be '*Painful Alienation In A Seaside Town Where No One Recognises The Genuis Of Kurt Cobain But Me*'" before begrudgingly admitting the band *do* know about showmanship and that "history might yet prove them right."

Good or bad, Muse weren't being ignored (the greatest indignity a band could suffer). Although the UK media were still resoundingly undecided, at least they were now regular features in the music press. Their debut album went into the UK chart at Number 69 and a loftier Number 8 in the independent chart. More important were its slow-burning sales figures – *Showbiz* would go on to sell over 300,000 copies worldwide in the course of the next nine months – in the process laying the foundations for one of British music's truly international fanbases.

There were signs that Muse was a band that was really about to succeed. This was not the new gadgets that their advance afforded them; nor the rapidly changing wardrobe of clothes; and not even the growing column inches they'd accrued throughout the year in London's weekly music press. No, it was the sudden increased interest from local paper *The South Devon Herald Express*. After years of anonymity it took successful national and international tours before the band had finally come to the attention of the *Herald Express*. Although a story of October 6, 1999, acknowledged the band's growing potential – not least because they were rumoured to have signed to Maverick for a reported £1 million – far from being hailed as conquering local heroes, remarkably the first local scoop was of a negative bent.

It was in a Muse publicity biog – a band's story distilled down to the simplest terms for lazy journalists – that the peculiar chastisement of the prodigal sons began. In charting the trio's origins Teignmouth was described as a typical seaside town – *"barely breathing in summer, stone cold dead in the winter. If you're aged between 13 and 18, a living hell the whole year round."* The biog also referred to a big drugs problem in the sleepy seaside town.

When word filtered back to the local council and its leader, Mayor Vince Fusco, the Teignmouth old set were not happy with the portrayal of their town. Not least coming from three lads whom he happened to know on good authority came from decent homes.

"To say I am upset and disappointed is an understatement," commented Mayor Fusco at the time, photographed dumping the band's newly released debut *Showbiz* CD into a garbage can. "Teignmouth is no worse than anywhere else as far as drugs are concerned, and a darn sight better than many.

To start being rude about their hometown, where a lot of

people helped them with their music shows a lot of ingratitude now they are about to break into the big time. There are far, far worse places to grow up in and a lot of places do not have anything like our facilities. It does not do our image much good when this sort of tripe gets dished out in the national media."

Yet despite his vocal complaints, the mayor couldn't help but mask a strong sense of civic pride. At least Teignmouth was being talked about. "But for all that I still wish the lads well and hope they reach the top!"

Local councillor and youth worker Mary Kennedy was less knee-jerk in her reaction, recognising the universality of that teenage desire to see the world, to escape, whilst inadvertently denigrating the place that spawned them in the first place.

"We shouldn't over-react, a lot of young people go through a phase of being unhappy at where they live," she said. "It is all part of the growing up process and is quite normal. But it is surprising how many want to come back after they have travelled around a bit and seen other parts of the country. I think we should listen to what young people say about the town and try to make it more appealing for them, rather than constantly criticising them as some senior figures in Teignmouth do."

"The mayor was pissed off that we said Teignmouth was dull and it's no wonder kids turn to drugs," Chris later told *Kerrang*! "There was an article in the paper a week later saying how we'd apologised. He wanted to shake our hands. It was a weird situation."

"It got blown out of proportion," said Matt. "One quote from a magazine article and the local newspaper treats it as a sound-bite and judges your whole personality on it."

"A lot of people probably had a laugh at it really," reckons Dom. "I mean, it *is* dead in the winter. All you've got is the local pubs where you get the same old men who sit in the same chair night after night, repeating the same conversations."

"There were gigs to do," remembers Matt, "but when you'd do them, they'd say, 'don't ever come back' because it wasn't really a venue. I understand, if I was in a pub, sitting there, having a pint, *happy*, and then some kids come on whinging about life..."[2]

NME added fuel to the fire when a visiting writer branded the resort "a black-hearted realm of eternal torment, decay and despair." One Teignmouth resident by the name of 'Brody The Windowlicker' wrote into the paper's letters page protesting that "I'll admit the town's hardly buzzing with entertainment but there are tennis courts, parks and in the summer it has the nicest beach and sparkling sea on the English Riviera." The response was appropriately patronizing: "Up here in Big Town, we call that 'humour'. Either keep up, or fuck off."

Muse were spared the stocks, although the irony of a band who had been howling into a void for a full five years now suddenly getting recognition on their own doorstep was not lost on the band. Ultimately though it *was* their home town, it was where their families lived and, despite the off-hands comments to journalists keen to pitch the band as bitter outsiders reacting against their environment, they *liked* the place and were quick to make amends. After all, if the mad circus ended tomorrow, they'd be back in Teignmouth eating a healthy portion of humble pie regardless of what they had actually said about the place.

"The comments were taken out of context, no offence was meant," Matt told the *Herald Express* by way of that aforementioned apology in a convoluted story with the strapline: "Sorry Teignmouth! The up and coming Devon rock group who caused a furore by apparently slagging off their home town, now claim it was all exaggerated."

Anyone who thinks it's just the tabloid newspapers of Wapping and the salacious rock press who go digging for a story, think again – a local paper is every bit as ruthless as the international in its hunt for a story. The band further made amends when Dom praised the former head of music at Teignmouth Community College, Jill Bird, for her encouragement of the band, while humbly – and truthfully – playing down the story of their newly-acquired seven-figure record contract. Matt was quoted as "complaining" that "it was a lot less than that, but the trouble now is every time I go back to Teignmouth people keep asking me for money because they suddenly think I'm wealthy!"

Eight days later, under the headline "True talent will shine", the same newspaper was editorialising on the recent resurgence of small town bands making good on a grand scale, namechecking Stereophonics from Cwmaman in the south Wales valleys and Catatonia and Radiohead from, er, Cardiff and Oxford respectively. Aside from mentioning the £1 million record deal that Muse had denied in the same pages the previous week the piece concluded that Muse's impact was proof positive that hard-work and talent were all that was needed for young people to achieve their goals – "especially if other temptations, many of them illegal and dangerous, so often dangled before you, can be resisted in preference for something that will bring lasting value and fulfilment."

At long last Muse had gained recognition and acceptance in Teignmouth – and Teignmouth had acknowledged that drugs exist. Safe in this knowledge, Muse embarked on their most important shows to date.

*

Muse's roadwork was relentless. Their rapidly balding tyres took them to different towns every day, drinking after shows in local bars and clubs, sleeping, then driving to the next place. The six months that followed the release of *Showbiz* would see Muse do close to a hundred gigs across Europe. But first came another trek round Britain.

October saw a support slot with Skunk Anansie that took in established mid-sized venues such as the Town And Country in Leeds and Nottingham's Rock City.

With the album out there, Muse were no longer finding themselves playing to crowds waiting patiently or otherwise for the evening's star attractions, instead noticing pockets of fans there purely to see *them*. It was not just at gigs that all the signs of a sizeable groundswell of support were evolving. Late 1999 was when the first Muse fanzines and websites were started in honour of the band. As the shows progressed, Muse began to drop new songs such as 'Feeling Good, 'Plug In Baby, 'Darkshines' and 'Screenager' into their set, their first post-*Showbiz* material.

Primed from these shows, Muse headed to Germany and

France for gigs with wonky alt-rockers Pavement. It was a slightly strange pairing, but Muse had been big fans of Stephen Malkmus's skewed songs since the Rocket Baby Dolls days, so were more than happy to oblige.

If Muse were pleasantly surprised by the instant reaction to the album in the UK, then nothing prepared them for the reception they were afforded in France, where *Showbiz* was selling five times as quickly as in the band's home country. They played Lille, Nantes, Toulouse and La Cigale in Paris with Pavement, plus the massive Bercy venue in Paris, this time with the Red Hot Chili Peppers.

"The French tour has been a bit of a shock, a very nice shock, especially the gigs in Paris," Matt wrote in a message from the road to long-standing website www.microcuts.net. "We did an instore at a Virgin Megastore I think, and it was so packed they had to stop letting people in, and there were hundreds more outside trying to get in. We also did a gig on TV from the MCM café and it was the same – about five hundred inside and five hundred outside trying to get in. The gig was fucking crazy, people falling all over the stage..."

Playing a handful of shows with the Chili Peppers provided Muse with the perfect opportunity to perform to massive crowds in virgin territories while picking up a few tips from the old funk masters.

"They picked up a hell of a lot from touring with such a big band, it made them men as it were, rather than boys," says Mel Brown. "It knocked them into shape – I mean, they were touring with some of their heroes! From early on they had a very good booking agent. From a publicist's point of view, they had some shit tours – shows with bands like [insipid American pseudo-spiritual-types] Live and Creed – because they just weren't that pressworthy, but they picked up fans. They built it up in the very best way."

If Muse were indeed becoming press-worthy, it was for one major reason: their live shows. Sure, the album was an impressive enough calling card, a fine introduction to the world of Muse, but it was on stage under the glare of the spotlight that they came alive, that they truly distanced themselves from the many other tempestuous souls wrestling with their guitars and proclaiming the end of the world was nigh. For the first time they were learning to adapt and enjoy their touring schedule, a way of life that can be not only mentally and physically exhausting, but achingly *boring* too. For every half hour of performance, there's another twenty-three spent hanging around in hotel lobbies, sterile dressing rooms or holed-up behind tinted windows, cruising along the Autobahn in the womb-like comfort of a tour bus.

"When we started touring the UK supporting other bands, although we liked them, it felt a bit like a school trip," reflected Matt. "Bands would do the gig, go to the hotel, go to bed, then do the same thing the next day. I went along with that way of doing it, but I just felt disconnected."

The dates with the Chili Peppers opened up new realms of possibilities for Muse. With the album finally out, suddenly they were playing large, well-equipped arenas to crowds respectful enough to listen to an unknown band who the headliners spoke approvingly of. They were eating and drinking well, staying in nice hotels, tasting the type of life they suspected existed, but had not yet experienced. Yes, they were first on and, commercially-speaking, far from reaching fruition even back home, but glimpses into the Californian party boys' dressing room was enough to suggest it was all theirs for the taking.

"The Chilis had parties every night for themselves and the people who worked for them. I thought 'This is what it's all about'. We made more of an effort to be much more interactive by getting people from the gig back, people from the crew, having a party, going out to bars, getting to see the towns you're in. Because that's what touring is about – experiencing the world, *really* experiencing these things. Some bands see it as a job. I never want to be like that."[3]

Between a show at the Patinoire Arena in Bordeaux with the Chili Peppers and one at Exeter Lemon Grove six days later, 'Muscle Museum' was given a deserved full re-release. This author's particular favourite, the song was given a big push by the band's various labels.

Not one but two videos were made to plug the single. The first captured the essence and energy (and splendid facial gurning, no less) of Muse live through footage shot at various European dates throughout the year and suitable for broadcast on the pop programmes if necessary; the second was a more cinematic clip made in LA for the MTV-led American market and directed by Joseph Kahn who had previously worked with Korn, Faith No More and Janet Jackson.

Shot in a dilapidated high school gym in downtown Los Angeles, the concept for this second video features a surreal mix of disturbing imagery that owes some debt to David Lynch's' dark journey into psychological hinterlands, *Blue Velvet*. Sifting through treatments (short synopses) concerning torture, hospitals and similar such things, even the band found some of the proposed ideas a little too weird or too suggestive for their tastes.

"They were some really perverted ideas," Matt told *MTV*. "One involved an eight-year-old boy walking around with a syringe with milk in it, squirting it in people's faces. I thought that was pretty dark, so it got a big no. I think directors just read the title 'Muscle Museum' and think it's supposed to be this twisted, dark Marilyn Manson thing. But I liked some of the weird suggestions too – the one I wanted to go with starts with us drinking out of petrol pumps..."

Filling the various formats for each Muse single release can't have been an easy task. The hectic touring schedule allowed for little time to constantly write and record B-sides, while also thinking about album number two. 'Muscle Museum' was backed with 'Do We Need This' and a live acoustic recording of the lead track on CD1 and 'Pink Ego Box' (aka 'Instant Messenger' off the original 'Muscle Museum EP') and 'Con-science', which began as a simple four-note piano song and ended in a splendidly chaotic montage of noises. The seven-inch was backed by 'Minimum', a song aired at most of that summer's festivals.

On the strength of its lead track alone, 'Muscle Museum' was C-listed on Radio 1, therefore guaranteeing a minimum number of plays per week. It reached Number 43 in the charts – the band's best placing to date and three places higher than the then much more successful Bush, a band Muse was to support around Europe in two month's time – although in a time when singles sales had been in steady decline, this was nothing to open the champagne about just yet. It would have been a massive success for a three-piece local group, but perhaps was not so fantastic for a hotly-tipped band with a bagful of record deals and the patronage of Madonna. Success in music is a relative thing.

"I don't care, it's just numbers," said Matt about the single's chart position. "I don't really follow the charts. I think it would be better to stay out of it. Sometimes you can cut yourself off from your original people and just get fat. I think, as a single, it's typical of where we are now. The reason I wanted to put it out is that it's one of the newer songs on the album [oddly not strictly true – it had been released already]. It's the way I see us moving."

By the end of 1999, Muse had enjoyed their first full year as major label recording artists – a 'proper' band who, despite years of preparation, had still been thrown in at the deep end. Nevertheless, they were already swimming with style and grace. The list of achievements was impressive: successful tours in the UK and Europe, the release of a critically-acclaimed debut album, the endorsement of Madonna and a growing legion of fans, including people like ex-Nirvana drummer and Foo Fighters frontman Dave Grohl, who talked about them with an almost embarrassing degree of reverence at any given opportunity during interviews. In their end of year poll, *Melody Maker* readers voted Muse second in the 'Best New Band' category, just missing out to the more established Travis. In *NME* they went one better topping the same category, beating the likes of Britney Spears, Eminem and, ahem, Gay Dad along the way. Little over a year on from those important showcases in Manchester and Manhattan, the plan was coming together nicely.

When I caught up with Muse again they were supporting US arena rockers Live at the cavernous Brixton Academy in December, as that enormously eventful year drew to a close. They were certainly a changed band – undoubtedly for the better. The road miles and the need to *project* in the large venues had honed them into a taut, fraught and overwhelming live act, but one unafraid to slow things down mid-set with their more downbeat piano moments (a definite risk for little known support bands). In the following seven nights, they went on to play club shows in Holland, Denmark, Belgium, Sweden and Norway.

"With a rhythm section carved from granite and howling, shadowy figure of a frontman," I wrote for a *Kerrang!* review, "Muse's move to bigger stages within twelve months of the release of their debut is admirable. Tackling balls-out rock with the deft touch of neo-classicists, they tweak out grandiose mini-operas from the ether, pummelled with stock-piled riffs of pure thunder – senses engorged, hair on end, wired to the gills..."

Perhaps most significantly, their music had affirmed the trio as appropriate soundtrackers of the historic passing of one millennium and the birth of another. The world was fretting unduly over computer bugs, internet viruses, power cuts, natural disasters and Judgement Day-style religious reckonings (a paranoia soon to be replaced by the unseen terrorist threat following the events of September 11, 2001); here was a form of high-tensile music built on frenetic highs and emotional lows, driven by its own sense of urgency, confusion, volume, aggression and celebration, capable of evoking devotion across the globe. This felt exactly like what the world's airwaves needed.

To celebrate the much-hyped Millennium Eve, the band went their separate ways: Matt headed to Iceland for a week's break (where he particularly enjoyed the fireworks displays: "They were amazing, much better than in England,"); Dom went skiing and Chris kicked back at home in humble Devon.

"New Year's Eve went down the pan for me after the Millennium. It was crap wasn't it?," Chris laughed. "Because my daughter's birthday is New Year's Eve I'm confined to Teignmouth for the rest of my life. You can't really leave town on her birthday, can you? Mainly though, I realised when you go out in Teignmouth it's still the same people sat in the same seats in the same bars – only this time they're wearing fucking Superman outfits or something."

A decade that had exploded with the underground cacophony of Nirvana, witnessed rock music crawl out of the gutter and into the arms of the mainstream and subsequently fragmented Kaleidoscope-like into a thousand sounds, each crossing themselves at various junctures – a musical cross pollination of metal, punk, Britpop, hardcore, alt-rock, dance, rap, trip-hop and jungle – had come to an end.

The Nineties were over.

The century was gone.

The Second Millennium was no more.

With the world turning unsteadily on its axis, all thoughts turned to the future.

8. ON THE ROAD AND UP THE RIVER

"It's a new dawn, it's a new day,
It's a new life for me…"
Lyrics from 'Feeling Good' by Bricusse/Newley

SAME SHIT, different millennium.

The reward for Muse's workload in 1999 was a growing legion of followers and a full two weeks off. This rare fortnight's rest was barely enough time to reflect on their achievements, let alone re-acclimatize to the snail's pace of Teignmouth and how little anything changes. Before the post-touring bends kicked in, their suitcases were packed and the operation was ready to roll again. With Muse's many labels making the band priority in their respective countries, on January 6, 2000, Matt, Dom and Chris flew to Europe's sin city – Amsterdam – where they played to a sweaty and enthusiastic Paradiso crowd blitzed on the local skunk weed; they then made an overnight drive to France, where the album was still sitting pretty in the charts, for six shows. On the last day of the month, they were back in London for an *NME* show with Irish buzzsaw punks Ash (also part of Korda Marshall's stable).

"That period was a real turning point for the band live," remembers Mel Brown. "The day it all turned around, when you could see real change, when they found that extra *something*, was The Astoria show. Matt started performing in the way you see in latter shows – something that just wasn't there in the early days. By this point they'd played with the Chili Peppers, they'd played with the Foo Fighters [on the same bill at the Paris Bercy] and it was really beginning to show…"

In combining intimate club gigs with arena shows with ready-made crowds, Muse's agent was cramming in as much of the live experience as possible. February saw Muse covering the middle ground in Germany as back-up to Bush, playing such halls as the Offenbacher Stadthalle, the Grosse Freiheit 36 in Hamburg and the Haus Auensee in Leipzig, then blitzing Switzerland and Austria before swinging through Germany again, where they were picking up increasing amounts of radio airplay.

When Muse arrived in Austria to play the Orpheum Theatre Graz on February 4 and Libro Music Hall in Vienna on February 5, it was during a particularly tense time. Jeorg Haider's Neo-Nazi Freedom party was making substantial political gains and there was growing unrest on the streets. The band were beginning to feel the effects of four weeks straight playing similar-looking venues and seeing little of the cities they visited (despite their best intentions); the schedule was simply too tight for sight-seeing. Vienna was something of a lost weekend for Matt, who disappeared with some people he had met when drunk, only later to find out they were possibly Austrian Nazis. It wasn't unusual for the singer to slope off to his hotel room to enjoy a bottle of fine red wine by himself, but this time he wasn't seen for a couple of days.

"That was funny," remembers Mel Brown. "Matt's a slippery character in that he likes to do his own thing. He's sociable, but sometimes he likes to do his own thing. He's naturally inquisitive."

"I was hanging around with people I didn't know, Matt sheepishly explained afterwards. "I didn't sleep for forty-eight hours." The gig they played was a mess of nerves and frustration. Matt ended the performance by smashing up his guitar and slamming a mike stand into a bouncer who – incredibly – had been caught dozing. Smashing guitars has long been a part of rock 'n' roll since The Who's Pete Townsend first jammed his head stock into a Marshall amp in a pique of galvanized energy, and had long since passed into cliché for a band. This time though, like Nirvana's Kurt Cobain before him, Matt's act of wilful destruction seemed to come from a genuine place of tightly-wound frustration and disillusionment brought on by increased pressure and an endless schedule, the first sign of a crack in the otherwise increasingly slick sheen of a Muse live performance. "I just lost it," he explained. "Dom said that I looked possessed."

The same week, 'Sunburn' was released as a single in the UK. The first CD featured 'Ashamed' and a live version of 'Sunburn' recorded – appropriately enough – at the Libro Music Hall in Vienna three months earlier, while CD2 was backed by the storming 'Yes Please', a song that saw Matt heavily replicating the breathless moan of the Deftones' Chino Moreno very closely. The final song was a live cut of 'Uno' recorded for London's alternative radio station XFM at the capital's Sound Republic.

A clear vinyl seven-inch single was released with an acoustic version of 'Sunburn' that was recorded at a radio show in the States as a B-side. A month later a three-track promo-only twelve-inch surfaced featuring three remixes of 'Sunburn': the shitty 'Timo Maas Sunstroke Remix', the 'Breakz Again Remix' and the 'Steven McCreery Remix'

The aforementioned shows with the Red Hot Chili Peppers had clearly endeared Muse to the Californian quartet and from this rapport they got their biggest break yet, a US tour support with two of the biggest bands in rock. Not only the Chili's but the Foo Fighters too. *On the same bill.* As mentioned, they'd done it once before at the Bercy in Paris, but this time they were on the two other bands' home turf, playing not to the cynically-minded New York/LA elite but to America's rock heartland, where musical nourishment was drip-fed straight from MTV and their regionalised state-wide radio stations.

After a half-decade of below-par recordings, the Red Hot Chili Peppers errant guitarist John Frusciante had kicked a heavy drug habit and returned to the fold the previous year. Subsequently, their new album, *Californication*, saw a rejuvenated band back on form and very much in favour. The tour was a summer-long trek taking in most of the major sports arenas, hangars and air-conditioned, popcorn-scented cowsheds that Uncle Sam had to offer.

A month into it, ever-ebullient Foo Fighters frontman Dave Grohl described the trek as "beautiful, the best thing that's ever happened. I don't think the Chili Peppers actually like touring. They do three weeks on and then take ten days off, so that's why it takes five months to do the whole of America."[1]

For Muse, this momentous tour began March 22 at the Double Door in Chicago and ended fourteen dates later at the UTC Arena in Chattanooga, Illinois. They were only playing a small portion of the tour, but a significant one, reaching between ten and twenty thousand musically malnourished potential fans each night – as many as they could hope to enrapture on an *entire* UK tour.

"Meeting Dave Grohl was a bit of a moment," said Matt. "It wasn't just meeting him, it was him, like, jumping on Chris's back and going 'Yeeeh, man! How's it going?!?' But it changes your perspective of bands like Nirvana. Seeing Dave Grohl on a daily basis demystifies your perception of someone you grew up listening to."

"They went over really well, great," says Grohl. "We did [that] one show before with them in Paris with the Chili Peppers. When I heard they were on this tour, I thought they might be kind of over people's heads. Americans are raised on convenience and Muse aren't something that's easy to understand, but they went over really well. The audiences were blown away by Matt's vocals and his guitar playing."[2]

Support bands suffer at the best of times. US arena crowds make life even more arduous. These large gatherings in huge venues usually comprise people who only check out big bands on rare occasions and have little interest in watching the opening act when they could be out in the car park slamming Buds and huffing on nitrous oxide – or, worse, parking the SUV while the kids stock up on popcorn. Bad enough then for an American-born support act, but some unheard-of weirdo skinny-ass English noisenik boys?

"A lot of the venues were seated and it was a very controlled atmosphere," explained Matt. "There were aisles through the middle with security guards being heavy-handed with the fans if they dared move from their seats. They had signs up that said, 'No Moshing'. But the thing with Middle America is the people are very warm to you... especially if you have the right colour skin."[3]

Muse fared well though in front of this conservative middle-American rock crowd and gained invaluable experience in preparing them for headlining such cavernous places in years to come. Each night their set was short, early and as direct as possible. In Grohl's home state of Virginia, Muse watched on as their show turned into a free-for-all when the crowd started ripping up the ice hockey rink's floor during their set. The Foo's couldn't play until things calmed down. In the end, Grohl brought his mother, a former teacher, onstage to quell the potential riot.

"Because we were on the Bible Belt leg of the tour, we also got into a lot of religious debates," said Matt. "I had a lot of people trying to indoctrinate me into Christianity. This one guy wrote a ten page letter to me about how I was trying to fill the hole in my life with music, when really I should turn to Jesus."

In Dayton, Ohio the boys also got to do some socialising with their new tour buddies. "We all went out [the Chili's, Foo Fighters and Muse] looking for a good time," Matt remembered. "We ended up walking past this karaoke bar and they happened to be playing a Foo Fighters song, so Dave Grohl ran in and pushed the guy out of the way and said, 'This is how it's done!' And the whole place went mental."

The party continued through to an after-hours lock-in that lasted till early the next morning, the three bands drinking heavily and singing old rock anthems with the pissed locals who included a few off-duty policemen. At some point during proceedings, MTV turned up and started filming.

Another feature of this memorable tour was that other staple of the big-league rock star's world: the groupie. Hanging out with two of America's most famous bands rubbed off on Muse, rendering them automatically desirable.

"They say things like, 'Can I come back to your bus?' or [adopts American accent], 'D'you wanna come and smoke some pot with us?'" said Matt after the tour. "That's the most times we've been approached by groupies, in the US. After each of the Chili Peppers shows, there would be thirty or forty girls just waiting to be plucked for them. It was weird."[4] Just twelve months earlier, Muse were playing to a hundred people in a pub in England.

After the final show with the two Nineties rock titans in Chattanooga, Illinois, Muse flew south to Atlanta, Georgia where they were to play with Stereophonics, a fellow Brit band also often dismissed as small-town outsiders even back home. On this occasion, they had little time to get to know each other. Far from becoming kindred spirits, their paths were to cross again a year later in a farcical and publicly played-out difference of opinions.

*

Muse were feeling the effects of being on the road more or less solidly for a full year – yet they were still facing a packed itinerary that stretched on for the next *eight months*. On May 3, *NME* ran a news story under the headline, 'Muse: Reaching Burnout' in which their frontman reflected on the band's punishing schedule down a crackly phone-line from the States.

"Some record companies get bands to fall into that trap of touring all the time – it makes for bad music in the long run," he explained. "I think at most you can get away with doing two albums before you need to get some more life experience, take a break and learn, so that you can then reinvent yourself."

He then went on to tantalise readers by mentioning the new songs that were arising out of improvisations each night during their shows with the Red Hot Chili Peppers and Foo Fighters. "We've been calling it 'alien funk'," he said proudly. "It sounds like a cross between Michael Jackson and Nirvana."

All talk of alien-funk aside, Muse, of course, were doing just fine, albeit feeling a little frayed around the edges. There was no actual mention of exhaustion or fatigue and the 'burnout' news story somewhat paradoxically concluded with details of new single 'Unintended' (released June 5), as well as their forthcoming European tour and a just-confirmed headline slot on the second stage at the Reading festival. Go figure. Perhaps it was a quiet week for news.

That week I saw the band back in London supporting another big arena (well, in America at least) rock band, Bush. Muse were middle on the bill between Belgium's Soulwax and the headliners, who were touting their regurgitated grunge on the home turf they were named after, Shepherd's Bush. It was one of a handful of gigs that Muse would play supporting Gavin Rossdale and Co. across Europe.

"What delighted me about seeing Muse night after night was finding out that they were twice as good live as they were on record," enthused Rossdale. "And I think that by the time they get to make their next record, they'll be able to capture all the energy of the live show in the studio. And it helps that they're really nice individuals. Touring is bad enough without having to hang around with a bunch of dicks. It can be hard for support bands but they're such capable musicians, I don't think they could ever do a bad set."

The gig was part of MTV's annual 'Five Night Stand' set of shows filmed for broadcast. I remember thinking that the plush extravagance of The Empire Theatre, with its multi-tiered balcony lay-out and original old-time flip-up, worn velvet seats were perfectly suited to the baroque splendour of Muse who, only a year on from their show in Cardiff on *The Evening Session* dates, were now clearly a far deeper and darker proposition. It was the first time I became aware Muse were a ROCK band: "Matt's whole body electrified and contorting whenever he steps away from the mike, his guitar, swirling, hammered, abused... sound crystallising into an orchestra of metallic chaos – joy and despair battling it out to the death."

"I'm caring less about how I look onstage these days," said Matt. "One thing I'm getting into is prolonging the ending of a show, staying onstage longer than we're welcome. I'm starting to have private moments playing in public, playing with the strobe lights, lying on the floor until I get really comfy. One night, on the tour, I ended up on the floor with these smashed speaker cabinets around me, got really comfy and just lay there for about fifteen minutes. The tour manager had to come on and ask me whether I was asleep or not! That's my aim – to fall asleep onstage at the end of a gig. Smash everything then huddle down and appreciate the peace."(5)

The band were due to play a similar German equivalent of the MTV shows, only for it to be cancelled at the eleventh hour. Deep in road mode, the band reacted by smashing everything they could get their hands on in the dressing room – to the tune of £3000. "We were fucking ready for that gig," Matt said afterwards. "The energy was there! So when it was pulled we were fucking gutted. The level of negativity which set in at that point was immense, almost as if that was it, the end of the fucking band."

If the band *was* close to burn out, well...tough shit. A summer touring schedule stretched ahead that even a fit and healthy Pope would find a little excessive. The US dates with the Chili

Peppers had led straight into a short club tour on the east coast (New York, Washington, Atlanta etc), before the band had flown back to play two dates in Ireland with a flagging Elastica and string of shows with literary-minded Scots rockers Idlewild throughout France and Germany. Already another month had passed and only two days later Muse embarked on yet more British dates, this time with three rising British guitar bands, old *In The City* rivals Coldplay, plus My Vitriol and Twist. The trek had kicked off at Portsmouth Pyramids and culminated in two sold-out nights at The Astoria in the heart of London's West End in the first week of June.

"When they booked the first night at The Astoria I was trying to get them to cancel," Matt spluttered at the time. "I was thinking, 'Will we fill it? Not a fucking chance!' Seriously. I don't want people to think we are bigger than we are. So selling out two nights there is something of a shock."

The band's worries were unwarranted. "They don't just sparkle, they shine like a thousand midsummer sun beams," wrote Ian Fortnam in *Kerrang!*, of the first of the two shows. "It's the rather more reserved and mannered material that will ultimately earn Matt Bellamy his inevitable Caribbean tax haven; 'Sunburn' is a full-blown knicker-stripper, a sultry, seductive serenade worthy of an excessively oily Bryan Ferry on heat, while 'Uno' tangos like Rudolph Valentino on industrial-strength Viagra. Hell, even the pathetically trembling 'Unintended' sounds heroic when presented in the context of a full-tilt live performance."

On June 5, Mushroom/Taste Media decided to release another single in the shape of the lush, angelic 'Unintended', the song that most effectively revealed Muse's soft underbelly. Coupled with the meandering minimalist instrumental 'Nishe' and a live acoustic recording album track 'Hate This & I'll Love You' on the B-side (from a session at Oui FM in Paris), it made for their mellowest release yet. The second CD featured 'Recess' and an acoustic working of 'Falling Down', plus the 'Unintended' video.

A further two-track cassette and a clear vinyl seven-inch single were also released, both containing 'Unintended' and 'Sober' (live). Perhaps unnecessarily stretched out over four different formats, the band were testing the loyalty of their fans and their willingness to part with cash for any new variation of old or recycled material.

The video was confusing. If there was a concept, it was a little unclear. It essentially showed the band in a room, melting into other people and poncing about in what might be a castle.

"Whenever we come up with an idea, it just never comes out the way we'd expected it to," Matt said. "I don't get the video. Making videos is something we're not very good at. At all. We're shit at it, actually. Really shit. It's the one thing about this band that is bollocks. Our video-making abilities, it's embarrassing. Embarrassing."

"I wish we could make videos like Aphex Twin. But we just can't. I definitely want to take some time to make at least one good one on the next album. Something that's interesting, something that isn't just bollocks."

"The 'Unintended' video was trying to do something that just fitted with the pace of the music," added Dom. "But, you know… nothing happens, does it?"

The single reached Number 20 in the charts. It was their first time in the upper half of the Top Forty. Proof that if you build it, people will come. Or rather, if you sell it, people will buy….

Four days after the pivotal London shows, things *really* got going when Muse travelled to Rock Am Ring in Germany to play the first of forty European festival dates. Since the late Eighties, the festival circuit had grown in strength, particularly when larger American and British bands had leant weight and kudos to such events. By now, there were enough large established outdoor shows to keep any band busy for two months solid so long as they had the backing to fund the pan-international jaunt. Bands such as The Prodigy and Foo Fighters had certainly reaped the rewards of playing a different country every day to large crowds of drunk-and-sunburnt and/or drunk-and-soaking wet Euro-nutters, taking unknown territories in one fell swoop and moving onto the next big field with a power supply.

In typical Muse style, nothing was going to be so simple for them. On the flight out to Germany from London City Airport in late June, the engine of the Lear jet the band was travelling in was engulfed in flames during take-off. Fortunately no-one was hurt as the plane was vacated on a grassy area next to the runway – another casualty in the band's quest for greatness.

A typical run for Muse would begin when they left Rock Am Ring on Thursday to play Holland's Pinkpop on Friday. Sunday would take in a turn at The Heineken Jammin' Festival in Italy, followed by an overnight flight to play Israel on Monday. If it's Wednesday then they must be back in Torquay to play a local thank-you show for a thousand hardcore fans (complete with glowing review in the *South Devon Herald Express*), before a slot at the week-end at Glastonbury, then from the beastly mud and *oomska* of Somerset to France the following day, then Switzerland and Norway, back to France, on to Scotland for the *Braveheart*-esque T In The Park crowd, then Greece... Portugal... Austria...

On and on, fuelled only by backstage festival catering, service station snacks, beer and raw adrenaline... senses distorted, nerves frayed... the journey relentlessly guiding them further and further away from reality... up the river like Brando's General Kurtz... the question was, who was pulling the strings?... and when would they make it stop?

Not any time soon. When the mind and body are flagging from fatigue and an alter ego rises from the subconscious to absolve all sense of responsibility, there's really only one thing to do: go East towards the rising sun. Head for Japan.

*

Many British bands claim to be big in Japan, but it's rarely true. One club show in Tokyo does not a fan base make. Yet even though overseas releases only count for 5% of all record sales within Japan, it is often the first country to pick up on the cream of British music in much the same way fans of alternative music in Britain often pick up on little known American bands like The Strokes and first turn them into true stars outside of their own country.

Japan then is an increasingly vital port of call for any rising band with one eye on the first flourish of homegrown success, the other on the fire escape that leads to bigger, better things. Increasingly, the more ambitious of bands – or those with a strong financial backing – make it their business to sign deals and go to Japan as soon as possible, often finding fervent followings and fan-clubs upon their arrival. With Japan having adopted – or co-opted – so much of Western culture as its own, it's up to the rock bands to offer something different. Maybe it's the flash and swagger and sense of occasion that comes when a band from a land far away rolls into town, or the fact that, by comparison to the staid politeness and air of repressive Japanese society, Western bands are more socially subversive and outwardly sexy. Whatever the reason, the fact is cities such as Tokyo and Osaka have been traditionally kind to British rock bands. In particular, acts like Suede, Manic Street Preachers and Placebo – interestingly, three bands who all flirted with Geisha-like androgyny, and whose respective *oeuvre* combined fragility and vulnerability with confidence and hyperbole – all built strong followings in the land of the rising sun from very early on in their careers.

Muse loved Japan instantly – and the love was reciprocated. The neon glitz of Tokyo, the energy, the futuristic infra-structure all appealed to Muse's lustful, worldly sensibilities. Reciprocally, their emotive musical crescendos that transcended language boundaries and lack of inhibitions appealed to Japanese teenagers. Japan also gave the band their first stalkers.

"It's hard to say why exactly, but they seemed to inspire the most obsessive of fans," says Mel Brown. "There's just something about them as people. When we went to Japan there were groupies hanging around. In the hotels, *everywhere*."

Girls took to appearing in their hotel lobby, peeping round corners and giggling when the band acknowledged them, always keeping a respectful distance. Just quietly observing these boys they'd seen on MTV and in the imported British music magazines.

"I was in a lift with two girls and when they realised who I was they fell to their knees," said Matt. ""They weren't offering anything – if you know what I mean – but it was very strange. Fascinating as well."[7]

Little wonder then, that Japan welcomed Muse – with their

charming English ways, all-round rock pomposity and willingness to return the love offered to them by their new fans in the East – with open arms.

Back in the rather more grey urbanity of the UK, at the start of August Muse played an intimate seven-song set at The Barfly in Camden Town, for broadcast on Channel 4 alongside Coldplay and Badly Drawn Boy. The previous four weeks had entailed a gruelling schlep around the European festival circuits, taking in places like the Festival des Eurockéennes de Belfort, France where they were received as nothing short of rock gods, the Doctor Music Festival north of Barcelona, near the Spain-France border, and The Rockwave in Athens, Greece. Aside from the public airing of Matt's new cobalt blue hair colour, the band encored at the Barfly with an interesting new song called 'Plug In Baby'.

After the show, Matt went drinking with a couple of new female friends and got hammered, later vaguely recollecting standing on some scales and playing air guitar while everyone laughed at his weight, then crawling in the road and waking up at eight in the morning, one hour before a flight to Germany. He made it to Heathrow – but only just. The next couple of hours were spent puking through his fingers as the plane followed the curve of the earth, a shifting mountain range of clouds below offering scant comfort to the mother of all hangovers.

Luckily the band had ten days off. Unluckily they returned for a humiliating last minute public appearance (these things can't really be classed as gigs) at Radio One's One Big Sunday event at Chantry Park in Ipswich.

"Wow! That was fucked," wrote Matt the following day on fan website www.microcuts.net. "What a farce. We turned up only to be told we had to mime, so we said 'No', then they said that Mansun and JJ72 were miming, so we had to. I said, 'At least let me do the vocals live' and they said 'OK' but when we went onstage there was no vocal monitor, and it was so sudden we didn't even have our instruments, so Dom ended up on some stranger's bass whilst Chris decided to batter [MOR Scot rockers] Texas' drums. I had no guitar at all! And to top it off, when I battered one of their mikes, they cut off the backing track and then started it again. It couldn't have been more comical and disastrous, so we said 'Fuck that' and left before we were supposed to play another song..."[8]

Later in August, the Reading festival more than compensated for this East Anglian debacle. Placed at a far more lofty end of the bill than the previous year's debut, the gig was a plateau of sorts. Increasingly, Muse were beginning to feel that their live show was now a grand, bombastic and musically refined spectacle on a par with any band who had previously trod the renowned festival's rickety boards.

Muse's headlining slot on the Radio One Evening stage on the Friday night coincided with an appearance on the main stage by the increasingly pedestrian Oasis, defenders of the button-down Britpop old guard. Singer Liam Gallagher, lairy and inanimate, had long since become a self-parody, while brother Noel delicately strummed his guitar like a man fearful of leaving so much as a scratch on his six-stringed mistress.

By stark contrast, playing to a tent packed with fans who had patiently endured Shed Seven (with whom Oasis had once toured), Muse were the very antithesis of the Gallaghers' musical conservatism and too-cool monkey swagger. Oasis pretended they didn't give a fuck yet they clearly did, otherwise they would have dropped their brash guard and *evolved* as a band since their remarkable 1994 debut. In performance, Muse truly didn't give a fuck how they looked and therefore pushed the boundaries, unafraid of ridicule or physical injury in their sonic abandonment. Their Reading performance screamed "Look at us!" In a lull between songs, Liam could be heard crooning from the main stage and Muse's crowd started up a chant of "Fuck off Oasis! Fuck off Oasis!", Dom joining in with a jaunty drumbeat.

It was a symbolic victory.

Those singles kept coming. Adopting a do-or-die approach, the record label was relentless in their promotion of the band. A second re-release of 'Muscle Museum' was to be the sixth – sixth! – release off *Showbiz*. Muse were playing the game and the game was playing them; a mutually beneficial relationship, although those of the opinion that band and label were milking their debut for every single penny they could…well, they might just have been right. At least Muse never made any worthy claims of conducting a career that adhered to any underground ethics or ideals – theirs was a masterplan with a world vision and the financial assistance of some of the biggest paymasters in the business. Any accusations of selling out – an over-peddled notion generally defined by how easily an artist will compromise their art in the pursuit of fame or financial gain – were pointless. In fact, Muse had stuck to their plan rigidly, watching as the pieces fell into place. Besides, they were one of many hundreds of bands suckling on the corporate teat, although with far greater success than most of their contemporaries.

'Muscle Museum' was again released over three formats, the first backed by a charged live version of 'Agitated' recorded at the London Astoria in June; a 'Sunstroke' remix of 'Sunburn' by dance-floor filling producer/DJ Timo Mass (which lead to Muse getting a play on Pete Tong's *Essential Mix* dance radio show!); and the live video. CD2 featured the same US mix of the single, a perfunctory 'Saint US' mix of 'Sober' and a storming reworking of 'Muscle Museum' by sometime touring friends Belgian group Soulwax who, under the guise of musical mash-up duo Too Many DJ's, successfully married a synthetic electroclash beat with that strangest of guitar sounds. The vinyl version featured a live recording of 'Escape' from the Paris Bercy show. The cover photos for the single, although capturing the band in full flight were far from spectacular and the lack of artwork, inside each sleeve – they were left blank – was disappointing, doing little to dispel the notion that singles had become nothing more than loss-making marketing exercises to sell albums.

On its third release, 'Muscle Museum' reached Number 25 in the charts – eighteen places higher than the previous year's effort. Ironically, while the song that boasted of playing in every toilet nestled in the charts, Muse were living it up overseas like three little Lord Fauntleroy's.

But, Christ, it really was time to record some new songs…

In October, the relentless tour took Muse back to Japan for one show each in Nagoya, Fukuoka, Osaka and The Blitz club in Tokyo. Used to teasing the crowds into a heightened frenzy, they were still trying to adjust to the innate politeness of their Japanese audiences where polite clapping was not the sign of a bad gig, but the norm.

"We were a bit afraid about being too over-the-top on stage at those shows," said Matt. "At one point I made some move with my guitar and the whole crowd seemed to gasp as though shocked. It was like there was canned applause between songs."

Nevertheless, the band were primed to work Japan, realising the potential of building a solid fanbase there. In between playing the four shows and discovering the joys of being asked absurd questions in interviews via translators (example: "Are you trying to start a religious cult?") – something they would soon have to do a lot more of – they did find time to visit ancient temples in Nagoya and Osaka.

"There were lots of girls and young women with their faces painted white, praying and chanting," Matt later explained suggestively. "It was just about the hottest thing I've ever seen."

It was just during these shows that Muse unveiled two further new songs, 'Bliss' and 'Futurism'. Somewhere, their record label executives were no doubt gleefully rubbing their hands together...

Mind-Bending Drugs And Bent Coppers

For anyone with a hunger for experience, Japan has many new delights. New Millennium Muse were happy to embrace everything, including the freely available magic mushrooms. "They're legal, which is very, very cool. Japan is very surreal and very intense anyway and doing mushrooms intensifies the whole Japanese experience."

The band's collective stance on drugs was relatively clear-cut – organic, natural drugs like weed and mushrooms were in, anything man-made was generally out. Their openness about this stance was refreshing too.

"Am I a toker?," pondered Matt in an *NME* drug debate. "I don't know. I used to rape nature by battery farming copious amounts in my loft when I was fourteen. It paid well but once

I fell off a cliff, stoned."

As if often the way, by the time the band were enjoying their first real signs of success, drugs only played a small part in their life. They simply didn't have *time* to get off their blooters on three-day narcotics benders. Back in the flat in Exeter four years earlier Matt, for one, had seen the effects drugs could have when they become the sole focus of your existence, rather than the recreational perception-changing enjoyable experience they should be. Their experiences among London's music industry merely conformed this belief.

"Drugs in regular social situations I find unpleasant to be around," said Matt. "I see a lot of it when I go out in London. In the music industry, and especially in the TV world, things like cocaine are just everywhere, and I find it a bit weird. The problem with drugs is they force you to become happy at a moment in time which is not naturally a happy moment... people take cocaine to force themselves to be in a good mood. So when you do other things that really should put you in a good mood you don't get the natural high from it that you're used to. Then it's catch 22, because when you go back to a social situation, you remember, 'Well, last time it was a bit better, wasn't it?'"[9]

But they did like to indulge. Sometimes it's rude not too.

"I remember one time in Japan [Muse] asked me whether they could borrow two hundred pounds so they could make a detour to a market," says Mel Brown. "It turned out to be a drugs market that sold every drug imaginable. But they were only interested in mushrooms. They forced me to have some, so I had half a mushroom which unsurprisingly didn't do anything for me. But it didn't do anything for them either – they'd been ripped off. With my money!"

Hallucinogenic Psilocybin mushrooms had always been the preferred drug of choice. Mushrooms eaten dried out or boiled down and drunk as a tea can have a profound effect, intensifying sound, movement and colour, inducing giggling fits and, sometimes, enabling a clarity of thought by tapping into previously unlocked parts of the subconscious. Mushroom season in the UK tends to be between August and October where in certain areas – school fields, farms, golf courses

– they're readily available, best picked at day-break when they're freshest. Historically-speaking they have always been a favourite of the thinking man's drug taker (or Hawkwind fan). Matt in particular still likes to find time to trip on a fistful of mushrooms once or twice a year.

"His drill is this," observed *Kerrang!* in 2003. "Make sure you have no stress clouds on the horizon, clear a few days from your diary – at least three of which should be free after the event – and be willing to surrender yourself to whatever may come your way."

Matt, Dom and Tom Kirk got to do exactly that earlier in the year when they had found themselves with a rare day off in London. Bored of the city, they took the first available budget flight out to Amsterdam, picked up some mushrooms and weed from one of the cafes and headed for the Vondel Park, where they stayed for a few days, eating at restaurants, staying out all night, getting recognised by the occasional fan and tripping their tits off.

"I guess the point of doing this is to dig into your subconscious," Matt elaborated. "To experience something that's not usually on offer. I'm not afraid of seeing something dark and seeing something horrible when I do this. In fact, I think the last time I did mushrooms I was actually looking for that to happen. But I think it's a way of connecting with yourself in a way that you can't do in everyday situations."[10]

Such drug-aided searching of the subconscious was part and parcel of Matt's interests and outlook on the world, a continuation of those childhood Ouija sessions back in Cambridge and Dawlish. Religion, science, drama, death, evolution, travel, dreams, hallucinations – all journeys of the mind or body, all topics that the singer expressed interest in and that he would soon be talking freely about in interviews. As Muse's sound developed, so did their collective identity as a band bursting with ideas and theories encapsulated by a fast-talking frontman who never claimed to be an authority on any subject – he was just *interested*.

Unfortunately, his loose tongue got him in trouble with the locals again. When interviewed for an *NME* section entitled 'Heroes & Villains' he named 'bent coppers' as one his pet hates.

"Well, I've had experiences with the drug squad, although I don't want to get into that, exactly," he explained. "They must have such a laugh, though, getting fucked-up on all these drugs for free. But the thing that really bugs me is that they sell it back. Especially down where I come from. You see the police bust it from all the ships that come in, they get all these massive hauls, and it's always on the evening news. But a few weeks after it happens you actually start buying it. And it's corrupt policemen that are making loads of money from it."[11]

A Detective Inspector Neil Treaby of the Devon and Cornwall Police professional standards unit counter-balanced Matt's theories with a standard, "There is no evidence to support the claims." The Muse singer later said he was horrified the remarks were printed and that they were taken out of context as they were based on hypothetical situations."

Aside from the women, the restaurants, the cheap gadgets, the licensing laws, the abundance of reasonably-priced state-of-the-art gadgetry and the mushrooms in Japan, Matt found another cultural difference to his liking: the clothes. Generally tailored towards a smaller, trimmer figurer, Matt would stock up on clothes each time he was there, instead of having to buy girl's clothes back in England.

The unwashed grunge look of the mid-Nineties and the-little-boys-lost-in -Burtons chic of *Showbiz* were long gone; in their place a slightly sharper more urbane look. Monochromatic colours. Cleaner lines. Tighter. *Sharper*. Nothing drastic but still way more stylish than the sartorial non-entities I had seen in early 1999.

"Luckily – perhaps because they supported these bigger bands – they picked up tips and began to really develop their own image," says Mel Brown. "The problem for Matt has always been his size. So when they came into money, he started to have his clothes made for him, particularly when they started going to Japan. I went with the band there a couple of times and Matt [would] come home with loads of stuff."

After Japan, the tour swung to Australia where Muse hooked up with Feeder once again for three shows, then playing a further two festival shows in Brisbane and Sydney (although they'd played a TV show in Melbourne back in March, this was their first proper tour Down Under) before flying to Europe to play Dublin, Helsinki, Oslo, Malmo and Copenhagen. And suddenly the year was over. Where the hell had it gone? Everywhere, actually.

*

By the close of 2000, Muse had a won the hearts of a lot of fans, many of whose unnerving dedication to the band was beginning to reach levels of new–found obsession. Websites were springing up all over the world, with chat-room cyber-communities forming to swap any snippet of information about the band and declarations of love being made on a daily basis.

"There was a lot of nakedness on the bus," Matt told *NME*. "I remember seeing Dom's bum running down the corridor and [a crew member] with a couple of women on his face. But when you're doing that kind of thing it never really feels like what you thought it would… No, it did actually. And it was brilliant. I think we realised we are normal people and people go for it when they're on tour because that's what it's all about."

It's always the way: the bigger a band becomes, the more attractive they are. Give a misfit a guitar and suddenly he's Don Juan. Fame suggests power, intelligence, wealth, aspiration – all attractive qualities. So as the band's fame grew, they were certainly greeted with more and more opportunities for some traditional rock 'n' roll shenanigans.

"It's difficult to talk about that sort of thing without sounding like an arsehole or a wanker because it's not something you do just to talk about," reasoned Matt. "But yeah, you get that sort of thing going on the road. I prefer to spend my time with people who are not necessarily fans of the band. I think it's a dangerous thing to do with people who are fanatical. Dom will tell you this. He's done it more than any of us. There's been a couple of experiences where they've ended up following him around, going to every single gig, then you realise you might've given the wrong impression. It's something I'm wary of."

"Well," smiled Dominic, when asked by *Select* about his reputation as Muse's resident party boy, "that's not for me to say. I tend to take life in my stride, easy come, easy go.

Sometimes Matt takes it in his stride. Sometimes he goes mental."

Partying aside, a year of foundation-building and hard work and hard partying was drawing to a close with no immediate sign of the excess drying up. "We started losing the plot towards the end of 2000 – having more parties, being a bit more excessive," Matt said that Christmas. "Maybe this year we'll completely lose it, just become full-on alcoholics and drug addicts and die at a young age…"[12] With fridges being stocked and drinks put on ice in venues around the world, there would certainly be plenty of opportunity to try…

9. LIKE THE NEW BORN

THE YEAR of *Space Odyssey*. 2001: the band were changing. The *world* was changing.

The extended gestation period of 'Muse: The Early Years' and the incubation of the *Showbiz*-era was over by that defining year of 2001 – in which we as a species were lead to believe we would have been living in splendour on Mars... in Bacofoil suits. Yet in reality, we couldn't quite let go of centuries worth of ignorance, bigotry, fear, greed and pointless religious dogma. For their part, Muse had metamorphosised from overlooked chicks hungry for a morsel of success to proud peacocks: colourful, confident and walking with the type of swagger in their stride which comes when thousands of people shout your name and hundreds want to fuck you every night.

If the sales of *Showbiz* were anything to go on, the band had gone from underdogs to serious contenders in the space of a debut album with the greatest of ease. As the band prepared to unleash their follow-up, with 180,000 copies of *Showbiz* sold in the UK in the first year, the figures for the slow-burning debut were highly encouraging, the album surpassing recent efforts by bands of far greater stature – trouncing Korn's *Issues* and Marilyn Manson's *Holy Wood (In The Shadow Of The Valley Of Death)* (85,000 and 90,000 copies sold respectively), shaming Slipknot's defining self-titled debut proper (140,000) and even going one better than The Offspring's pop-heavy punk album *Majority Of One*, which sold 165,000.

Despite the complexity and breadth of their international record deals, and their popularity across the globe's live circuits, on a worldwide scale Muse were only just beginning to make their mark. Sales in some countries were far lower than others – and other bands – yet in an ever-changing industry where a dip in sales can mean the end of a recording career, Muse were holding their own. Just take the UK alone. 180,000 copies at £12.99 each... well, it was more than enough to keep Muse in business.

Creatively, this initial flourish of eye-opening success and heavy road work had not only broadened the trio's horizons but twisted them into strange and wonderful possibilities. In two short years they'd seen and done more than most do in a lifetime. If that doesn't change a person, nothing will. And where some bands cling to their former pre-fame identities as if never changing or developing their identity is some sort of badge of honour, Muse, ever the modern band, seemed happy to embrace new ideas and new styles. Whether that meant espousing theories about politics, science and human development in interviews, namedropping mighty Russian composers like Rachmaninov or finally have the tenacity to experiment with hair-dye as Matt and Dom did with red, blue and jet black, and peroxide respectively.

At one point on tour in the middle of 2000, Matt was dying his hair every day and regularly inking the veins on his arm black "because it looked cool" and claimed it made him play better. He had talked of getting them done permanently but the tattooist he approached refused to do such a job, claiming the frontman would regret it for the rest of his life. At least that's what he told interviewers. The truth was his mother said she would prefer it if he would stay the way he was made.

Thankfully, Muse never got arrogant, didn't suddenly turn into wankers. They just got more *interesting*. Exciting. Unpredictable. Unhinged. Not only had their show turned into a big rock extravaganza capable of combining the layered dynamics and hyper-speed energy of bands like Deftones and System Of A Down and the technical and visual pomposity of prog rock, but Muse were now only thought of as *Muse*. Not the 'post-Nirvana three-piece from Teignmouth', not the 'moody, Buckley-inspired rockers' and *not* the new fucking Radiohead. They weren't an indie band. They weren't a metal band. They weren't – yikes! – a nu-prog band. They were all three and so much more.

"Matt Bellamy is a class-A, top-grade, split-personality psycho bastard top rock nutter in *excelsis*," observed Mark Beaumont in the *NME*, following a visit to the barge studio on the Thames where Muse had decided to work on new songs. "A full year of on-the-road mayhem, plus a string of mid-table hits from their

Muse aged sixteen.
*Photo courtesy of Santina Elena
@ www.rocketbabydolls.com*

Sweet Muse–ic in America...

Major labels are battling to win the signature of Teignmouth three–piece Muse. The band, who signed a management deal with Sawmills Studio owner Dennis Smith early this year, have been playing showcase gigs over in America.

And Dennis called tdb from Los Angeles, and said: "We have now got a bidding war going on.

"We just showcased for a label in LA and we got through the second number and the guy said he didn't need to hear anymore.

"The boys have now flown back over to England, but I'm staying over here to sort a few things out.

"I have always believed it would happen for the boys, but you never know in this industry. Now it looks almost definite.

"One of the labels was saying he believed Muse could turn out to be the next U2."

Muse started out life as The Rocke___ ____lls and most of their ____
of th___
Rec___
Cav___
in ___
on ___
b___
T___

PIC: DAVID GOODCHILD

Much touted Teignmouth band Muse have inked one of the biggest record deals of 1999.

For Matthew, Chris and Dominic have signed a massive six–album North American deal with Madonna's Maverick Records. The band have also signed a German agreement and, by now, should have a French connection in the bag. Then comes Japan and Australia, with the UK next.

The band were spotted by Madonna's partner while showcasing for several labels in Hollywood (as you do), Maddy was given a CD and she loved it. Muse were signed and everything's gone mad.

New single "Muse Museum EP" has gone into the NME indie album chart at number three, the band are potentially doing the forthcoming Gene tour and an end-of-year trip round America is in the pipeline. Oh, and the band are about to go and record their debut album as well. And they're due to play the Glastonbury and Reading festivals...and...and...and...

Manager Dennis Smith said it was one of the best deals signed by a band from this side of Atlantic for quite some time. But he said the boys were determined to keep their feet firmly on the ground. "Obviously, this is a very big thing indeed. The feeling here is that it really is all about to happen.

"The way we've gone about signing the deal is definitely the way forward. It gives the band control over their catalogue and provides some kind of security."

The album will be produced by John Leckie – the man responsible for the Stone Roses albums – and will be recorded at Dennis' Sawmills Studio in Cornwall and at a London venue.

t is hoped a single will be available nationally by late spring and he band's first album should be out late summer/autumn. But for

Some star spangled Muse–ic

Teignmouth's Muse have signed the biggest deal ever. This time next year, they will be huge.

now, there's still a lot of hard work to be done. "Obviously, everyone is absolutely delighted at what has happened, but the boys do realise that this is where all the hard work begins. Too many bands forget that, but Muse are determined and sensible enough to know what's needed," Dennis said.

Muscle Museum , which is currently being played to death by Radio 1's Steve Lamacq, features six tracks and is available from Solo Records in Exeter at £4.99. (See next month's tdb for an interview with the band.)

Muse live at the Cavern Club, Exeter

This is the sound of a band waving goodbye. Muse are going places. Places far away. Let's just hope they remember us. The Cavern is rammed for Muse's first local gig since signing their deal. The audience is very young and that's a good sign. And tonight this band, despite a couple of technical problems, play a blinding set which reveals just how far they've come on over the past few months alone.

Singer Matt's wearing a shiny top, which appropriately enough shines like gold. This boy must have been a choirboy in the past as he puts pre–ball drop Aled Jones firmly in the shade with a vocal display that shatters drinkers' glasses at 20 paces.

The people here know the songs, which is always a sign of a band on a roll, and Muse deliver each and every tune with the confidence of boys able to run up a department store down escalator. Muscle Museum is greeted like an old friend, while the likes of Intended seem destined for future greatness. Muse know its happening for them and so does everyone in the Cavern.

Matt says it's probably the best gig he's ever done. There'll be better, though. Just enough space to wish them all the luck in the world.

Early clippings on Muse, reproduced from the *South Devon Herald.*

Dennis Smith and Muse's first ever magazine cover.
Photo of Dennis courtesy of Liam Smith.

Musings behind the drums.
Photo courtesy of Santina Elena @ www.rocketbabydolls.com

Chris keeping it simple.
Photo courtesy of Santina Elena @ www.rocketbabydolls.com

'If I have to go to one more backstage party I might have to strangle myself...'
Photo courtesy of Martyn Goodacre.

Live at the London Arena, November 2001.
Photo courtesy of Brian Rasic/Rex Features.

Muse relaxing before a show.
Photo courtesy of Tina Korhonen.

Chris performing at the Bank of America Pavilion in Boston, August 2, 2006.
Photo courtesy of Robert E Klein/AP/PA Photos

'Successful album = Buy myself swanky acrylic drum kit!' August 2006.
Photo courtesy of Robert E Klein/AP/PA Photos.

Muse at Wembley Stadium December 12, 2006
announcing their show there in June 2007.
Photo courtesy of Joel Ryan/PAWire/PA Photos

Muse receive the Award for 'Best Live Act', during the Brit Awards
at Earls Court, February 14, 2007.
Photo courtesy of Ian West/PA Wire.

Matt during Muse's stunning headline slot at the 2006 Reading Festival.
Photo courtesy of Brian Rasic/Rex Features.

half-million-worldwide-selling debut album *Showbiz*, was like feeding the nervy insecure mogwai Matt of 1999 medicine after midnight and unleashing the slavering, razor-toothed monster Matt."[1]

Even the band's previous non-persona was now a point of interest: "He considers himself to be some kind of mental cyborg-cum-Etch-A-Sketch who can erase all elements of his 'bored and frustrated' pre-Muse personality and 'download' a brand new one from passing acquaintances."

So the gremlins had been exposed to sunlight and there was no turning back. In the same piece, Matt explored a particular favourite topic: conspiracies. He imparted the information that for a while he had been having hallucinatory dreams which involved a triangular metal blade piercing the back of his head, after which he would awake with a bad headache. A TV documentary on Psywar (psychological war-fare) prompted the thought that perhaps the government – or unseen forces – were trying to control him through items such as mobile phones and microwaves, therefore causing the headaches. While such methods of control *are* plausible, one does wonder why, given such a power as a government, they would choose to target the whippet-thin singer of a post-Nirvana Radiohead-copyists three-piece from Teignmouth. Ahem.

"It got to the point where I was thinking that maybe that's what real life is and this is all a dream," Matt admitted. "Then I thought it was one of a number of phobias I had so I went to the doctor and he told me to drink more water and that was that." The strange hallucinations had been a result of dehydration on tour, rather than some Big Brother personality control device. An extra bottle of Evian a night was all that was needed to remedy the situation.

Rock 'n' roll!

*

"The mood was 'Right, what are we going to do this year boys? Let's make a plan. Let's make an album to remember... let's change the face of music forever..."[2]   Matt Bellamy

If *Showbiz* was twenty-two years in the making and documented the trials and tribulations of the lives of three young men at the close of the Twentieth Century, complete with broken hearts and bitter disappointments, Muse's second album was to be a snapshot of the here and now – not throwaway like a fading Polaroid, but the perfect encapsulation of the world as they saw it, a work of art to frame and hang for years to come. Rather than developing and refining a set of songs over many years as they did with their debut, Muse were now faced with starting from scratch – and this time the ante had been upped. This time they had to work even quicker. This time they had even more to prove. Before, no-one had been listening. Now, everyone was watching.

After little more than a couple of weeks grace after Muse's final show of 2000 in Copenhagen in early November, work began on the traditionally difficult as-yet-untitled second album at a number of suitably conducive, expensively-priced locations – residential, state-of-the-art places like Sawmills in Cornwall; Ridge Farm studios in Surrey; Peter Gabriel's Real World Studios in Wiltshire; that floating barge-studio on the Thames; an old church; even Abbey Road.

At the production helm for seven songs was John Leckie, the success of *Showbiz* testament to the band and the knob-twiddler's easy working relationship.

Dave Bottrill produced the other four tracks that would make it on to the album. Bottrill was another well-respected producer best known for his work on Tool's genre-bending *Aenima* album – indeed, Muse and Tool certainly shared the same dark and technically-minded sensibilities – as well as production credits for equally musically-challenging artists such as particular Muse favourite Deus (who Matt had first seen supporting PJ Harvey in Devon as a teenager), Nusrat Fateh Ali Khan, Mudvayne, Paul Oakenfold and VAST, as well as latter-day prog types Dream Theater and King Crimson.

Some of the new songs had been born out of writing and rehearsing sessions snatched in stolen moments on the road, on the back of the tour bus or in anonymous practice rooms in middle America that had been booked on rare days off. The subject matter of the forthcoming album was heavily inspired by a book Matt had been reading called *'Hyperspace: A Scientific Odyssey Through Parallel Universes, Time Warps and the 10th Dimension'* by Michio Kaku, which picked up where Stephen Hawking's *A Brief History Of Time* left off. The singer later claimed, "I found that the truth about science is sometimes more fantastical and exciting that some of the lies of previous religions." Some of these songs has already made it into the live set, the band purposely trying to gauge public reception to their new ideas. This plug-in-and-play mentality carried over in the actual making of the new album.

In each studio, the band set up a large PA as they would at a gig and turned it up *really loud* in order to avoid the sense of detachment that comes when one member is in a drum room, another in a vocal booth and the third on the fire escape smoking a roll-up. They were also playing on far superior equipment than that used for *Showbiz* and had been taking production ideas from their old favourites Rage Against The Machine (Rage guitarist Tom Morello's guitar tech, who was coincidentally originally from Exmouth, had recently been working for Matt.)

"The first time we went into the studio we knew what we wanted to do," said Matt. "Initially we just recorded the songs live so they sounded like a three-piece raw kind of thing. We got all the stuff we knew we wanted to use and we knew what we wanted it to sound like. The first album we really weren't sure."

The plan for the session with Bottrill at Ridge Farm Studios near Gatwick had originally only been to record 'Plug In Baby', the oldest of the new songs and one which had been tentatively pencilled-in as a potential single.

Muse's love of magic mushrooms extended into the studio for the recording of the second album. Thankfully they weren't about to grow 'taches and float up the ceiling to record their own take on 'Yellow Submarine'; it was more a case of three young men getting mashed.

"We were off our faces on mushrooms when we recorded 'Plug In Baby'," Matt laughed. "There was this big field next to the recording studio filled with them. So we ate them all. I don't know what we were doing but we all ended up naked in a jacuzzi and I went deaf in one ear from falling asleep in the sauna."

When the hallucinations had subsided, the song was done, leaving the band with a spare week's worth of paid-for studio time. So they carried on laying down ideas and completed three of the album's strongest songs, 'New Born', 'Bliss' and 'Darkshines', before Bottrill had to leave to produce what would become Tool's *Lateralus*. Arrangements for the new songs were different by modern rock's more orthodox standards, the band proudly admitting that on some songs it wasn't relevant which was the verse and which was the chorus, even boasting of some guitar-free tracks which were nevertheless as heavy as hell.

"A lot of the songs on the album are about simplifying," pondered Matt. "About how all the exterior things you surround yourself with, like possessions and your job, can make people feel trapped. For me, making music all my life from when I was very young, put me in a blissful state of simpleness."

The recordings with John Leckie were equally as fruitful, a real bond between the band and producer formed from certain shared musical interests and a desire to make the most over-the-top, bombastic record possible.

"I like Muse because they sound fiercely modern," says Leckie. "I saw a band with a sound that could carry into the new millennium. In the studio they were very competent, so it was up to me to create the right mood for them to play in, getting things like the lighting right. Also, as an old fogey, I was able to introduce them to a lot of new stuff…"

At the end of a hard day's work, Leckie liked to dim the lights and pull out a few of his favourite records, introducing the band – and Matt in particular – to visionary artists like Captain Beefheart, whose disjointed *Trout Mask Replica* is a complex and remarkable reinvention of rock 'n' roll; and Tom Waits, whose throaty Beat-inspired low-life stories and grasp of the musical macabre was to prove an inspiration. Matt particularly appreciated the unique instrumentation that the latter used to bring his dark carnival to life, while the band would soon adopt Waits' monologue 'What's He Building In There?' as their intro music on their future so-called 'Hullabaloo' tour.

"I saw a Tom Waits concert and he was using the bones of dead animals and I really liked the sound of that," said Matt. "I want to get human bones, I really want to get them, but John

Leckie's not sure. Ideally, I want to get a set of human skulls but I think everybody thinks that's a bit too on the dark side, but to hear that percussion on the record, and to know that it's produced by dead beings, that will make it sound much more powerful, more vibey."[3]

Through Leckie the band discovered the aforementioned studio situated on a Thames river boat that was once owned by Charlie Chaplin but was now in the hands of Pink Floyd. They promptly investigated and made some initial recordings there. For the album closer, Matt located a church organ from St Mary's Church in Bathwick, bartering the resident vicar's proposed fee of £450 down to £350.

"Hopefully people will see us as a band who've got their own sound now," said Matt, emerging from the recordings like a mammal waking from hibernation. "Some people will think it's a load of pretentious wank and some people will like it because it's different. I can understand both points of view because I know we're a little dramatic for some tastes. So much stuff is dull and drab now – I am over the top and don't see any point in hiding it."

*

At this juncture, two-thirds of the band were living in London. For convenience sake, Dom, Matt and Tom Kirk were sharing a flat in Islington, North London. In reality, it was more of a stop-off point on the way to somewhere else – a studio, usually – and months after moving in, there was little decoration beyond the standard regulation furniture and a computer and a piano – two totems of the Muse world – in opposite corners.

"If I'm in the same place too long I can't write anything," Matt said when *The Guardian* paid a visit to the temporary Muse HQ. "When things are changing, that's when the writing kicks in, whether that change be moving house or losing a girlfriend, or making a new bunch of friends. Because that's when I get the urge with wanting to be in touch with the one thing that is a constant, which is the feeling I get from making music. That's why the second album is called *Origin Of Symmetry* – because it's important to have that base when everything else in flux."

To mark the passing of the wide-eyed Muse of old and show the world they were more than ready, willing and able to step up a gear – musically and sonically – on March 5, 2001, the lead single from their sophomore album was released, entitled 'Plug In Baby'. Things were moving along quickly – the band was still in Abbey Road studios wrapping up the final days of mixing the album when the first single from the project was released.

And what a single it was. A short burst of feedback gives way to the type of turbo-charged virtuoso guitar melody that easily gets under your skin; the type of swirling riff that you just know every budding smalltown guitar shop hero will be dashing out as some sort of mark of ability between the usual 'Stairway To Heaven' jams. The type of riff that screams a hearty 'Fuck You!' at anyone who may have suggested that guitars are irrelevant and rock 'n' roll is dead; 'Plug In Baby' was one of those songs that you can listen to once, yet find yourself full on vibrato-ing to in the bath after three months. Behind it all, the deepest bass and snappiest drums lock down the song, freeing Matt to do his best, *'God, what hast thou forsaken me?'* vocals. And all this in less than three-and-a-half minutes.

The mix was ingenious too. "The bass distortion is on that side and the guitars on that side," explained Matt. "Normally the bass is in the middle, but we wanted it to sound like we are on stage."

Lyrically, 'Plug In Baby' best epitomises early twenty-first century angst and melancholy, the plug in baby of the title an automated metaphor for something very much more real. The single was backed by 'Nature_1', one of their strongest B-sides and which makes good use of high-to-low vocals; and the head-banging 'Execution Commentary'; plus the 'Plug In Baby' video. CD2 featured the rarely heard tear-jerker 'Spiral Static', a bonus track that originally featured as an extra song on the Japanese release of *Showbiz* alongside the instrumental 'Bedroom Acoustics'. Two weeks later a low-key, limited edition seven-inch vinyl release appeared of 'Plug In Baby'/'Nature_1'. They also released a cassette version of the same two songs.

The new single's accompanying video saw the band playing the song while genetically-modified models mutated around them. Like the two high school geekboys in Eighties flick *Weird*

Science, it was really an excuse to let their imaginations run free; cyber-porn for a generation beating their meat to unobtainable 2-D monitor screen beauties.

"The idea came from a conversation we had about genetics and being able to design beings for their own purpose," said Matt. "In this case it's porn creatures. In the video, they eventually go wrong and fall apart. The truth is, we just wanted to hang out with a load of models all day. Making videos is boring, so from now on we want to get as many women in them as possible."

The porn creatures did their job. The single charted at an impressive number 11, Muse's greatest achievement yet.

*

Meanwhile Back In The Real World...

It was time to circumnavigate the world once again. This time the schedule was to take in either less frequently-visited countries such as Portugal, Turkey, Finland, Norway, Denmark and Sweden or playing more festival slots – always a valid entry point into previously uncharted waters.

Muse's second world tour began with an intimate warm-up show at Exeter Lemon Grove on April 4 to three hundred fans, including Matt and Chris' immediate families, the entire Howard clan and even some devotees who had flown in from Japan.

While the band were away on the road, they became embroiled in a handbags (and glad-rags) at dawn spat with the Stereophonics, a band they'd previously played with in the States, shared many a festival bill and whose respective careers had enjoyed similar trajectories.

Although either band would probably be loathe to admit it, there were many similarities between the two acts. Both were tight-knit trios who had grown up together, incubating slowly in remote and uncool towns (in Stereophonics' case Cwmaman in the south Wales valleys) miles away from any major music scenes and then being called hicks when they did get noticed. The success of both acts has also often been accredited to their music above all else – substance over style – both taking a workmanlike pride in being rock stars. Having interviewed both bands on a number of occasions, they certainly share that same sense of insularity and, particularly early on in their careers, the same sense of slight suspicion and cynicism. And both centred around two diminutive and savvy frontmen, who were the sole songwriters and spiritual driving force of their respective bands. Neither was known to take undue criticism lightly.

Speaking at a press conference held to unveil the line-up for their big-selling 'A Day At The Races' shows at Donnington race-track (supported by Ash and two retro-tripping bands in the form of Black Crowes and Proud Mary) Stereophonics frontman Kelly Jones launched an attack on Muse by revealing that they had been approached to support the Welsh band at the show but had demanded £25,000 for the privilege. He quipped, "You can get a Radiohead tribute band for less than that." Whether Jones was vexed because the band could command such a fee or because they were blasé enough not to care either way if they got the Stereophonics support slot or not, was unclear.

One important thing did separate the two bands and may have been the source of Kelly Jones's apparent rancour: Stereophonics were an increasingly conservative-sounding, backward-looking band – the epitome of a group afraid to become true flamboyant rock stars lest the boys back home in the village gave them a ribbing; Muse meanwhile were resolutely futurist in their approach, explosive where their newsprint rivals were tempered, progressing and diversifying at the same speed in which Stereophonics retreated/regressed back to their flat caps, corduroy and Rod Stewart records. This was something Muse was clearly aware of. As he-said/she-said comments went back and forth in the music media, providing minor titillation for as many as two weeks, Jones' barbed words and dismissive attitude to Muse's music seemed to bare a trace of bitterness – a reigning king nervously anticipating a peasant revolt – while Bellamy's was of detached couldn't-give-a-shit bemusement. A typical exchange:

Jones: "That bloke's got his head up his arse – he should get laid more."

Bellamy: "I wish I could get laid as much as Kelly Jones. He's so cool."

Jones: "He's just a fucking tool. He's got to realise that they might not be around for the next album because the music they play isn't music that lasts at all."

It was the type of inane exchange that rock stars do so well, which the eager weekly British press thrives upon and is more often than not used to wrap fish suppers the following week. Nonetheless, it was a symbolic victory for Muse. They knew they didn't have to diss other bands to stay in the press. With songs as good as the new ones they working on, they knew they had zip to worry about.

Good news of sorts also came that week – the band cashed in/sold-out 'Sunburn' by allowing Apple to use the song in a worldwide TV advertising campaign for their new iMac computers. The press speculated that the deal involved a five-figure sum. Reportedly more than they'd have been paid by Mr. Jones *et al* for far more effort. Nice work if you can get it.

*

A second single from *Origin Of Symmetry* followed at the beginning of June, the weird and wonderful album opener 'New Born'. The track was certainly an interesting choice for a single – not because it wasn't an amazing song that perfectly encapsulated their new-found apocalyptic rock direction, but because at six minutes it was *long*. And compared to the faceless parade of buff, crotch-grabbing mannequins, *utterly mental*. Beginning with an extended mock-baroque piano opening before soaring off into the cosmos, down a dirty black hole and crashlanding to a gratifyingly spectacular conclusion, it wasn't exactly 'Macarena'.

For the UK release, the song was backed by a song from the John Leckie sessions, the Muse-by-numbers 'Shrinking Universe', which sounded exactly like a song just a little too mundane for the album; and 'Piano Thing' (Matt tinkering about on a grand piano – hey, B-sides were lean) plus the 'New Born' video. The single's alternative release also included a song called 'Map Of Your Head' which featured what appears to be a folky mandolin and a jaunty backbeat, was something of a departure for Muse and, for once, all the better for it. It was also backed by a live version of 'Plug In Baby' recorded the previous month at The Paradiso in Amsterdam. A few weeks later, a three-track twelve-inch release surfaced, primarily aimed at plugging Muse's remix in the clubs. It featured a Paul Oakenfold/Perfecto remix of 'New Born', plus two Timo Maas mixes of 'Sunburn' ('Sunstroke' remix and 'Breakz Again' mix), all of which were, at best, unnecessary. All filler and no killer.

At least no one could accuse Muse of denying fans their music; releases were coming fast and thick. Just to plug the one song – whose function was merely to promote the far more profitable album anyway – the band had released a further seven songs and one video. 'New Born' was worth every penny, but the days of a two-track single sufficing were long-gone; this was big marketing budget stuff, a sign that if Muse ever had a deprecating indie mentality it was still kept well hidden. In keeping with the times, Muse had become more than a band. For better or for worse they were turning into a rock 'n' roll *brand*.

To promote the single, the band climbed aboard the colourful carousel that is music television promotion once again, playing on six shows in the space of little over a week. The appearances truly unleashed the three-headed rock beast to the wider population and, when watched back-to-back, display a hilarious unspoken insight into the band's state of mind, and opinion of such facile shows.

"I used to be like, 'Fuck off, we're not miming'," said Matt, "but now I've realised we can have fun with it and put our own stamp on everything we do."

It began with a performance on Zoe Ball's Channel 4 tea-time show *The Priory*, before they then performed less than half of 'New Born' on *T4* (the credits started rolling before the band had barely broken into a sweat). Then they moved on to *CD:UK* where, clad in demonic all-black with red roses dangling from their mic stands, they suffered the indignity of an introduction by the over-excitable guest host, Ritchie from boy band 5ive. "How rock n' roll!" quipped perma-grinning presenter Cat Deeley, when the song ended with some guitar-flinging action.

"We'll send them the bill later."

Getting to perform such an overblown and fantastic song as 'New Born' on kids' TV shows, however tawdry, was a healthy sign that music this wired was going to find affinity with anyone young, bored or angry. And if a few early-teen Westlife fans were converted to the dark side as a result, then even better.

Five days later, on Channel 5's *Pepsi Chart* show, the boys were tiring of the idea of miming along to another rent-a-crowd of day-glo pop kids and performed the entire song with Dom playing bass, and Chris, a mass of unkempt hair and flailing limbs, back to his first instrument of drums. The performance ended with Matt giving up all pretensions of actually *playing* his guitar and instead injecting a bit of anarchy into the proceedings by climbing his amps, clinging to a long white drape and dangling perilously atop a wobbling Marshall stack. As the band hit the (badly mimed) skronk rock freak-out finale, Matt hung like a monkey on a vine looking like it could go either way, like it could go badly wrong... *and cut back to the presenter.*

Two days later it was the turn of *Live & Kicking* where Muse stuck to their revised line-up once again, Dom clearly living a bedroom fantasy by cutting bass shapes and looking like he should be in Korn, Matt sneering behind shades and spikes like Sid Vicious on parole day. The song collapsed into a group pile-on, but not before a breakdancing friend had cut some backspins to the songs ending. 'New Born' reached the same conclusion on that week's *Top Of The Pops*, Matt unveiling freshly-dyed blood red hair, twitching like a Shockheaded Peter before taking a bow for the camera.

It's a shit business....

'New Born' made it to Number 12 in the UK singles charts which, although a slot lower than 'Plug In Baby', was something of a victory for any music which can't be squeezed into the three-minute pop pigeon-hole. In a climate dominated by Pop Idols and disposable music, very rarely do such unconventional songs do so well. The record buying public is a fickle entity, but Muse's strong increasingly obsessive following was serving them well.

The true purchase power of Muse's loyal followers would be

tested soon enough, with the release of the all-important, traditionally difficult (or so they say) second album on June 11, 2001. Aside from incorporating images and imagery from Kaku's *Hyperspace...* the title *Origin Of Symmetry* was a nod toward Charles Darwin's *The Origin Of Species*, in which the naturalist proposed his theory of human evolution from apes – still a controversial idea amongst many of the more conservative religious denominations today.

The cover artwork (a vast improvement on *Showbiz*) by unknown artist William Eager was an illustration of a series of what appears to be scattershot telegraph poles or rugby goalposts (or giant tuning forks...), casting parallel shadows across a featureless desert-like landscape beneath an intensely orange sky. The cover was part of a larger commission of works, all offering different interpretations of 'Origin Of Symmetry', ten of which were subsequently used to great effect in accompanying artwork. The images complemented the sound within, while encapsulating where Muse's heads were perfectly: a line of automaton-like people filing into a anonymous factory marked 'Chaos', a foreboding spaceship-like image against a black space-like background, the seemingly placid scene of a women in a garden subverted with images of satellites and the silhouette of a factory.

Two of the images were subsequently used as the alternative covers for the 'New Born' single release. Collectively, the art (and the music) portrayed a panic attack-inducing world, a sensory overloaded society of activity, chaos and confusion, or a species not evolving but disintegrating slowly in shopping malls and lonely rooms; the dissolution of communication – of conversation of the feel of flesh on flesh – a new-found sense of alienation.

Origin Of Symmetry opened, appropriately enough, with the aforementioned 'New Born', a new declaration for a new age. Tantalisingly drawing out the hushed and lush piano and vocals intro, the song lulls the listener into a false sense of security like a vengeful lullaby. There's a brief pause before giving way to a guitar sound that's pure *Bleach*-era Nirvana, then – boom! – the dirty guitar, rubber band bass and drums that hit like a suckerpunch to the throat transmute into a twitching writhing mess which, after such an electrical jolt, snaps into shape and races off into the distance. 'New Born' has more peaks and troughs than a stroll through the Himalayas, more emotional crescendos than *Carmen*, more ferocity than Rage Against The Machine on a bad hair day.

'Bliss' was something of a contrast, though no less exhilarating. The seemingly summery lyrics belied a kind of world-weary bitterness from a protagonist who has seen too much yet strives for the unobtainable purity of innocence. Musically, like a mysterious Fifties sci-fi machine, 'Bliss' twinkles and *throb*s, Matt's voice sounding like the last gasps of a stranded cosmonaut floating away from earth, doomed and alone. Little wonder it's still one of the fans' favourites today.

The rolling piano thunder of 'Space Dementia' could have been written about Matt's beloved flying machine and the extra, detached perspective he gained from hovering above mankind with a big fuck-off motor strapped to his back. The middle section of the song is particularly peculiar, a trippy, FX-laden middle-eight with vocals compressed until they sound like a scene-setting piece from *2001: A Space Odyssey*. The spacious, sweeping classical sounds that film's director, Stanley Kubrick, used in his many movies certainly seemed an influence on the album as a whole.

'Hyper Music' was no understatement. Chris's booming elastic bass sound was fast becoming a trademark and this live favourite was underpinned by the enigmatic one's bottom end fury. "This one really rocks out," explained Matt. "It's really full-on but the lyrics are just plain negative, just pure anger and disregard for affection, the opposite of 'Bliss'."[4]

Staying true to the album's themes, 'Plug In Baby' criticized new technologies such as the internet which are supposed to encourage people to communicate but which actually serve to emotionally isolate us even further.

'Citizen Erased', aside from being a great title for a song, novel or movie was as foreboding as its title suggested, a possible reference to Orwell's *Nineteen Eighty-Four* where non-comformist citizens are erased and the state is ruled by lies.

"It's an expression of what it feels like to be questioned," was

Matt's explanation. "I spend more time than most people being asked about purpose and it's a strange feeling. I don't really have the answers and I have to respond with the knowledge I have obtained so far, but the problem is that it gets printed and by then something else has come along that's made you completely disagree with what you said."

'Micro Cuts' was about the dream Matt had had where he was in a desert and the sky was raining down huge blades upon him, the strange feverish visions forming a blunt poetry of sorts. The song also saw Matt taking his falsetto to new extremes, his voice piercing like Diamanda Galas. It was an amazing and somewhat faintly ridiculous vocal performance topped by a brutal finale.

Formerly known as 'Razorblades And Glossy Magazines' and featuring different lyrics, 'Screenager' begins as if it was recorded in the narcotic fug of an opium den, dreamy, dark and close to comatose. The quiet after the storm of earlier, more insurgent songs, 'Darkshines' was similarly arched like a lounge lizard with a mariachi twang; lascivious and slinky. 'Feeling Good' was their version of a song made famous by Nina Simone, and a particular favourite of Marilyn Bellamy. Matt too was a big fan of Simone, whose voice was one of the twentieth century's most recognisable. Where others may have ruined an unbeatable song Muse retained its air of sophistication.

'Megalomania' was not one of *Origin's* strongest tracks, although the intention was interesting. It was a song for which Matt located that church organ and which had a suitably funereal and cataclysmic quality to it. "The lyric is directed at the church," he said. "I went to church a couple of times when I was younger and I was always drawn to the church organ, the sounds coming out of it. I didn't want some geezer telling me how it should be. I saw this barrier, and how people use religion and things like that to attain power over each other. [I got the church organ] went in there and recorded this song, which is extremely anti-Christian, under a statue of Jesus. It was a dark moment in my life."

And a fitting end to a very dark album.

In the space of fifty minutes, Muse had shown us their world, their universe. We'd had our toes dipped in the Sea of

Tranquility, suffered dementia amid meteor showers and been sucked down soul-wrenching black holes.

"Their reinvention of grunge as a neo-classical, high gothic, future rock, full of flambed pianolas and white-knuckle electric camp is a precarious venture," wrote Roger Morton in a 9/10 review of the album in *NME*. "Yet as the bloody abattoir riff kicks in on 'New Born', colliding with Bellamy's fairy dreamtime piano, it's apparent that Muse can handle their brutal arias... Thom Yorke's least favourite word is 'angst'; Matt Bellamy's is about to become 'psychotic'. We're the lucky ones who get to look at the pretty shapes as the blood hits the wall."

"Unlike the band's *Showbiz* debut, *Origin Of Symmetry* has no weak tracks; no fillers and not a whiff of the hesitancy which once made Muse sound uncomfortable with their heavier moments," noted Dom Lawson in *Kerrang!* "Best of all, Muse have got better songs than virtually anyone operating in the mainstream at the moment. Combine that with a new-found heaviness and a penchant for deeply unfashionable prog-rock influenced extravagance, and you're looking at one of the year's most intriguing albums. It's also one of the best."

Muse had set out to shatter preconceptions and had succeeded. The general reaction amongst critics was 'Hmm, perhaps they do rock after all...' However, not everyone was as receptive to *'Origin Of Symmetry* though.

Writing for website *Playlouder*, Everett True gave his reasons for disliking the album: "First, my old violin teacher used to scream like that. Gave me nightmares, she did. Hair standing on end, bow raised ready to strike. Second, atmospheric guitar parts like those on 'Darkshines' are best left to Dire Straits and former members of The Pretenders. Third: little keyboard noodles like those on 'New Born' and 'Bliss' should be strangled at birth and left in a sewer alongside the decomposing body of Rick Wakeman...."

And still the increasingly redundant Radiohead tag was dangling like a name-tag on a cold mortuary slab corpse. Only at least now it was occasionally meant as some sort of veiled compliment: "If you want to sound like Radiohead when even Thom Yorke doesn't want to sound like Radiohead, you might as well take it to such preposterous, bombastic, over-the-top levels," admitted authoritative website www.allmusic.com. "Church organs, mental electronics, riffs bouncing off each other like monolithic screams so that you'd finally be in position to crack skulls like coconuts and make the world's speakers ooze gooey blood."

The occasional scathing review was nothing compared to the reaction to *Origin* in the US, where the ascension of Muse was slowed considerably by a series of obstacles, many seemingly from the band's label, Maverick. Following a lack of airplay for lead-off radio single 'Plug In Baby', a label representative suggested the band re-record the track "without the falsetto vocal", to which Muse are said to have replied, "Stick it up your arse you fat cunt."

Many US observers said the album was just too weird. Each to their own of course, but this came from a nation that had, after all, brought us the music of Captains Beefheart, Milli Vanilli, William Shatner, Deicide and Funkadelic.

Whoever was right, it didn't bode well for a healthy-working relationship on the eve of Muse's big push – the album that would elevate them from cult, college-level and support band status in America to bigger things. The label stood their ground, even going so far as to suggest *Origin Of Symmetry* was lacking in singles – a decision that in time will surely be utterly regrettable. Muse's career in the country that had first recognised their talent was also the place where they were to flounder first.

In the UK, the album considered too weird for America debuted in the charts at Number 3.

10. FEELING GOOD

"When I sing certain notes that take so much physical force to get out, it can feel like you're floating, moving out of the body, it's quite strange....and sometimes when I'm playing a song live, I can experience what it was that inspired me when I wrote it. It can be experiencing a particular experience with a particular person."[1]
Matt Bellamy

THE PROMOTION of *Origin Of Symmetry* was to last all year, taking in France, Germany, Spain, Holland, Switzerland, Italy, Germany, Austria, Sweden, Belgium, Denmark, Luxembourg, Finland, Russia, Japan and a couple of extended tours of duty in the UK. Those involved knew that Muse had just made a killer record, now they had to go out and convince the already-loyal following – and beyond.

In April 2001, old friend Tom Kirk, fresh from a college degree in Brighton, had visited the band at their aforementioned show at The Paradiso, a converted church in Amsterdam. He was soon approached about working for them full-time taking care of what might be called 'the Muse aesthetic'.

"We'd always kept in touch but they'd been away working in America for a while," says Tom. "They were aware that they needed someone to handle their multi-media. I had a camera and started filming some bits and pieces and a couple of days later I was quickly fired from work for not returning from the tour. Three years later I'm still here. I love it all."

It was around this time that Chris nearly had the rock world's most absurd death since a member of Toto met his end in a bizarre gardening accident – although it did take place on a tour bus, so it could have at least been classed as rock 'n' roll-related. While chewing on an empty tube of Smarties he inhaled the round coin-sized plastic cap and starting choking as it lodged in his throat. Something of a first aid expert, Matt was just about to step in and administer the Heimlich manoeuvre when his friend coughed the cap up again.

"I was paranoid because I've got this friend who, when he was five years old, did the same thing with the propeller from

145

one of those foam aeroplanes you used to get, and it punctured his lung," said one embarrassed bassist. "His lung collapsed and everything. Thinking about death though, you think I could have died but then you think 'Why do I smoke and drink every day?'" After some careful deliberation, he chose to give up neither.

Mid-way through the previous year, Matt had split with his girlfriend of six years. The sudden realisation that he was single again certainly had an effect on his lifestyle, as he found himself having to account to no-one for his actions. By time of the *Origin* world tour, Muse hadn't quite reached Motley Crue-esque levels of excess or de Sadian-style degradation, but for a while they were taking advantage of the many beautiful women who presented themselves to them on tour buses in dressing rooms or night clubs in a different city each night. With women who otherwise wouldn't give them a second glance. Or at least Matt and Dom, the bachelors of the band were – Chris was unerring in his love and dedication to his family and childhood sweetheart Kelly, happy to sit back and watch his bandmates indulge themselves.

The band had a handy solution to overcome any shyness when entertaining the fairer sex. "How we dealt with it initially on tour was wearing masks backstage," remembered Matt. "We'd have aftershow parties, where we'd make everyone wear something of a mask-type nature. So no-one could really see each other, which kind of freed up inhibitions a bit."

While there's surely something totally empty, cheap and devoid of meaning about such a random, short-lived exchange, it's also visceral, spontaneous and slightly comical – the fact that the three boys from Devon had become text-book clichéd rock 'n' roll fanny magnets (but always with impeccable manners). And that in itself is perhaps the essence of rock 'n' roll, the only lifestyle option that gives licence to do things and see places and be with people that painting and decorating or cleaning toilets just doesn't afford: it's the chance to live a fantasy. Of course, unless you're Mick Jagger, it never lasts. Which is probably just as well....

"I'd been in a relationship from sixteen to twenty-two, so

I always had that stability," Matt explained with hindsight. "But when that stability stopped and we split-up right in the middle of the *Origin Of Symmetry* tour I thought to myself 'Actually, being unstable is much better!" Before, touring was a bit of a jading experience, but when I was free it was the opposite because I'd never really experienced anything outside of the life that we had in Devon."

The on-going road party was still in full swing when *Kerrang!*'s Paul Brannigan joined them in Copenhagen, Denmark in June 2001 for the final show of a string of Scandinavian dates, gaining a rare insight into what Muse really get up to – the side of them which they talk about but rarely show. The band and their entourage enjoyed a foray into Christiana, a former military base on an island in the centre of the city which is now home to anarchists, hippies, radicals and tax-dodging drop-outs, a place where soft drugs have been decriminalised and sold freely. For the first time on this tour the band didn't have to share their temporary home – their trusty tour bus – with their road crew. Again, another sign, if one were needed, that Muse had 'made it'.

"It's great, especially when it comes to having guests," explained Matt while giving a guided tour of their palace on wheels. "You'd have to ask Dom about that. He'll deny it of course, but I've got the footage to prove it. Seriously, after a party one night, I went back to the dressing room and it was all dark. I heard some strange squelching noises in the corner, so I went out and got a video camera with night vision on it. I went back and got the last ten seconds just as he went..."

At this point the animated frontman enthusiastically mimes cumming over a girl's back. "I got the money shot on tape," he laughed. "Can you believe that? I played it to him the other day and he didn't even recognise his own dick, he thought it was me. I was quite insulted actually...."

That was only the start of things. Buoyed by alcohol and those ever-present mushrooms (in this case bought legally from a Christiana vendor) the aftershow party spilled out of the band's dressing room and on to their bus.

"We try and get as many women in the shower as possible, then we film it and whack it on this bad boy here," boasted

Matt, slapping the television beside him, before noting that tonight was going to be a quiet one. "If this is quiet, I'd hate to see them when all hell breaks loose..." observed Brannigan, before describing a scenario in which "tequila and mushrooms are being passed around, in full view of the bus's occupants, a Danish girl is on the toilet with her knickers around her ankles and upstairs, some of the most attractive women I have seen are draped around assorted members of the band and crew..."

With Chris, the band's resident drinks man, mixing vodka, tequila and cherry cocktails, Matt was busy getting intimately acquainted with two – that's two – new friends...

"As it said in the subsequent feature, there were about ten *incredibly* attractive Scandinavian girls surrounding them," recalls Brannigan today. "Clothes were disappearing with alarming frequency and I suddenly realised that even with Matt and Dom having two women each, there were still two or three 'spares' and I was about the only 'free' male. Now, in the real world, there would have been absolutely not a snowball's chance in hell that I'd have been in with such young ladies but under the influence of mushrooms, pot and tequila... well, you know, some people don't think straight.

Having a lovely girlfriend, I basically bottled it and ran away," laughs Paul, "and passed the girl with her panties round her knees having a piss in the toilet, while necking a bottle of Tequila. This was after Dom had videoed me promising not to say anything about the night. The next day we ran into them at the airport and Matt was casually telling us how little sleep he had what with those two girls being so frisky..."

In August, 'Bliss' was released as a single. The release also featured an instrumental 'The Gallery' and 'Screenager' (from The Paradiso show in April) and the 'Bliss' video; on the second CD was a more reflective acoustic reworking of 'Hyper Music' re-titled 'Hyper Chondriac Music' and a version of 'New Born', recorded live at the BBC's Maida Vale studio for *The Evening Session*. A 'Bliss' DVD was also released featuring a Muse photo gallery, lyrics, discography and the making of the video. One for the fans. 'Bliss' entered at 19 and fell out of the charts soon afterwards.

Another thing happened that summer: Labour won their second term in a landslide general election. Although not a remotely political band – they were away touring and couldn't vote – Matt nevertheless began to address wider issues and theories about the world.

"I'd vote for the Yellows [Liberal Democrats] or the Greens next time" he told me. "Get some of those yellow boys so maybe people will start taking it more seriously. I think that's what we'll see in the next election – more of a protest vote."

At the end of month, Muse were back at the *Kerrang!* Awards where they beat Ash, Feeder, Cradle Of Filth and – oh, yes – Stereophonics to win 'Best British Band', as voted for by the readers of the magazine. Presenting them the award was a *bona fide* Muse hero and genuine musical influence: clog-wearing lady-haired Queen guitarist Brian May. With the same operatic qualities as singer Freddie Mercury and a neo-classical approach to guitar playing similar to that of former chemistry student May, Muse had picked up a fair share of comparisons (which would continue with third album *Absolution*) to the stately Godfathers of British arena rock. Some had suggested they were natural successors to the throne of a band many had considered to be the best in the world on certain nights.

"The things we have in common with Queen are the things I'm really proud of about this the band," said Matt. "We have a big sound, and we're not afraid to put on a show. In the past seven years, the most famous English bands have seemed incredibly self-conscious on stage. Their performances have been based around trying to break down the barriers of rock stardom and say, 'We are just normal people.' The problem is that in order to break through to thousands of people and relate to them on a 'normal' level, you have to remove everything that's interesting or characterful [sic] about yourself. You have to strip away your own individuality, and individuality is what makes for a great performance: the audience gets to see something they don't normally see in everyday life."

To the strains of 'We Will Rock You', Matt was up and out of his seat almost before their name had been announced, bounding onto the stage like a gazelle only to notice the crosshairs of rock's drunken royalty pointed straight at him.

"Nice one! What do you say? Wow…cheers…" he stammered.

He managed to pull himself together in time to thank Paul Brannigan "for seeing the truth of what we do on tour" (despite asking him not to tell *too* much truth). They then moved on to the after-show party and got suitably banjaxed.

*

Then things hit warp speed.
On September 10, 2001, twenty-four hours before suicide bombers attacked the Twin Towers of the World Trade Centre, Muse were in New York, back playing the Mercury Lounge three years since their first appearance there. Then they moved onto Boston that night, narrowly missing the Apocalyptic scenes of the following day.

It followed a run of festival shows including the V2001 festival in the UK, Pukkelpop in Belgium and the Lowlands in Holland. If Muse's self-created musical world was one of bitterness, betrayal, confusion, anger, then this shocking atrocity only heightened their natural paranoia and gave credence to many of Matt's theories; the world is a fragile place, of that there is no doubt. Man is responsible for all that is wrong. And things will probably only get worse.

The next month brought a number of milestones in Muse's career. While other high-selling (predominantly American) bands promptly cancelled all tour plans – like terrorists are really going to want to bomb a Pantera concert – Muse merely upped their workload.

At the end of September, they travelled to Moscow to play a show. Russia has a booming bootleg business and although official Muse sales weren't massive, they found a large clued-up following who'd been tracking the band's every moment since the early *Showbiz* days. It was a country to which they would return to experience in greater detail

France adored Muse and the love was reciprocated when on October 28 and 29 they played shows at the seven thousand-capacity Le Zenith in Paris. The shows were being filmed for a forthcoming live Muse DVD and accompanying soundtrack album, both called *Hullabaloo* – more of which later.

In November, after a short seven-date UK tour, they headlined the English equivalent of Le Zenith, the cavernous Docklands Arena in east London, supported by rising British post-hardcore five-piece Hundred Reasons. With a concrete floor, metal roof and all the life of an open grave, it's about the worst place for a rock 'n' roll show, but by now Muse were old pros. It was three years since those first arena shows with the Red Hot Chili Peppers and the band had advanced immeasurably. For once, it wasn't sold out and come show time the touts hustling outside were letting their spare tickets go for cheap – not because the show was badly-attended, but because, for once, Muse may well have over-stretched themselves. Indeed, attendance at concerts, sporting events and other such large scale public gatherings had been adversely effected by the events of September 11, a mere two months earlier.

As with the gigs at Le Zenith, the show was an extravaganza of shapes and sounds, of giant confetti-filled balloons falling from the rafters (inspired by cult Sixties TV show *The Prisoner*), of silhouettes throwing over-the-top rock shapes, of guitars cocked at acute angles and bodies twisting and whirling dervish-like to the glorious noise. In the centre of it all, ringmaster Matt Bellamy running around the stage in a flared, satin shirt like a de-spectacled Harry Potter. Pretending to be a Hobbit. Understatement just did not feature in the Muse lexicon. It was their biggest show in their home country to date. Another landmark.

The double A-sided single 'Feeling Good'/'Hyper Music' was released to coincide with these British dates. "One song's really negative and about almost wanting to destroy a person you've loved," explained Matt of the contrasting brace of songs, "while the second is about looking to the future with hope."

Never ones to lessen their chances of airplay, two videos in one were filmed over two days at Black Island Studios in Acton, west London with director David Slade (of 'New Born' and 'Bliss' fame). A hundred hardcore fans had been invited down to take part as extras in footage that would be a departure from the usual robotic models and plug-in babies.

As Matt explained on the set: "The first video ['Hyper Music'] is supposed to be really fast, really full on. Then the walls come in and crush me, and then open back out again as we go into the next song. Then this unusual looking sky appears and petals start falling from the sky, and everyone who was dancing violently in the first half starts chilling out. All very surreal."[2]

The first CD lead with 'Hyper Music' and was backed by 'Feeling Good' (live in Bologna, Italy), 'Shine' and the video for ' Feeling Good'; while CD2 featured the Nina Simone cover, 'Hyper Music' (recorded at the same Bologna show), a cover of The Smiths' 'Please, Please, Please, Let Me Get What I Want' and the 'Hyper Music' video. Muse's version of The Smiths' song would also later be used on the soundtrack to the self-explanatory *Not Another Teen Movie*. The seven-inch single kept things simple with just the same two lead tracks. 'Hyper Music'/'Feeling Good' charted at a number 11, a higher placing than previous single 'Bliss'. Muse's equal best ever.

Muse did get further mileage from the release when their version of 'Feeling Good' was later adopted by Nescafe for a TV advert, presumably in an attempt to equate the vocal dramatics of Matt Bellamy with the warming effects of a nice cup of freeze-dried joe, all this despite the band refusing permission. After objections were made, the coffee company was forced to replace the soundtrack with a pale imitation of the song performed by someone called Eon John. Coffee remains the highest grossing commodity in the world.

An eventful 2001 ended for Muse with three glorious nights in Japan before flying back to England for *six months without a single live engagement*. Only minutes short of midnight on New Year's Eve 2001, Chris's girlfriend gave birth to their second child, a girl named Ava.

"It's difficult being away from them for weeks at a time," he said. "But at the same time I could never picture myself doing a nine-to-five job, so when I am at home I have absolutely no work to do, it's like a holiday. Lots of people go to work before their kids are even up, or get in when they're in bed so only spend a couple of hours a day with them. With me it's pure quality family time.

"I really like living a life of total opposites. One half of my life is crazy, travelling around and playing to thousands of people, the other involves going back to Teignmouth to a load of old biddies. It's two very different takes on life."

In early 2002, two-thirds of Muse relocated to Brighton to live in a house formerly owned by Winston Churchill, in which he used to keep his many dogs and hunting hounds. Although *Origin* was barely a year old, the band knew they had to start to come up with a third album. Yet they had grown accustomed to writing and recording in plush residential studios where it takes a mere sixty seconds to get from bedroom to vocal booth. To rent shared accommodation with the necessary recording facilities in London was out of the question – property-wise the city was currently the second most expensive in the world. The flat Matt and Dom shared in London for a while was nothing but a stop-off point between tours; the place where underwear got washed and mail got sent to, and little else.

So that's why Matt, Dom and Tom Kirk moved to Brighton, where the latter had gone to university before joining the team. The seaside boys were back on the coast again. "I've thought about moving to London, but I don't want to bring children up there and we'd miss little things like the beach," the bassist confided. "In the winter it is dull, but it can be beautiful in the summer: surfing, nice pubs on the river."

The band had made good use of their stay in the UK's hippest town – they filmed the video for new single 'Dead Star' in the basement of the Churchill house.

Ostensibly a reminder that, despite the lack of recent releases, Muse were alive, well and active (not that people needed reminding – the last four years had seen a positive deluge of Muse products), the double A-sided 'Dead Star/In Your World' was their one and only exclusive single to date. That is, songs that didn't appear on any of the studio albums, hadn't been released as live acoustic radio cuts nor even been remixed in five minutes by some anonymous, overpaid DJ. The single certainly bridged a gap between the hyper space rock of *Origin* and the anxious Armageddon arias of the forthcoming *Hullabaloo*, 'Dead Star' being as heavy as thunder, inciteful, turbo-charged and reminiscent of the layered musical darkness of Tool.

"I sort of got into that kind of thing of looking into space and all that – a bit embarrassing, really. I'm a bit of a *Star Trek* fan in secret, but don't tell anyone," Matt told www.inmuseworld.net of the origins of 'Dead Star'. "The song is kind of about how everyone reacted to September 11. We were in Boston at the time; we got stuck there, and that's when we recorded those songs. So, in some ways, the lyrics are a little bit about the hysteria around that time and how people were really quick to point fingers at everyone else when they should have pointed fingers at themselves."

'In Your World' featured a guitar riff that seems inspired by Bach's 1708 smash hit single 'Toccata & Fugue In D Minor' and a vocal described by *NME* as "oddly reminiscent of Brett Anderson being burned at the stake."

Aside from 'Dead Star' and a live version of 'In Your World', the CD also featured the 'Dead Star' video and 'Futurism'. Singing of possible negative futures where society is little more than a collection of individuals lacking emotion and all servants to a higher system, 'Futurism' fitted in with *Origin Of Symmetry*'s themes of gut-wrenching alienation, Matt's voice wavering with plaintive despair. The only reason it hadn't been included before was because the band had been unable to do it justice live.

A 'Dead Star' EP was released with the same tracks, but also a version of Andy Williams/Englebert Humperdink's 'Can't Take My Eyes Off You' and the two videos. In June the single entered the charts at a respectable Number 13. The Top Ten still eluded Muse.

In the meantime, the band were finishing up lovingly piecing together footage for the live DVD, a work that would be called…

11. HULLABALOO!

THE OXFORD English dictionary defines a hullabaloo as "a loud commotion, or uproar", while the Cambridge Dictionary has it as "a loud noise made by people who are angry or annoyed." It's a good word – funny, child-like and rambunctious. It seemed a fitting word to describe the Muse live experience and therefore a perfect title for this live album. Two albums into a career seems rather early to be releasing a live album – traditionally it's what some say bands like AC/DC or Rush do when they've run out of new songs. However, Muse were always about the live show. Even the pristine production and unbending grace and power of *Origin Of Symmetry* paled when seen in the live context, so with album number three a long way off, in the first half of 2002 the band worked alternatively on this DVD release and writing new material.

Over the course of the live/B-sides album and a two-disc DVD, *Hullabaloo* played to Muse's strengths by not only showing how kick-ass the band had become to any of those still thrown by the sub-Radiohead comparisons, but also in capturing the sense of occasion and opulence of a Muse show – what *NME* would describe as "Moulin Rouge ridiculousness. If these songs have moustaches they'd be twirling them..."

The DVD featured nineteen songs with six of them having the added option of being viewed through various camera angles etc. A second DVD disc featured forty minutes worth of footage shot largely by Tom Kirk – who was producing the release – ranging from the sublime (Tom filming from the heart of a stage-smashing end of set melée complete with stage-diving exits) to the ridiculous (dressing up in ill-advised top hats for the photos that would promote the release in the press – not their best artistic decision). With cameras fastened to guitars and swooping overhead, they'd turned a potentially staid affair into one of the better live shows of the DVD age.

The *Hullabaloo* album was equally as worthwhile in converting more people to the Muse way. Listening to it, it's hard not to gasp at the outrageousness of it all; the fact that Muse make the playing of complex music sound so fluid and easy, or that what shouldn't work – a humble young trio sounding like Thor conducting Led Zeppelin with vocals supplied by the Archangel Gabriel – does completely, unquestionably. The inclusion of the many B-sides in one place also meant that anyone who hadn't been suckered into buying all the formats each time could still get to the flipside of the band in songs like 'Map Of Your Head' or the Tom Morello-sounding 'Yes Please'.

The *Hullabaloo* soundtrack charted at a respectable Number 10 in the UK charts – pretty good going for a live odds-and-sods collection, albeit it a highly lavish one. Reviews varied greatly. Thanks to the accompanying DVD, for the first time many of the snub-nosed UK critics actually got to see Muse in action (although still from their comfort of their own home) and how they viewed such precociousness was down to each reviewer's personal taste – and their willingness to accept the fact that Muse were already huge without or without their approval.

While many praised Muse's very un-English sense of grandeur and inflated ambition, *NME* weighed in with an outright dismissal for the very same reasons: "Their idea of grandeur is one huge delusion: compare these circus-freak hysterics with the cosmic humanity contained within work by The Flaming Lips or Spiritualized and Muse's flaws are obvious. Despite Matt Bellamy's reputation as a strange young man, there's not a moment of sensitivity here, not a moment of convincing emotion – and not enough milk of human kindness to cover a bowl of cornflakes."

But even then, reviewer Victoria Segal conceded, "For all their unlikeability, there's something undeniably impressive going on here." In a review marked three out of five, *Q* magazine's Roy Wilkinson was more forgiving, noting that: "A Parisian venue called Le Zenith is a suitable source for live recordings of Muse's exotic, sci-fi-gilded cyber-grunge. The effect is enhanced when singer Matt Bellamy announces, 'Bonsoir, Paree!' like some angst-rock version of dear dead Larry Olivier. Such theatricality is one of the elements that make Muse such an audacious young guitar band. They are as ridiculous as they are brilliant, something rammed home on hysterical, Total War-dimensioned versions of 'Muscle Museum', 'Space

Dementia' and 'Megalomania'."

After six months of writing and recording throughout early 2002, checking out new music on the fertile Brighton club scene and travelling to and from London for endless meetings and sessions working on footage in editing suites for *Hullabaloo* – Matt often doing the journey to the capital in his new black Lotus sports car – it became apparent that, for the money spent and travelling time wasted, they might as well be living in the capital. So the trio moved back there – Matt in with his girlfriend, and Dom and Tom Kirk first sharing a flat, then too moving in with their respective girlfriends, all in the Islington/Hackney area of north London. With two kids (and another on the way – he'd been making good use of band down time) Chris avoided London's over-inflated prices and soaring crime rates by continuing to unpack his suitcase in Devon.

Anyway, the *Hullabaloo* DVD would only satisfy people for so long. It was time for some more shows. Muse could afford to be more selective now, or at least didn't have to undertake massive slogs playing eight, nine or ten consecutive club shows in almost as many European countries, instead playing major festivals where they were increasingly honoured with top-ranking slots.

At the end of May, Muse travelled to Russia to play the Stunt Festival in Moscow and then the Leningrad Youth Palace in St. Petersburg. That Muse had a fan base in a country they had played only once before and which was far removed from the trio's own experience was one thing; that they were met with such open arms was amazing, although not that surprising. After all, music by its very nature transcends basic language and cultural differences. Russian kids get Muse for the same reason as people in Australia – because their music was fuelled by raw emotion and sounded like the past, the present and the future all at once. Whether or not you understood the words Matt Bellamy was singing didn't matter, you *felt* them.

In September 2003, I travelled to Zagreb, Croatia with Placebo – the only other British band with a devoted fan base as far-flung and geographically varied as Muse – and was humbled by the reaction the band got playing a beautiful city in a beautiful country that only gets on average two Western bands per year (so even Teignmouth has more gigs per week than Croatia does per annum). When I asked young fans and people working in the embryonic Croatian music business why they liked Placebo so much, the answers were simple enough: because they have made the effort where others never have.

The same can be applied to Muse, whose rigorous work ethic was taking them to such varied and musically undernourished places as Istanbul, Leningrad and Ostend, as they did in July. In just turning up, half the battle of convincing a brand new audience was already won.

In June, Matt wrote an erudite and illuminating account of his Russian experiences for *The Guardian*. Under the headline 'And The Crowds Went Wild', the piece went on to give a valuable insight into the frontiersman-like mentality the band embraced and the all-round absurdity of fame and life on the road. Matt revealed their surprise on their first visit to the former Soviet Union at finding themselves as the sole band playing at the 'Stunt' festival – quite literally an event centred around madmen riding around metal cages on their motorbikes, launching into rivers and tearing around dirt tracks in tractors.

"I have absolutely no idea why Muse are considered a suitable musical accompaniment for these activities," wrote the frontman, "but I feel like shaking our Russian booking agent by the hand and congratulating him."

Few Western bands visit Russia, so the effort Muse made was clearly appreciated, even if most of their sales were on the black market – that highly lucrative (for the bootleggers, at least) highly illegal outlet that accounts for huge percentages of sales in Russia, South America, Eastern Europe and Asia. Matt reasoned that if you've sold 100,000 records in Russia, the actual figure was probably something more like four times that. The day after their bizarre festival appearance, at a press conference held in the band's honour in Moscow, Matt tried to dazzle the assembled press representatives with his knowledge of Russian classical music.

"Some Russian classical music has been a really big influence on Muse's sound," he said. "I love Rachmaninov and Tchaikovsky. I've always felt that our sound could be a mix between their piano music and really hard rock. I thought that perhaps the Russians had picked up on that influence, that maybe they recognised something of their own culture in it, and that was why we had taken off over there."

At the press conference, however, Rachmaninov doesn't get a look in. Instead the journalists enthusiastically compare Muse to Seventies progressive rock bands like Yes and Rush, particularly bewildering to Matt as he has never heard these bands. "It's clearly intended as an enormous compliment. Perhaps they get the Rachmaninov stuff on a more subliminal level..."

The band spent their nights in Moscow lurking in 'Eurotrashy' nightclubs where they kept stopping the bad pop music to hold competitions to win vodka. Once in St. Petersburg, Muse went in search of edgier more underground entertainment, ending up, literally, underground in a club held in a disused nuclear bunker. Inside, Matt later revealed, the place was full of people injecting drugs and discarding their syringes on the floor. The band stayed just long enough to not look like horrified Western tourists, then took their leave. The subsequent three thousand-capacity St. Petersburg show made up for the less-than-pleasurable after-hours entertainment the city had to offer, crammed as it was full of excitable fans, the greater percentage of them female.

In St. Petersburg, there were about fifty women waiting outside the dressing room. "One of them comes up to me," wrote Matt. "She's obviously a psychopath. She has a gift for me – should she go and get it? I'm used to Russian fans giving me roses and teddy bears, but she comes back with a huge, incredibly intricate oil painting, which she says took her five months to complete." The bizarre picture featured Matt naked and horribly emaciated, with birds on his shoulders, holding a glowing heart in front of his genitals. "It's such a disturbing image that I decide to get some air, a bit of peace and quiet, and gather my thoughts. I step out on to the balcony of the dressing room. There are ten girls outside screaming at me, which hardly soothes my nerves."

The next day, as Muse leave for home, Dom is seen walking around the airport with the painting, showing it to complete strangers. None of them seem as bothered as Matt. "As I said, rock stardom in Russia has a unique way of revealing its idiosyncrasies…"

Festival dates continued with the Fuji festival in Japan while back home on July 8 *Hullabaloo* charted at number ten. In August, after an upbeat set from Ash, Muse took to the Reading Festival main stage just as the heavens opened and the light began to fade. What came next was a show-stealing performance in front of a massive crowd; a dark carnival after a jaunty crowd-pleasing set by Sum 41, The Hives and A. Afterwards, headliners the Foo Fighters looked somewhat dreary by comparison. "Reading definitely felt like a turning point," says Tom Kirk [they also played the sister gig at Leeds]. "Being on the main stage was a huge, huge gig for them."

By end of the 2002 summer festival season, the band felt ready to resume their personal lives away from all things Muse – writing, recording, touring, just generally being around one another 24/7 – and maybe even sleep in the same bed for more than one night. "I've been trying to get that side of my life together because I didn't really have a personal life until after Reading," Matt told writer Catherine Yates the following year. "I felt during the whole time of the *Origin* tour – and maybe it's going to happen again, but I hope not – that I'd lost any sense of having a personal life, any sense of having something that is mine. I didn't really have a sense of home. So I began to try to appreciate the simple things, really. Trying to build up something that feels like its private, that is mine. To go into the details defeats the point."

"We'd spent four or five years either on the road or recording or making the DVD or whatever with little more than a week off at a time," was Chris's explanation. "It was nice to be able to finish all that, go off and do our own things for a bit, than get back together in more of a homely environment, rather than desperately trying to find a rehearsal room on a day off in the middle of a tour or quickly jam something out in a soundcheck. It was the first time in five years that the three of us spent a lot of time together as mates, outside of the tour bus. It was almost a case of getting to know each other all over again, like starting a new band. A whole new approach."

The new approach would involve the unthinkable – almost an

entire year off the road. After a month's R 'n' R – that's rest and relaxation – Muse began rehearsing regularly again, something they hadn't had time to do since before the recording of *Showbiz* nearly four years previous. They'd just been too busy actually playing and working to practice – not necessarily a bad thing.

"If one us turned round and said they wanted to go on holiday for a couple of weeks, then we could do it," says Chris. "We needed to do our own thing. It was certainly the first time I was able to have a family holiday. I had a nice week in Majorca doing the typical tourist thing."

"We got a room in Hackney," explains Dom. "It was an open plan loft space. It was good just to have one space for us just to make music. We were doing demos too [in a warehouse space in Hackney formerly used by metalwork sculptors] which is something we hadn't done before. It just felt good to feel like we could experiment as much as we wanted to with each song or track. We didn't have a fixed idea of what it would sound like. Because we had time to experiment, a lot of the songs changed, we found out different ways of playing them."

"We spent the three months after the Reading and Leeds shows writing music, three or four days a week," adds Matt. "It felt good to concentrate on just making music again, for ourselves. It felt like going back to what it was like before we started touring loads and getting a record deal. *Showbiz* and *Origin Of Symmetry* felt like one long tour – we went straight from touring to the studio. We love touring so much that for a number of years we did every tour that was offered to us. We pushed it to the point where we were doing everything and just ending up totally knackered. This time we wanted to take it easy and take our time."

An unexpected diversion came during the band's writing period when they locked horns with Canadian 'songbird' Celine Dion. The latter was about to embark on a three-year residency in a Las Vegas hotel and had revealed that she planned to called her forthcoming show 'Muse'. The show was to be an 'extravaganza' and tickets would cost up to $1000 each. The band had wisely bought the worldwide rights for the use of the word in any music-related services including live shows, so Dion had the option to make a payment for use of the name. Still

Muse refused. After a press release from Muse and on-going disagreements, the songstress was forced to come up with another name, claiming that Muse had only ever been one of a number of possible names on a shortlist. Carnal Mayhem was not believed to be one of them.

It was Stereophonics' Kelly Jones who reckoned come the third album Muse would be trouble.

Boy, was he wrong.

By now Matt had a new girlfriend, an Italian lady called Gaia. Similarly Dom was seeing a girl from Pennsylvania. Chris was ensconced in his family life back in Teignmouth with Kelly. The band were in love and it is was starting to show. Matt joked that his new relationship had inspired some uplifting songs that were less chilling than *Origin Of Symmetry*. He wasn't married yet but he was in love – "Some of the songs sound like ABBA!" he laughed.

Muse have never been a pessimistic band, never prone to Joy Division-esque levels of despair, but they were effected by everything that was going on in the world. Matt's sponge-like ability to soak up information and rationalise the confusion of modern life is one of their strongest points; that which endears them on a global scale. So when the outside world began to encroach on his little love-bubble, it was time for a re-think. The sense of optimism in the new songs was short-lived.

The beginning of the darker times that would change the shape of their forthcoming third album began for Matt that Christmas. His well-deserved break with his girlfriend in Italy didn't turn out as planned. The day they arrived they received the tragic news that her ex-boyfriend had died.

"It was an experience," says Matt. "Italian funerals are berserk and I really felt like I shouldn't be there, like people were looking at me as if it was my fault. I was an outsider and it was the worst Christmas I've ever had. On the actual day I'd had enough of it so I drove off up into the Alps by myself in the empty roads and it was the first time I saw a white Christmas. So it was the best and the worst day, all in one."

*

Hooray For Hollyweird

The Sunset Strip feels like heaven and hell at the same time. A long stretch of road perched just high enough to look down across LA and the brown carcinogenic cloud malevolently hovering over it, but not so high as to encroach on the closed community of the Hollywood hills. By day the Strip hums with the constant stream of traffic, big polished cars driven by upwardly-mobile West Hollywood types – wannabe actors, models, screenwriters, porn stars, studio guys; all visiting expensive boutiques, Starbucks, flashy diners, tattoo parlours or bars. At night it comes alive, a snake of headlights winding into the distance driven by groups of rich girls from the valley, bling gangs in from east LA and people from the music and film industries visiting bars like The Rainbow, The Viper Room and On The Rox. Tower Records stays open late and Larry Flynt's *Hustler* store does a roaring trade in life-sized forearms and cock-rings. Nobody walks on the strip. They valet park their cars and tip heavily. Everyone is tanned, buff, silicone-static, oiled. On weekend nights, cops cruise constantly, pulling people over with a loud-hailer every hundred yards or so.

Then there are the hotels and the pretentious bars and pool-side areas where the true playas hang out, starting early, around midnight, sipping drinks, swapping phone numbers, hooking up, moving on to the next place. Being seen at the right places – The Whisky Bar at the Sunset Marquis, The Sky Bar, The Chateau Marmont, The Mondrian, The Standard or, for a bit of old school action the Hyatt House aka The Riot House. The Strip was where The Doors were discovered, where Motley Crue flourished, punk got nasty, *Swingers* swung, River Phoenix died and where the LA elite party *hard*.

In June 2003, Muse took rooms at The Standard, right in the heart of the West Hollywood end of the strip, an aggressively chic hotel where bikini-clad models recline for hours at a time – human eye candy – in a perspex box behind check-in. DJ's spin perfectly-volume dance tunes in the lobby and everyone presses the flesh on shag pile rugs beneath deliberately flattering lighting. On one visit to The Standard (on someone else's expenses) I passed Justin Timberlake on the forecourt, exchanged nods with a lost-looking Badly Drawn Boy in the lobby, had breakfast next to Angelina Jolie and Billy-Bob Thornton on the terrace. It's one of those places. At The Standard everyone works it hard; and you better believe that waitress's smile is going to cost you. It's a great world to step into, but one which will make demands on your sanity if you let yourself get sucked into it. A bit like Teignmouth.

Matt, Dom and Chris were staying at The Standard while they put the finishing touches to their new album – working title *The Smallprint* – at nearby Cello Studios. They has been staying in a rented apartment further away but relocated to the Strip more for convenience than a need for round-the-clock revelry and too-cool room service (raw tuna, carrot and Wasabi pizza a snip at $16).

Despite the many potential distractions in the delightful Sodom and Gomorrah made-flesh that is the Strip, Muse were focused on the new album, keeping socialising to a minimum in order to mix the album down. Old road mentors and LA scenesters the Red Hot Chili Peppers had a permanent set-up in Cello during Muse's stay, Tom Petty was working next door and System Of A Down frontman Serj Tankian had taken to dropping by the studio on occasion to say a bashful hello. REM, Green Day, Stone Temple Pilots and Elton John were all regular Cello clients. The Beach Boys recorded *Pet Sounds* there – and the equipment they used is still there to this day.

Fortunately for the band – what with all the distractions of Los Angeles around them – lots of the work on Muse's third full studio album had already taken place in early 2003 before they had even reached California – first at Beatles producer George Martin's Air Studio in Hampstead, London, a place often used by the likes of the Manics, U2 and Madonna, then at southern Ireland's only residential recording studio, the charmingly-named Grouse Lodge Studios near the village of Rosemount in the county of West Meath. Recordings went well enough that by the time they reached California most of the songs were in place, old friends Paul Reeve and John Cornfield having contributed their skills to nascent version of album track 'Blackout' back in

England. Such was the flurry of recording activity that the final stages of the album were a relatively relaxed and enjoyable affair.

"We were pretty chilled making the album," Matt told Channel 4's Colin Murray. "We had pretty much finished the album in Ireland but then we said that we needed to record some more backing vocals in that studio that the Beach Boys used for *Pet Sounds*, so we ended up going to LA pretty much to hang out on the Sunset Strip for a couple of months!"

At the helm of the recordings in LA was Rich Costey. Costey began his career in music playing guitar in bands while he was in high school, but his interest in recording soon took over. After producing bands in Boston and New York for various independent labels, and engineering for avant-garde composer Philip Glass, he re-located to Los Angeles. Once there, his work with Fiona Apple brought him to the attention of Def Jam/American Recordings all-round rock producer big-wig Rick Rubin. Costey was soon engineering and mixing Rubin projects, including Rage Against The Machine's covers album, *Renegades* and went on to work with some of the biggest, or more interesting, major label acts of recent times – The Mars Volta and Cave In. For Muse, he was producing, mixing, engineering and *informing*.

"They're one of the few bands who really seem like they're trying to do something different," Costey said of his reasons for working with the band, "and I thought that was fantastic."

"He's done nothing but bombard us with daily, jaded information about America and world politics," laughed Matt. During the recording, the experienced Costey marvelled aloud at how the trio had developed such a definitive sound and sense of direction so early on in their career, while they responded by declaring Costey a genius.

Muse had been recording in LA for seven weeks straight and staying at The Standard for twenty-four days when they were interviewed by *Kerrang!* between bouts of table tennis. Reflecting on *Origin Of Symmetry*'s Olympiad of excess, Matt admitted to having been irrevocably changed by being thrust into the spotlight and the new experiences that fame had afforded him.

"It had a very big effect on me," he admitted. "I changed. Very much. And I haven't really gone back to who I was before. When it all started kicking off, I made a point of going forward and forgetting about it all. I don't know why. But I think… I mean… I can't really remember who I was any more. There's whole sections of my life that I can't remember – everything that was my life up until I was about twenty is gone. So I'm trying to have things I'm going to remember in my life other than touring and making albums."[1]

Behind the scenes, changes were being made as the band brought in two new managers to oversee their day-to-day running and business affairs: accountant Anthony Addis in Stockport and Alex Wall in London. Tom Kirk was also now part of the management team while Dennis and Safta, who own a share in all the band's output for a number of albums, were now credited as the band's executive producers. Among other changes, publicist Mel Brown was suddenly exchanged in favour of Hall Or Nothing, the company who also look after Oasis and, ironically, both Stereophonics and Radiohead. Their next tour would be run by not one but two tour managers. Things were getting complicated. The list of people on the Muse pay-roll was now beginning to look more like a board of directors.

To be fair, the band were clearly moving forward. There was no signs of a stalling career or a below-par album on the way; no conflicts within the band itself. For the making of forthcoming album, it was as if, in the eye of the storm they had opted for self-preservation by closing ranks again and turning back in on themselves, back to the struggling outsider band of the mid-Nineties. They may even have been – whisper it – calming down.

"We honestly had a go, we really did try to socialise," Matt said between playbacks of the album. " We were so overwhelmed that people were into the music, we wanted to turn music into something more that was more than just a gig and a goodbye. It worked for a while, but as we got bigger, the crowds got younger and the parties just turned into signing sessions. Besides, I can't think of anything more unattractive than someone wanting to have sex with you for what you are onstage."[2]

It wasn't all introspection and self-analysis though. The band had taken time off to tool around in a couple of "ridiculously fast" cars which they opened up on the coastal roads between LA and San Francisco, (which were later crashed by their hotel valets).

"LA definitely affected the importance of some of the songs and the title of the album," Matt later explained. "We felt a bit different out there, we were going to gigs and walking down the street and you just get the impression that no-one really gives a toss about what's going on in the rest of the world. At the same time we were there, there were millions of people protesting [against the war in Iraq] on the streets in Britain. It made me see that... it's fucked up and there's nothing that anyone can do about it."[3]

A band disillusioned with the more tawdry aspects of fame and the retrogression of mankind and the world at large? Pre-millennial tension giving way to the post-millennial realisation that *this really is it*? Hmmm. Sounds like the perfect inspiration for a new set of songs.

12. SING FOR ABSOLUTION

absolution ~ n. *priest's formal declaration of forgiveness of sins.*
absolve ~ *clear of blame or guilt; free from an obligation.*

THERE'S A man who stands outside Oxford Circus tube station in the heart of London's West End. He's there everyday with a loud-hailer and battery back, berating passers-by with tales of hellfire and brimstone, death and damnation, pointing his finger and whipping himself up into an excited, spittled frenzy of the usual evangelical clichés. If you ever passed through there, you'd know who I'm talking about.

He's been down there about three years now, and when he's not on his usual patch he's to be found outside gigs intimidating people for giving themselves over to Satan ("But Satan has the best tunes!" I once replied, stealing a Bill Hicks one-liner). This manic street preacher's philosophy on life has been condensed into one choice phrase: "Don't be a sinner, be a winner." Give yourself to Jesus while there's still time. In other words: we're all fucked, the end is nigh and only a total devotion to Jesus can save our souls.

That he's a proper mad Scouse bastard who once revealed he had done many bad things in his life and prefers to use his fists than turn the other cheek to detractors is of no consequence here. What is, is that it has been suggested that if Matt Bellamy wasn't the greatest rock star in Britain he'd be down on Oxford Street at rush-hour prophesising the exact time and date that it's due to turn to shit, while acting as a human conduit for life forms from far beyond the galaxy, piecing together messages with a Ouija, improvised with a grubby bit of cardboard and a cut-up copy of the Ikea catalogue.

Instead he chose to write an album about it all. War. Religion. Death. Destruction. Our inevitable demise. It was to be called *Absolution*.

*

"*Absolution* is an album about relationships between you and other things, whether it's you and God or you and your girlfriend," says Matt Bellamy. "Contradiction is in everyone. If you look immediately around you, you've got your friends and loved ones but if you look at things on a more global scale, it all becomes a bit jading.

It could be about the fact that war was breaking out, it could be about the fact that in four hundred years there's going to be an ice age. I think within our lifetime we're gonna see some dark stuff. But the reactions aren't all negative. There's a few tracks that are trying to find that strength, the raw energy that keeps you going through that jadedness, as opposed to just resigning."[1]

Lest we forget, during 2002 Matt had been revealing to crowds and press alike that the new material was uplifting, heavily inspired by falling in love with his new Italian girlfriend and was "a bit like ABBA". A few months later it was an entirely different story.

The bulk of the third studio album was written and recorded in the months leading up to the US and UK's invasion of Iraq under the pretence that they were hunting out weapons of mass destruction. Critics said it wasn't a war as such – that requires two opposing sides – rather a vulgar display of American power, with Britain taking on the role of the little shit who always sticks close to the playground bully at school for protection. With the authority of the United Nations undermined and America adopting the role of righteous Christian crusaders fighting a quasi-Biblical world of Muslim terrorists, the implications were potentially massive. By 2003, the world had become a more unstable place than it has possibly ever been.

When you have even half a brain it's hard not to be affected by such cataclysmic events. Muse's reaction was an emotional rather than a political one. "There were moments when the war kicked in when everyone was watching TV for those first few days and it was a pretty dark atmosphere in the world," explained Matt. "It was a bit of a weird vibe. I think that inspired a bit of doubt in the album as well. Some songs became more important than others, like 'Apocalypse Please'. That song set the stage for the whole album. Religious fanaticism and religious stupidity are going to cause everything to fuck up and the whole album is about what goes through your mind at the last moment. Are you pissed off and jaded or are you happy you've done everything you could've done?"[2]

Such was the change in mood of the world as a whole that the band dropped three of the first five songs they had recorded for the album, keeping only 'Blackout' and 'Butterflies And Hurricanes'. The other songs had been considered inappropriately cheerful.

On July 14, Muse broke with convention and released 'Stockholm Syndrome', the lead-off track from *Absolution* but as a download-only single. For once people weren't faced with a deluge of multiple formats often containing the same songs recorded in different places. Although this disqualified it from the charts, the number of downloads it received would have equated to a Top 3 place – effectively their most successful single to date.

The song itself was beautiful metal and arguably Muse's hardest moment yet – and certainly their most brutal-sounding single so far – a thrusting display of Metallica-like virtuoso guitars providing a stark contrast to Matt's tempered vocals. Actually, it bears something of a resemblance to the indulgent fretboard masturbation of Steve Vai, only this time it had soul and wasn't afraid to slam-dance and solo at the same time. 'Stockholm Syndrome' was the first download-only single to feature in a significant number of end-of-year reader's and writer's magazine polls. It was also just about the perfect teaser for the new album.

*

The first thing you heard on *Absolution* was the rhythmic stomping of jackboots before the ominous stabbing piano chords and crashing drums of opener 'Apocalypse Please' thundered from the speakers. It was nothing short of a Biblical start, Matt a howling prophet pointing the finger as Babylon burns around him, the spotlight of truth beaming down on him from unknown dimensions.

"The message of that song is that religious inaccuracies lead to the re-enactment of ancient prophesies," explained Matt. "That's what's going on right now – that knobhead in America and with Islam. Between them all they're believing in some ancient prophesy, when all that was was a couple of people in robes improvising. The fact that the modern day world is still influenced by these ideas is outrageous. I'm singing from the point of view of a religious fanatic saying, 'C'mon God, come down to earth and sort it all out.'"[3]

All pulsing bass-lines, the intro for future single 'Time Is Running Out' sounded tactile, but the chorus was anthemic – an urgent mini-melodrama about a relationship that feels like suffocation. Perfect single material. "This song is about the feelings of being monopolised by someone," said Matt. "'Time Is Running Out' makes a reference to the fact that we tried to break this enclosure."

Dull muso fact: the electric piano on the song was originally used by U2 on 'New Year's Day' although unlike when Muse used it, it wasn't distorted to all hell. "We definitely worked to find new sounds, and we tried rubbing our hands together and slapping and clapping, all that kind of thing, which is something we'd thought about doing and features quite heavily on this song," said the singer. "You know, finger clicking and stuff."

'Sing For Absolution' was the centre-piece that prevented the album from succumbing to the Doomsday forces powering its harder moments. It was the eye of the storm, the necessary respite which, although dream-like actually, carried a heavy religious message about accepting that we may well already be beyond redemption.

"This song is completely different from the rest of the album," said Matt. "There is something oppressive in this song, with a gothic sound. The couplets speak about some kind of a dead relationship."

The title of 'Stockholm Syndrome' concerns a psychological scenario whereby someone falls in love with the person who had kidnapped them – a typically Muse-like way of looking at a situation. The term itself comes from a failed bank robbery in 1973 at Kreditbanken in Stockholm in which four people were taken hostage. Within just six days the hostages were actively resisting rescue from the authorities, then not only refused to testify against the robbers but subsequently raised money for their legal defence. One of the hostages even went on to become engaged to one of her (by now imprisoned) captors.

What is intriguing is the psychology behind such a U-turn in behaviour. 'Stockholm Syndrome' – that sudden shift of allegiance – is believed to come into effect when a person is isolated and forced to consider their own possible death, but yet, confusingly, is shown acts of kindness by the captor, therefore giving them a God-like position of power. It only takes three or four days for the kidnapped to relinquish all control to their captors, to such an extent that they will actively defend those who have put their life in threat in the first place. The lyrics here almost refer to the most notorious case of Stockholm Syndrome when Patty Hearst, kidnapped daughter of publishing magnate Randolph Hearst, who, despite being tortured, changed her name to 'Tania' and took up arms to join in the fight with her captors, the Symbionese Liberation Army.

'Falling Away With You' was a tender song, hushed like a late night Evensong choir. "It's kind of singing about when you have flashbacks to things," said Matt. "It's only things like scars, pictures, photos and videos and stuff that really make you understand that the past really did happen. I find the past can blur itself up a little bit, especially when it comes to relationships."

To remind us that Armageddon was just around the corner, a forty second 'Interlude' of symphonic post-rock noises followed, before a bit of bass arpeggio-ing and siren-guitars announces 'Hysteria' (the introduction sounded almost exactly like 'Cochise' by Tom Morello's Audioslave). The song's title was the most downbeat aspect of a song that was the closest Muse had come to replicating the pomposity of Queen – the chorus of "I want it now...." recalling Mercury and Co's 'I Want It All' – 'Hysteria' stealthily pulsed along, a dense slab of rock.

Of the swooning 'Blackout' Matt says: "That song came from a combination of influences, really. It's obviously influenced by the more classic types of songs that were going round before the Sixties and Fifties. I'm talking about the times of Frank Sinatra, that type of era where classical music was combining itself with popular song." It was soon to become a staple part of Muse's live set and a chance for a breather with Chris playing keyboards and the pace stepping down a gear. Toilet time.

'Butterflies & Hurricanes' was an epic counter-piece to 'Apocalypse Please', a hopeful-sounding high-drama that masked a truly pessimist view of the world that could have been spoken by both George Bush or the Osama bin Laden/Saddam Hussein's 'axis of evil'. By-passing dogma for a pan-international, religiously impartial emotional response through the language of music, it was the personal-political at it best.

Already part of their live set, 'TSP' aka 'The Small Print' was another scorcher, a song that embodied Matt's opinions on the myth-making and manipulative nature of organised religions for the purpose of mass social control (*"I'm the priest God never paid"*). Drawing from a variety of sources of half-read books and TV programmes, Matt never openly admitted to taking information and forming his own political/religious theories, which he was more than happy to share during the many interviews conducted for *Absolution*.

"Jesus wasn't a Jew or anything," he expounded. "Basically, Jesus didn't die on the cross. He got taken down. He was taken down and he was resuscitated, not resurrected. It comes from the same Hebrew word, resuscitation and resurrection. It's important these guys know this stuff, because Judaism says that the Messiah will come down to Earth and sort it all out. But he didn't sort it out, did he? He came down, multiplied some fish and did this, that and the other and died. He was obviously not the Messiah. My point is, he was a great bloke and the real story is much more interesting than some weird fantasy. Because the real story is, the most important religion in the Western world is actually influenced by Eastern ways of thinking. The things that I'm saying now, in the years 900, 1600, people who said that got quartered and burned at the stake. And if I was saying what I'm saying now in America then I think I would be quartered too..."[4]

By virtue of the strong competition, 'Endlessly' was one of the album's weaker tracks, a downbeat ethereal forlorn love song. The Smiths-influenced 'Thought Of A Dying Atheist' had originally been written and recorded as part of the *Origin* sessions of late 2000, but for some reason the title seemed a little too bleak and so the song was held back. It was classic Muse, where a tempered, tightly-controlled breathless verse plunged into a glorious surging melody of a chorus. It was also typical example of the band's canny knack for painting lyrically bleak scenarios then injecting them with a life-affirming sense of optimism through the sheer musical abandonment of the song. They are that rarest of bands that have mastered the art of traversing the highest peaks and the deepest, darkest lows in the space of seconds.

"It's about the idea of a guy who comes back to his office at work and he's killed everybody," Matt explained. "He's ripped them all apart with his bare hands. The mindset of the song is that someone has done that and gone home to their wife with blood on their hands. It's not the ending of his life as such, but the end of his sanity."

Drawn-out for full funereal atmospheric effect and with a discordant baroque piano jolting like the last reflex of rigor mortis, album closer 'Ruled By Secrecy' was at least enough to suggest that a career as a theatrical or cinematic soundtracker surely lies ahead for Matt Bellamy should he chose to pursue it.

An album that opened with the lines: "Declare this an emergency/Come on spread a sense of urgency..." closed with the final words: "Changes in the air and they'll hide everywhere... and no one knows who's in control."

It sounded like a nail being driven into a coffin.

Like the death-knell for something sacred.

*

In combining the timeless romanticism of classical music with the most inventive and defining rock sounds around, while thankfully never once sounding like 'The London Philharmonic Plays Rock Classics', with *Absolution* Muse had made an album with a broad appeal, where pomp-rock, punk rock, metal and classical vied for space in the mix, the end result being something far more palatable, more *believable*, than it appears on paper.

"I do love rock music," said Matt. "But when I hear that Romantic stuff, it sounds like the meaning of life. It's as though the composers were using the peak of their intelligence to express the deepest of emotions. And this gives me hope – hope about everything! When I heard choruses singing that Palestrina stuff [an Italian composer of sacred music who was an important musical figure of the Renaissance; known for his "seamless texture" of polyphony], I think there is a God – there is a heaven."[5]

The cover artwork for *Absolution* was as interesting and evocative as the music within. It depicted a lone man standing on cold grey earth, seemingly grasping a gas mask in one hand, agape at the sky as the shadows of a legion of humans pass over him like silent stealth bombers.

On first glance – to this author's eyes anyway – it gave the impression of falling bodies, a shower of soul descending earthwards, yet conversely could also just as easily be humans ascending up to heaven. As in image it was perfectly ambiguous, an *is-the-glass-half-empty/half-full* image? that relies on individual interpretation, but either way was completely in keeping with the themes of absolution, forgiveness and human mortality. It particularly seemed to complement the album's title track (play the song while studying the images to feel the intended effect). The back cover showed a similar manipulated photograph, but this time the man was replaced by a child. The images of shadowy other-worldly sceptres was carried over into subsequent singles releases from the album. Inner sleeve photos of the band were taken by trendy rock photographer Perou.

On its release, critical acclaim for *Absolution* was widespread: "The conspiracy theories of *Absolution* are wrapped in delicate, intimate cloaks, an album where personal happiness has an Uzi-frenzied face-off with those issues that remain out of our hands," noted *The Fly*.

"Like *Ulysses* or *The Matrix Reloaded*, *Absolution* makes as much sense as you decide it's going to, " wrote *NME* reviewer Dan Martin. "There's been no record released this century with stakes so high, but one man's prog is another man's progress, and every guitar here sounds like it's from the future, every movement and score orchestrated with the celestial vision... chartbusting tunes really do fall from the sky."

These fourteen songs seemed to signify the passing of people's outdated preconceptions about who Muse were and what they did. Gone were the interviews where you could have a wager with friends about the frequency of the words 'Radiohead' and 'Devon' in the same article.

The album appealed to those critics and tastemakers who previously had dismissed Muse as a generic indie three-piece resigned to forever live out their existence on the tour circuit treadmill and the lower regions of the Top 75. When working on this book I had a number of older (though not necessarily wiser) journalists comment that "that album's not bad actually, it sounds like Queen." Similarly the broadsheet press discovered the band, lavishing them with praise and recognising their rightful place in the British rock canon alongside the dusty bands of yore.

Absolution definitely marked a changed status within wider public opinion. Critics finally realised that they may well have a classic band in their midst – the type whose absence they have been lamenting since the Seventies when the new broom of punk rock rightfully swept the floor clean. The year 2003 saw some embarrassed backtracking and the perfect coalescence of opinion. *Absolution* was the album that united classic rock fans with metal kids, indie kids with contemporary-minded prog fans – songs like 'Stockholm Syndrome' managing to straddle that Metallica-Wagner- R********* divide with ease. In fact, with their third studio album, Muse's musical cross-pollination and catholic tastes seemed liked the most natural thing in the world. Whether you like Led Zeppelin or The Aphex Twin, System Of A Down, Billie Holliday or Rachmaninov, *Absolution* and its attendant live show had something for all-comers.

"People seem to be asking a lot more questions about what we think about things in the world," laughed Matt in late 2003. "There's more to journalists' questions than just Teignmouth now! To be honest though, I get asked things in interviews, respond and don't remember any of it. I read it back and it doesn't make sense even to me, but it doesn't matter. It's funny."

When asked about sounding so gigantic so young, Muse were Dinosaur rockers before their time, Matt's response was resolute: "No. We're the opposite. We have the possibility of changing everything. It's not just making music, it's showing people what music is all about."

Only three British rock bands had number one albums in 2003. Despite initial quantities of *Absolution* containing a manufacturing error (tracks seven and eight, 'Interlude' and 'Hysteria' were listed the wrong way round) upon its release on September 22, *Absolution* was one of them (rivals Stereophonics *You've Got To Go There To Come Back* and The Darkness's *Permission To Land* were the other two). It went straight in at number one on the UK albums chart in the strongest-week for album sales in two years and fell out of the Top 30 five weeks later.

Muse had officially gone mainstream – without ever having to sound it. "Yeah, I'm pleased we sold 71,000 copies of our album in a week," laughed a self-deprecating Matt. "But Dido's new record sold more than that on the first day of release..."

But Dido hadn't written an album about the end of the world.

The staggered release of *Absolution* in other countries over the coming weeks yielded Number 1 chart positions in France and Iceland, as well as success in Holland and Belgium (2), Ireland and Switzerland (3), Italy (4), Austria and Norway (5) and further Top 20 slots in Germany, Denmark, Australia, Finland, Spain. In troubled times, Muse had sung for absolution. The people had listened. And the people liked what they heard.

13. MASS HYSTERIA

"Making music puts me in a simplistic state of realising what it is to be alive. My life has involved a lot of upheaval, with my girlfriend, money, my friends, jobs, possessions, family. I was always moving house, but I realised that all of these things were quite fickle. They can all change as life goes on. People move on."[1]

Matt Bellamy, November 2003.

MUSE KNEW they'd made it when they finally had a say in how they toured. Up until now, the military-like precision of their unrelenting touring schedule – a schedule that had served them very well – had been out of their hands. Now, with fame and success came just enough power to be heard when it was time to decide how they were going to be spending future chunks of their lives.

Muse eased into their third album campaign by combining a heavy promotional work-load with private shows in each town they travelled to – Amsterdam, Paris, Brussels etc – eschewing the tour bus for long train rides between full days facing the media.

"The day after the Amsterdam show, we were up at 10 o'clock and went to this old church in the middle of the red light district, some twelfth century church, and did all the interviews there," said Matt. "We've never done that many interviews in one day. We started at ten and finished at six, I think. It was bit more interesting doing it in a church. At one point I found myself playing one of the biggest church organs in Europe while being filmed by MTV. So that was a bit weird. There was all these graves everywhere. It was a bit morbid, actually."[2]

In Paris the band managed to blow the sound system of the small Trabeno club during opening song 'Butterflies And Hurricanes'. During the twenty-minute black-out, the band compensated by handing out their backstage rider to the audience. When the power was regained, a frustrating performance ended with Matt trashing the drum-kit and flinging his guitar across the stage, gouging a chunk out of Dom's head in the process. "That hasn't happened for a while…" quipped Matt afterwards as Dom went to hospital to receive a tetanus jab.

This brief promo trip culminated with a show for five hundred competition winners and industry schmoozers packed into the Carling Islington Academy for an *XFM*-sponsored show.

By late 2003, Muse had reached further than most British bands, many of whom suffer for their own parochialism. As previously mentioned, their's is a universal outlook, a sound that deals with emotions that need no translator. They never wanted to be the big fish in a small pond, they simply wanted to *be*. By the end of 2003 they were a fully functioning business, employing managers, publicists and A&R men. They were also running an office of two people in London – one friend organising promotional material and Tom Kirk running the band's website, artwork and live visuals.

Their autumn/winter European tour saw the band employing twenty-eight people for a stage show that was massive by any British band's proportions: a crew of bus drivers, truck drivers, caterers, lighting men, tour manager, roadies and riggers whose belt-loops proudly clink with an array of over-sized calipers and allen keys and who work for *no-one* when the football scores are read out on Saturday afternoon. All were there to make sure the show happened.

"The only reason we've made money on this tour is because we've sold way more tickets that we or anyone else thought we would," explained Matt. "We saw how much money we had managed to save so far and decided to spend all of it on equipment, staging, lights and a crew to put it all together. We actually over-spent, just to tour bigger and better places.

An example of their far-reaching popularity: at 9am on November 16, tickets went on sale in Reykjavik, Iceland for the band's show there the following month. Some fans had been waiting all night and within the first sixty minutes, all six thousand tickets were bought up (not bad considering the city only houses a total of 120,000 people.)

"There are two sides to the band that people respond to, depending on whether we're in the north or south of Europe," explained Matt. "In the north they treat us as a very serious band and they take us very, very seriously, whereas in the south they just see it as 'Let's fucking rock!'"[(3)]

Johnny Sharp of *The Guardian* met up with the band in France at one such show in the Loire town of Angers. The tour saw them leading a refined rock star's life that befitted the international success of *Absolution*, the band electing to spend a day off at a wine-tasting session at a rural fair, where they managed to sample all thirty-six wines on offer, awarding marks out of ten and noting down such words as "mould" and "Christmas". It was a far cry from sending Chris to the bar for pints of snakebite in The Cavern. The wine-tasting continued into Italy.

"There have been some crazy gigs so far," wrote the band in a fan-club message in November. "Milan, Geneva, Lyon, Berlin and Brussels really kicked off." On one day off, the band were personally invited to visit the Mayor Of Florence's palatial spread as his daughter was a big fan. After a couple of phonecalls the band found themselves exploring the secret tunnels beneath the city that otherwise were prohibited to the general public. Another anecdote saw them meet 'Ice' from 'Transylvania', who took them to his Italian rock/goth bars to meet a collection of people "that can only be described as difficult to describe..."

In Spain they paid a visit to Salvador Dali's house – "Pretty surreal," deadpanned Dom. In Germany they went, um go-karting. After a flurry of shows, the band did their recovering back in Florie, France with a spot of wine-tasting and a look at the local vineyards.

"The show at the Bercy in Paris was a particular highlight for me," recalled Chris. "I remember playing there with the Chili Peppers and the Foo Fighters and until that point the biggest crowd we'd seen was five hundred people. In fact, in the UK we were only drawing an average of two hundred people so at the time we couldn't quite comprehend eighteen thousand people going to see one band. So to go there and headline five years later and see the crowd go nuts was beyond what we thought was ever possible. Most of the British bands we grew up going to see – Senseless Things, Mega City Four, even early Radiohead shows at places like The Lemon Grove in Exeter – seemed massive to us, so we'd have been content playing to one, two thousand people a night like they did. But eighteen thousand..."

*

A quick word on prog rock – if that's not a contradiction in terms: by 2003 Muse were not alone in their prog rock tendencies. While never as dippy or self-satisfied as those Seventies progressive musicians capable of indulgence on a grand scale (Rick Wakeman's 'Knights Of The Round Table' on ice at Wembley anyone?), a tendency towards grandiose and groundbreaking sounds had recently re-emerged in alternative music, causing the erroneous phrase 'nu-prog' to crop up on more than one occasion.

Again, Radiohead were a central force, the band most responsible for stealing rock music back from no-brainer bands like Oasis, unafraid to flaunt their degrees and make music that incorporates new technologies into a rock 'n' roll setting. In which case, they could be called progressive.

The difference this time is that this 'nu prog' (yuk) was as much influenced by sounds as disparate as hardcore punk rock and electronica as Dungeons & Dragons; artsy instead of anal, political rather than pretentious. The new generation of progressive bands were not interested in musical one-upmanship, but treading new ground and rocking out. And so alongside Muse, majestic – but very different – sounding bands like The Mars Volta, Mogwai, Tool, System Of A Down, Sigor Ros, Cave In, Godspeed You Black Emperor and A Perfect Circle all contributed to the development of rock. Without dressing like wizards.

All further proof that some music can be called progressive once again without it being directed as an insult. Whether we'll yet get to see Matt Bellamy's *Waiting For Godot: The Opera (On Rollerblades)* remains to be seen – but it's hard to see the band either toning down or settling in for an easy and unoriginal passage in middle adulthood. Thankfully they're still too young and too energetic to be susceptible to acts of musical idiocy.

Where British big-name contemporaries like Oasis, Travis, Manic Street Preachers, Coldplay and Stereophonics all seemed to have settled for the easy option of formulaic, watered-down music or half-hearted attempts at controversy (often unwittingly becoming everything they once hated), others have flourished.

"Rock, strangely enough has been one of the most conservative genres around. And it's meant to be the opposite," spits Matt. "It's been a relatively simple formula since the Seventies and very few bands are willing to push away from that. If you look at the most successful bands in rock from the last ten years, they don't touch upon an ounce of the creativity of rock bands from the Seventies."[4]

Over the years, however, a few homegrown bands like Led Zeppelin, Pink Floyd and Radiohead have all made the leap to arenas, retaining at least something approaching artistic credibility or, failing that, a badass lighting rig. Others like U2 may have taken it even further, but they have also lost something important along the way – their souls. Bands such as Placebo and a recently-disbanded Suede (hardly rock, agreed) have enjoyed sustained success, albeit it lacking the initial press fervour they once courted, and with the odd receding hairline. Newer acts such as Hundred Reasons and Lostprophets are building followings but look unlikely to conquer the heartland of America, nor carve out long-lasting careers. More recent success The Darkness may yet make that arena leap too, tongue-in-cheek or not.

"I think the main criticism we got last time was that it was all overblown and over the top and prog-influenced," said Matt. "I think it's only in the realm of current times that we seem OTT. If you look at the history of rock, there's bands that have gone way farther than us, in every decade except for the Nineties, whether it was the image of bands in the Eighties or the experimentalism of bands in the Sixties or the whole prog rock thing in the Seventies. Towards the end of the Nineties it went more towards wanting to appear like normal people. Personally though, I don't think we are that over-the-top. Yeah, we play up to it a little bit but when I listen to us I don't think it's in any way extreme, compared to a band like Slipknot."[5]

Still. It was up to Muse to show everyone how it was done.

*

If Muse were now happy to be seen as latter-day *bon viveurs* by day and lip-curling, thunderous rock Dyonisees by night, the shows played in support of *Absolution* testified to a toweringly dramatic live band of Led Zeppelin proportions. Each night on the tour saw them coming onstage to a heavy military drum beat in front of a backdrop of the *Absolution* silhouette figures – either ascending angels, people flying overheard or falling bodies, depending on which way you look at it. Matt would take his place behind a huge red piano "like Freddie Mercury playing the Wizard of Oz" (*The Guardian*) with each key, when played, lighting up white neon lights seemingly in homage to *Close Encounters Of The Third Kind*. Matt saw the humour in their imaginative theatrics, joking that he had nearly gone onstage one night in Dracula cloak and fangs, until nerves got the better of him. It's certainly one to bear in mind for the future though...

Matt admitted to me, "We used to have a lot of parties on tour but learnt last year that you just can't do it every night if you're playing to crowds this size, because it's much more about the music than the lifestyle. Three hundred capacity pubs – that's where the good times are.

I think once you go beyond crowds of two or three thousand, you do sort of lose that intimacy of being close to the crowd, but it gets replaced with something that's much bigger, much more overwhelming," reasoned Chris. "When you go onstage and sixteen thousand people scream at you at once, the sheer volume can't really be beaten by anything."

The set-list largely remained the same each night, the band opening with the triple-whammy of 'Apocalypse Please', 'Hysteria' and 'New Born', then closing with 'Plug-In Baby', before returning to encore with 'Black Out' and leaving with a brutal 'Stockholm Syndrome' as a parting shot. Older tunes like 'Cave' and first 'proper' single 'Uno' were now only being played on odd occasions.

The European tour was punctuated by a night at the *Q Awards* where they won the first ever 'Innovation In Music' category.

"Dom has spilt a glass of red wine over Dexy's Midnight Runners," hiccupped Matt at the party afterwards, "and Lemmy from Motörhead has invited us to his gig at the Hammersmith Apollo."

For the award ceremony, the band had flown in from Milan where the previous day they had played an hour-long live set which provided the climax to MTV's 'Muse Day'. Yes, a Muse Day. Yes – Muse, an oft-derided band who had lived through Britpop, nu-metal, garage rock and any number of musical fads, were now big enough to warrant two days-worth of scheduling on the cultural vacuum that is empTV. The channel aired pieces on the making of both *Hullabaloo* and *Absolution*, a live show at Leeds University, old videos and the band's own video selections.

*

Maybe it was the way the fans in Manchester burst the giant *Prisoner* balloons with their cigarettes; in Cardiff they stood in drunken mute wonder, utterly enraptured. Or maybe it was the clusters of fans that appeared everywhere the band went – at backstage exits, in hotel lobbies, in the pissing rain, on Monday mornings when they undoubtedly had to be elsewhere. Or perhaps it was the pasta *fruits de mere* they were serving in catering.

I still can't decide on the one abiding memory of the Muse shows I witnessed when I joined them on their UK tour in December 2003. I think the overall impression I took away from it all was of a band on cruise control, a band finally able to reap the rewards of five years solid work as major label recording artists, ten years as a band and fifteen years after first learning to play their instruments.

The whole tour was a grand operation. Straight off the back of a mammoth European tour, it was running as smoothly as a well-oiled machine; all the components – whether roadie, bus, driver or frontman. It carried with it an air of luxury, comfort, confidence and total adoration for the band.

"We still don't get recognised that much, we're just not that kind of famous," laughed Matt. "We can go out anywhere as long it's not a rock venue or an indie club, which means we have to go to dance clubs and start raving away, pretending we're into that kind of music! Where I live in London, the Hackney/Islington area, no-one recognises me at all."

With expensive on-stage screens, carefully edited visuals and Tom Kirk down in the pit with a digital camera, even those in the cheap seats had something to watch as the band filled vast venues such as Wembley Arena, the *Manchester Evening News* Arena and Birmingham NEC – as big as indoors venues get in the UK. During 'Space Dementia' the huge screens showed a film of stars and planets rushing past at warp-speed, cut over shots of Matt's bony fingers dancing over the keyboard, a regular Captain Kirk of his own little space pod.

"We spent about a week working on everything beforehand and Matt got very involved coming up with visual concepts," explains Tom. " There's always a lot of preparation goes into this band – they're a lot more focused on keeping well, looking after themselves and being mentally prepared. The strength of the performances they've been giving has been amazing. They've really stepped up a gear."

That day I saw Muse play in Cardiff International Arena 'Hysteria' was released as a CD and DVD single, charting at Number 17. The CD and vinyl single were backed by 'Eternally Missed', while the DVD featured the 'Hysteria (Director's Cut)' video, the audio track, 'Hysteria' live at MTV2, the making of the video plus a fan's art picture gallery.

It's true, Muse were living in the lap of the Gods, but they also appeared to be more serious than ever about their live show, relishing it rather than going through the motions before settling into a stadium-sized rut.

Sitting with Matt just a few minutes before he strode out on-stage in front of 14,000 people in Manchester, he told me how, "the buzz comes from getting extremely nervous before we go on," said Matt. "I'm really nervous now, already. I think that when you get to half an hour before, the nerves turn into adrenalin. It turns into pure excitement, as opposed to just shitting yourself. I'm nervous all day, pretty much."

Backstage at the *Evening News* Arena in Manchester, the

atmosphere was celebratory, as the dressing room buzzed with well-wishers, all unwittingly standing in neat little circles around each band member. Matt's brother Paul was there – they don't look similar but share the exact same mannerisms – as were the band's new managers, their publicist and many of Chris's relatives from Rotherham and Sheffield. Someone pops open some champagne. Someone else tries to light their cigarette the wrong way round. Despite various gifts and cards containing girls' phone numbers and interesting propositions being scattered around the dressing room, things were relaxed, civilised and infinitely more sedate than the on-tour madness I'd seen three or four years earlier.

The fancy dress backstage parties of former days had long gone. "I have to be honest with you, I've gone off the whole thing anyway. I can't think of anything more unattractive than someone wanting to have sex with you for what you are onstage."

"It's a shame people might think that they've become arrogant, particularly Matt, who is misunderstood anyway," says Ronnie Kerswell. "I think he still feels weird when people come and ask him for autographs, because I think he still gets a bit overwhelmed."

Amongst the many well-wishers backstage at Wembley was a funny looking older guy with yellowy-blond hair. He and his daughter, a big fan of the band, invited the boys to their house for a party, but not being in the habit of disappearing with strangers (well, not quite as much as they used to) they politely declined. They later found out it was Rick Wakeman, progmeister general, the bane of many a Muse review. When relating this tale Matt complained that he'd never even heard of Wakeman's music in the first place.

"Is it really bad?" he enquired.

"Not if you like dragons on ice skates," was my reply.

And I *swear* I saw the spark of a new idea flicker in Matt Bellamy's eye...

God help us.

*

"I have become used to change and more addicted to this feeling I get from music, because the one thing that's been the same all my life is the process I go through when writing or playing music. All those other things just peel away and disappear. It's the only thing I say is truly me. Everything else is interchangeable."
Matt Bellamy, 2003

And Amen To That
At the time of writing, Muse's future is bright enough to warrant the wearing of shades indoors. Matt, Chris and Dom are in the enviable position of having a secure home at a number of different labels, have built a vast following of fans – but only if 'fan' still stands for fanatic – across the world, huge sales from three studio albums and, most importantly, a live show that lifts them way above the indie circuit that spawned them.

February 2004 saw the tenth anniversary of Muse, celebrated in style on tour in Japan as part of their 2004 Australia/Asia jaunt. In that decade of playing together Muse have had their passports stamped in France, Germany, Austria, Australia, Belgium, Demark, Finland, Spain, Greece, Hungary, Turkey, Iceland, Italy, Japan, Luxembourg, Norway, Holland, Portugal, Russia, Sweden, Switzerland and the USA. Some thought they'd never make it out of Teignmouth.

"It didn't feel like ten years," Matt told me. "Probably because for the first three years we only did about twenty gigs and were tied to school or college. In terms of really going for it, it only feels like we've been together since we were nineteen, twenty. We're still a young band."

And so long as the world is in turmoil the ideas will keep coming. "We've always had the idea of getting a fuck-off boat and sailing it around the coast of Britain with a stage on it, docking at a different port each night and playing a gig, in a tour round the coast of Britain," ponders Dom. "Maybe if we hired a supertanker – they're about a mile long aren't they?"

And if it all ended tomorrow?

"I'd go and buy an island and live off a rebreather [scuba diving apparatus] with Kleenex boxes on my feet," giggles Matt. "I think I'd go in the berserk direction, I think I'd end up like

Michael Jackson, but without the children! I'd become an obscene recluse to the point of discomfort. I've found a good balance at the moment, where I can walk around and still get on with what I want to do. Creatively I'm pretty balanced. But I'd be worried if that changes..."

For now, phase one is complete. There are other characters in this story. There are many unsung heroes and plenty of villains. There is much that goes untold and plenty more to say; there are plenty of loose strands left dangling, tendrils pulling us into the future where the tale will further unfurl itself. Muse's muse has been summoned and is here to stay. Somehow you sense that the second half the story will be equally as compelling.

Then there are the various myths, half-truths and lies that are all part of the Muse world. At some point in writing this, I arrived at one question: does a fact exist if it goes unconfirmed or unrecorded? It's something I came back to time and time again.

Ask three people about one gig and they'll all tell you very different accounts: one will tell you how bad it was; one will tell you how jaw-droppingly amazing it was; another will tell you about the fight they had on the way home. I asked dozens of people what their defining Muse moment was and no two people gave me the same answer.

Even the band offered conflicting information about dates and times and places. But ultimately it doesn't matter. Know everything and there will be nothing to look forward to – the mystery is what keeps us returning to worship at the altar of music time and time again, even when it lets us down. What matters is what you take from it all – the music, the ideas, the energy, the inspiration, the experience, the soundtrack to our lives.

And then there are the fans, each with their own reasons for falling head-over-heels in love with this most peculiar of bands; each with a book's worth of opinions in them. We only live once and who we choose to invest our faith in during these godless times is not to be taken lightly. Music is a religion and it is the bands who should feel blessed for the millions of stars shining down on *them*.

This is just one of an infinite number of perspectives.

14. RETURN TO PLANET MUSE

Mid-May, 2006 and the summer has finally revealed itself.

London's Oxford Street is awash with tourists, workers, homeless drinkers and the ubiquitous street preachers all jostling for space on the warm pavements. Cutting down a side street a mere two minutes from the hectic Oxford Circus tube exits, we come to a hotel. The interior is modern and the lobby sparsely populated with affluent looking businessmen. Walking across the clean marble floors and the neat lines of the restaurant, we come to a back garden terrace complete with sprinkling fountains and Japanese-style decking.

There at a table sits Matt Bellamy, smiling, sharply-dressed and looking healthy. His hair is freshly dyed and a new, long, black overcoat sits folded by his side. He looks ready for action. He looks like he means business. And he arrives protected.

"I got given this weird charm that some scientist made for me," he explains, fingering a curious-looking amulet that hangs from his neck. "It shields you from electro magnetic micro waves and all that stuff. I only got it a few days ago so I'm just trying to find out if it works."

But how will you know if it does?

"Apparently there's this special camera that can takes pictures of radiation and if you take a picture of someone who has worn one of these for a few days, you're supposed to be able to see some sort of shield around them, protecting. It's got some special gold and crystals in it that shields you from the radiation. A bit weird, but you never know…"

Fittingly, 'A bit weird, but you never know…' seems like the perfect soundbyte to sum up the approach to Muse's fourth studio album, unveiled to the UK press just the previous day and the subject of the round of interviews the band are starting in earnest right now.

Between us on the table sits the ephemera of such obligatory press and promotion days: half-drunk cups of coffee going cold and tall glasses of freshly-squeezed orange juice, a dictaphone and various cassettes, Matt's palm-pilot which rings incessantly throughout ("our techs are pulling their hair out about how we're going to do the new stuff live," he laughs), and a much sought-after set of headphones that mysteriously plays Muse's brand new album at the click of a button ... after the signing of a hefty contract of confidentiality, naturally. There are no wires or extra consoles, just music pumping out, currently the only way to hear the album that the band have just decided to call *Black Holes & Revelations*. Things have truly gone space age. Clearly we are back in Muse world.

At the bar, Dominic Howard and Chris Wolstenholme click their way through a lap-top's worth of new press photographs taken by the esteemed snapper Perou, carefully selecting the images that will accompany *Black Holes...* throughout the coming summer, on into the autumn of 2006 and long after that. Pictures to be wired around Europe, to Japan, Australia and the US. Pictures which – it has been decided – will not feature top hats and massive balloons.

Nearby, the band's manager, his assistant and publicist talk business while chatting to the odd journalist also here get the lowdown. The mood in the camp is one of steady readiness masking the inevitable mayhem that always bubbles beneath the surface of an international rock band with an intensely loyal following. The band knows things are going to get wild in the coming months. There will be riotous scenes at personal appearances, show-stealing festival headline slots, trips to new and unfamiliar lands, but all concerned know it pays never to think too far ahead. As Dom points out, you study the itinerary of forthcoming engagements at any great length and you're liable to lose your mind.

Let's step backwards in a time for a moment. You can do that in Muse World.

Two years have passed since the last chapter ended, easily their busiest and most fruitful yet. It has been a period of extreme highs and severe lows too, triumph followed by unexpected tragedy. Looking back from the future, for Muse, the years 2004 and 2005 will be remembered for a selection of key events. Any band worth their salt comes with a set of such moments in their history, achievement or events that define their purpose, their contribution, their buzz. Over time, when the small details or accountants statistics are forgotten, it is these instances by which bands are remembered, those occasions where all those varying factors – mood, weather, ambience, sound, smells – temporarily coalesce into a moment of near-perfection. For a little over an hour in a field in Somerset in June 2004, one such landmark came for Muse when they closed Glastonbury with their best ever live performance.

After heavy road work in Japan and Australia (at the Big Day out festival) then more European dates, Muse hit the British ground running. Headlining the daddy of all festivals in a country where you can't move for booming PA sound systems, the smell of frying onions, watery lager and the ubiquitous Joe Bananas stoner supply stores during the summer months, was an almost ridiculous notion to Muse. Being last band on at the Pyramid stage at Glastonbury was a career pinnacle, a notch on the cultural bed-post that few bands can ever claim. In fact, only three bands a year do it – in 2004 the other two were Oasis and Paul McCartney, the latter of whom Matt hoped to meet backstage.

"My dad met him once – apparently he did a gig supporting Rolf Harris and The Beatles at Manchester Apollo years ago," he told BBC radio just prior to the festival. "There were so many crazy fans outside that they had to call police security and my dad's band ended up getting off with a whole load of female police officers – they were the good old days!"

Muse had the hallowed festival-closing Sunday night slot, an appearance to seal the Glastonbury experience and send the punters home on their merry, stinking way. Previous Sunday headliners had included big-hitting rock royalty such as Bob Dylan, David Bowie and Rod Stewart, worthy of a mention as a sign of Muse's new status.

By the time the band arrived on site on the Sunday, the mystical Vale of Avalon looked more like a war-zone after the festival had been hit by the near-traditional weather extremes. Friday had seen a fierce storm and flash-floods that swept away tents and belongings before the festivities had barely begun. Such was the ferocity of the elements that Radio 1's backstage set-up, from where they broadcast radio and TV coverage, suffered sufficient damage that broadcasts had to be temporarily halted as a make-shift studio was hastily re-erected amid the rain and mud and lightning. Footage of people canoeing to their tents was shown on that evening's news broadcasts amidst much talk of the British "Dunkirk spirit." By Saturday, the sun had come out to help solidify the torrents of muddy water into glue-like swamps that were near-impossible to navigate through without losing footwear or contracting E-coli; the usual British festival scenario then.

By Sunday, festival goers had been through the gamut of weather systems and human emotions, many now in the tranced-out zone of not caring about the dirt or toilets or their jobs they'd have to be back at by Tuesday. They had entered the Glastonbury mindset, a state that requires the greatest of live soundtracks.

Enter Muse, stage right.

"I remember watching Morrissey and James Brown on before us and there was a real end-of-the-festival vibe where you suspected everyone was feeling a bit jaded and just wanted to go home and have a shower," says Chris today. "And it really was fucking disgusting. Mud everywhere, three days of festival madness, and I arrived with just a flimsy pair of trainers. Just stepping out of the tour bus was an ordeal. I was caked in mud up to the waist within minutes, covered in shit just trying to get to the stage. It wasn't nice. Maybe it was us looking at it in a negative-way, but we really didn't think we were big enough to headline the festival and sometimes you tend to amplify that negativity unnecessarily. Mainly though, we were nervous as hell. It was our biggest ever gig and we were shitting ourselves."

Given the band's recent schedule and Glastonbury's relatively close proximity to Teignmouth, many of the band's family and friends had also travelled to the site to witness the trio perform to their biggest ever crowd. The festival attracted over 110,000 people, half of whom were seemingly gathered to see Muse.

"All I remember is looking out and seeing all these flags from around the world, a real international presence," remembers Chris. "People had come from all over the place to this little bit of land in Pilton. We'd done a few other big festivals that summer, but Glastonbury is always the one. Playing big outdoor shows, it's rare where everything falls into place at the same time – whether it's the crowd reaction, the sound or our playing – but it seemed to be one of those nights. From the moment we walked on stage and played the first note, we knew..."

Of those in attendance and those who watched the simultaneous live TV broadcast from the comfort of their homes, few disagreed that Muse delivered a staggering set full of guitar heroics, showmanship, glitz and glamour and pure sonic rock thunder. With Matt clad in a long, flowing white coat, Muse put on a display of musical fireworks that began with 'Hysteria', closed with a jaw-dropping closer of 'Stockholm Syndrome' and in between played a set of *Absolution*-heavy songs that seemed to suit every mood of Glastonbury – from ecstatic surges of sound that ran up the spine and straight to the cortex, to introspective post-sunset moments. Muse's closing performance at Glastonbury made even their most ardent critics humbly nod in approval.

Days later, Amazon's sales of *Absolution* CDs increased by 240%. Muse had very much made it.

But perfection never lasts and the brief post-set high was broken in the most tragic of circumstances, as all in the band and entourage faced two extreme emotions within the space of minutes.

At 1.15am, as the band were coming down from the adrenaline rush of their show and the unwashed Glastonbury masses were celebrating the final night of the festival with fires and parties right across the vale, Dom's father Bill suffered a heart attack in close proximity to the stage which his son had just vacated in dramatic style. Bill was rushed to the festival medical centre but within thirty minutes had passed away. He was 62 years old.

To lose a loved one so unexpectedly is always hard to deal with, but for the drummer to lose his father straight after the band's finest moment to date made it all the more devastating. Once can only imagine what Dom, his family and all of Muse's friends went through that night as the sun broke over Glastonbury the following morning and another festival has passed. One thing we can be sure about though: Bill Howard witnessed a performance by his son's band that they may never match. Everything they had dreamt of and worked towards had reached spectacular fruition. He surely died a proud and happy man.

In light of this unprecedented turn of events, Muse issued a statement confirming the tragedy and requested privacy for Dom and his family. The band cancelled their next show in Bergamo, Italy.

Subsequent reports have suggested that Muse were pushed "close to break-up" during this period, but it doesn't appear to be the case. Despite grieving and working around the logistics of a funeral, the band soldiered on, visiting three high-profile European festivals the following week, culminating in Denmark's Roskilde, playing much the same fifteen song set each night. Three more festival appearances happened in late July, in France, Spain and Switzerland.

It didn't stop there, either. Perhaps you know this by now.

It never stops.

On July 28, at the personal request of the headliners, Muse joined The Cure's Curiosa tour in the US, a travelling package headlined by Robert Smith's back on-form goth marionettes and a supporting cast of challenging acts, such as dazzling post-rock architects-of-sound Mogwai, the monochromatic, indie doom-rock of Interpol and the rhythmic post-punk of The Rapture; all bands to whom some debt to The Cure was owed.

Though Muse played on a second stage on a rotating bill that also featured the likes of Thursday, Melissa Auf Der Maur and Head Automatica, they certainly shared certain characteristics with the headliners – most notably that they were outsides even within the rock scene of their home country, one step removed from the tittle-tattle of the *NME* bands and their barometers of cool, yet simultaneously adored in countries that newer, hipper bands couldn't get arrested in. Both had hardcore fans who would kill for them, and both bands had been doing exactly what the hell they wanted since they first inked a record deal – in The Cure's case, two decades before Muse.

It was while on the Curiosa tour that another disaster struck – albeit a far less important one than that fateful night at

Glastonbury – when Chris broke his wrist during a kick-about with the spectacularly coiffured Reading sextet The Cooper Temple Clause. As young Brits together on a US-heavy tour, the two bands had bonded; Chris's injury was caused by nothing more than a badly timed tackle, but for a bassist with a string of obligations over the coming months … not good. The band soldiered on without their dynamic bottom-end man by drafting in Morgan Nicholls (formerly of the Senseless Things, more of whom shortly) to play the parts until Chris's injury had healed enough for him to resume playing with a cast.

"It's made me feel like this is something that really is worth fighting for, which maybe I've missed," Matt told *NME* of a triumphant year punctuated by unavoidable traumas such as these. "Sometimes you take for granted that things are going well and everyone's healthy and suddenly a few things happen and it makes you realise that you should make the most of it when you're there."

Eleven US shows later and Muse were back in England to play the V2004 festival, a couple of shows in France – all with the unflappable Nicholls on bass – then on to Australia in August, when Chris returned to the fold.

A huge US tour throughout September and October took in all the major cities, and some of the lesser ones too. It was beginning to feel like no-one would be spared a chance to enjoy the full Muse live experience, as every corner of the globe was visited.

In December, the band closed what had been an action-packed year with a big blow-out to send revellers into Christmas when they played two sold-out two high-profile shows at London's Earl's Court, the type of arena venue closely associated with rock behemoths such as Led Zeppelin and Pink Floyd, the two bands Muse most closely resembled in terms of international, transcendental stature. Over the two nights, they would play to a total of 34,000 people.

Even this far down the *Absolution* trail though, the band were still experimenting with their set-list. While they pulled out all the stops visually – the usual glitter canons, sci-fi film clips and dazzling light display – they opted to play two different sets. Critical consensus was that the first show on December 19 was slightly muted, possibly because of the sterile atmosphere of a venue made from steel and concrete. But by the next night, adjustments had been made and Muse played a show that was one of their best yet, the ninety minute performance infused with a sense of seasonal magic and homecoming triumph. "During 'Blackout', Matt asks the audience to thrust their illuminated mobile phones in the air to make a bobbing sea of twinkling Christmas lights," wrote Luke Lewis of *Kerrang!* "It ought to be a grim spectacle: 17,000 people in a concrete shed, mobiles aloft – modern Britain in all its ugly, WAP-enabled glory. But somehow, in Muse's hands, it just looks utterly, heartbreakingly beautiful."

That seemed the perfect full-stop for the long *Absolution* cycle of activity; a trans-international trip that had taken the band to vertigo-inducing new heights. 2004 ended with Muse appearing in all manner of end-of-year magazine polls, the trio featuring highly in various categories that recognised not only *Absolution* and its attendant singles but also the band's assured status as one of the best live bands to have come from Britain in a long time. Further evidence of this would be available with the release of the *Absolution* DVD (late the next year), a collection taken from the highlights of shows during the past eighteen months.

The last vestiges of those days when the band were viewed with cynicism and suspicion from their home country's ever-critical press were gone. Muse had made themselves impossible to ignore, and unlike many of their hyped contemporaries had done things backwards – the best way. Fan base and sales first, then critical acclaim. It set them up nicely for any future activity.

In the meantime, Matt, Dom and Chris – and their extensive support crew – took a few much-needed weeks off. They later returned to dive into a rehearsal studio with the intention of working on ideas for songs that had been taking shape while on tour during soundchecks, tour bus jams and, occasionally, during the live set. Then, in February 2005, Muse were offered a tour of the American mid-West.

"It was something we couldn't refuse," Matt told me. "When most bands tour America, they play the main cities but we wanted to hit the rural towns that form the heartland of the country."

The tour was with Brit quartet Razorlight, a band peddling a more traditional, rootsy, punk-inspired type of guitar music compared to Muse, yet with similar success. On their first album, the band were post-Libertines press darlings and had achieved a high profile through singer Johnny Borrell's many declarations of his own genius and a pursuit of a textbook rock 'n' roll lifestyle – not long after the tour with Muse an appearance at Live 8 had some critics wondering if Razorlight were heir to U2's faux-passionate arena rock, Borrell an impassioned, motormouth frontman in the Bono/Geldof mould. Live though, Razorlight paled into comparison with Muse, their fairly rudimentary combination of early Springsteen anthems and new wave punk energy no match for the Teignmouth trio's awe-inspiring performances and musical virtuosity. Nevertheless, the pairing of two up-and-coming (to US audiences, at least) bands made some sort of sense and during March the tour wound through the smaller cities and larger towns of America playing to crowds of between two and three thousand per night. Of similar ages and backgrounds (though Razorlight's hedonistic lifestyle was in slight contrast to Muse's more seasoned, long-haul approach to touring), the two bands got on well and in Philadelphia they peaked with a crowd of five thousand people.

In April, Muse returned to the UK and were beginning to rehearse and write when they were interrupted again – this time with an offer to play at the Paris leg of the aforementioned Live 8 shows. Twenty years on from the Live Aid concerts and organiser Bob Geldof had decided to resurrect the idea, this time using his celebrity connections not to raise money for impoverished third world countries but to increase awareness about the wider problem of Third World debt. He called it Live 8 because of the timely G8 Summit Meetings that were taking place the following week in Gleneagles, Scotland.

Though ostensibly a benevolent affair, critics naturally questioned the motives for many artists taking part in the all-day, televised concerts, the main one of which was being held in London's Hyde Park – not least because of huge career benefits gained by artists who took place in the original 1985 concerts.

Recognising the importance of being involved in an event that was nobly attempting to tackle problems that the band had often made references to in their music (élite rulers, economic skullduggery, a mass displacement of people power), Muse avoided such criticism by playing in Paris and therefore swerved the main media spotlight centred on the London show. Also, Paris was their crowd – their historic *Hullabaloo* DVD had been recorded at Le Zenith and France was almost a second home to them. "We couldn't really say no...." was Matt's reasoning for their guest appearance on a mixed bill that also included mainstays of the European music scene such as Andrea Bocelli and Zuchero and internationally popular British artists such as The Cure, Craig David and Placebo. Putting on another flamboyant performance, Muse went straight for the jugular with 'Hysteria' and 'Bliss'.

"I'm glad we didn't do the London show because we were on an off-tour sort of vibe at the time," said Matt. "The London Live 8 show looked pretty intense, whereas Paris was more laid-back, more casual and with a little less attention on it. We enjoyed it. It was a good laugh playing to a huge outdoor crowd."

And that really was it for the *Absolution* shows. It seemed appropriate that Muse's tales of Armageddon and a world run by shadowy despots, and the human, emotional and musical responses to them, were being performed to a concert concerned with the age-old problem of the rich getting rich and the poor getting stiffed.

Finally Muse had a rest.

15. BLACK HOLES & REVELATIONS

Chateau Miraval is located in the heart of Provence in France's wine-making country.

Set in a wooded valley whose gently terraced slopes are covered in productive award-winning vineyards, the 17th century castle is also home to a recording studio that has been used by the likes of Pink Floyd, Sting and Chris Rea but, until recently, was no longer in use.

Miraval was remote – the driveway alone was a few miles long and there was little or no telephone and internet access, nor any mobile phone reception. There was, however, beautiful countryside, an agreeable climate, good local food and wine and plenty of opportunity to achieve the solitude necessary for the creative process.

Hearing about Miraval as a potential new recording base for the band, Matt flew out there on a brief reconnaissance mission and reported back to Dom and Chris that the place would be perfect for their needs. After some persuasion, the owners of the Chateau were persuaded to re-open the recording facilities and their residential quarters for artists and in August 2005 the trio decamped to Chateau Miraval to begin work on their fourth studio album.

It was only when they arrived at Miraval that its rich and colourful history became apparent. Though its wine cellar had been well-stocked and exporting since 1850, Miraval actually dated back to the 12th century when it was first inhabited by monks, then in the 1400s the Prince of Naples joined the French Court and settled there. The Estate was in the hands of the Orsini family for centuries until the early 20th century when it became home to the celebrated inventor of reinforced concrete. More importantly to Muse were the lesser known tales of shadowy figures and the air of mystery that surrounded Miraval's past – perfect fodder for their fertile imaginations. According to Matt in an online message, in Miraval they had been "around the ghosts of the Knights Templar ... apparently Jesus's ex-girlfriend was hanging around these parts once."

"The intention was to reinvent ourselves or find a new direction in some way – we just weren't sure how," Matt said in May 2006. "We needed time to do that but it wasn't until that summer that we were able to. On previous albums, we had wanted to capture the live thing because it hadn't come across as well on, say, *Showbiz*, but this time we wanted to remove ourselves from what we do live in order to reinvent ourselves in the way we play as a three-piece."

In the idyllic French countryside, Muse began writing. As mentioned, a few ideas had already been developed during their last US tour – one of them with the working title of 'Demonocracy', later re-titled 'Assassin', and other new tunes such as 'Glorious' and 'Crying Shame' – but unlike previous albums where they arrived with four or five finished songs that they had toured extensively, the band were starting relatively afresh. Also along for the ride again was producer Rich Costey who joined them part-way into their sojourn in Provence.

Slipping into the slower, rural pace, Muse adopted a routine in which they pieced together ideas and began recording the new songs on equipment that had not been in use for a number of years. For a while, it was going well. It was grape-picking season at Miraval and the band did their share of sampling the home-grown wares and helping out with the wine-making process on occasion.

But after a few weeks, the lack of distractions and external influences began to have a less positive effect. Cut off from girlfriends and children, they were getting bored. There was a pool to swim in and Chris used his spare time to go running around the vast estate, but little else.

"I'd go for a run but after an hour I would still be on the driveway," he grins. "It was five miles long and I'd be going nowhere! I felt like Forrest Gump. But if he was in *The Shining*."

The band also rented a satellite dish in order to check e-mails and find out what was going on in the world, but found the slow connection next to worthless. "I'm an internet berserker," said Matt. "I like the fringe stuff, the alternative news websites and the sites that talk about the things you don't read in newspapers. The internet provides more access to more information – and also to more crazy stuff too. The only down-side is that the factual stuff can get mixed up with the crazy stuff."

"But it was a cool thing to do, cutting ourselves off from the world like that," he continued, fingering his amulet again. "You'd be surprised how much all that stuff influences you – being around TV sets or technology in general, it really gets inside of you. Which is why I'm wearing this around my neck."

As has been proven in the past, a bored or restless Muse generally produces some improvised entertainment. The devil makes work for idle hands and all that.

"The place was so remote and there was only the three of us and loads of insects and creatures hanging around," said Matt. "After a while the insects were making us a bit phobic. Weird, big spiders, bats, all sorts. At one point, we stuck a stick insect – actually it was a Praying Mantis – to one of those rockets that you can build from a kit which has a little camera on it to take a picture from up in the air, and shot it into space. But as soon as it was up in the air, we felt really guilty because we had just tortured or at the very least seriously psychologically disturbed it. But when the rocket landed, the Praying Mantis just jumped off the rocket and wandered off. We have it all on film so no-one can accuse us of cruelty to animals. In fact, we expanded his mind and universe. It was probably a bit like going on holiday for him."

A few weeks into their stay and the band were clearly getting increasingly restless without having produced a great deal of material they were happy with to justify their growing sense of unease. "Obviously our intention was to not only record the album but also create ideas, find a new direction and dismantle people's expectations of us," added Matt. We wanted to see how far we could push it and it turned out that such identity-exploring took up most of the time and we didn't actually get much recording done."

Many of the ideas laid down were at the more extreme end of the Muse spectrum – the type of music pieces Matt had been writing for years, but which generally never made it onto albums for fear of being too weird for commercial success.

"Yeah, some stuff was too 'out there'," laughs Matt. "If you imagine just the piano solo in 'Butterflies & Hurricanes' – but ten minutes long; music very much in the classical genre but extreme and difficult to translate into songs. A lot of that stuff really opened up something quite different for us, but it was a whole world of pain that we thought we should maybe leave for the future. We did have some electro-based ideas which worked, songs such as 'Supermassive Black Hole' which come from the shallow end of Muse. By that I mean as a band we have a tendency to move between the deep end where you get into very sub-conscious emotional stuff that ends up very proggy and conceptual, and the shallow end, where songs are based on a cool riff or the rhythm. The tough thing about *Black Holes* ... was trying to decide which area to work in. And the deep end stuff was becoming very *Dark Side Of The Moon*, very long-winded, extended and liable to have featured four songs across the album if we'd have continued in that direction..."

This tendency towards the indulgent had, of course, always been there. In fact, it is one of Muse's strong points – that willingness to boldly go where other bands are too cool or technically incapable to go. But their prog tendencies have always been tempered by an understanding of contemporary concepts such as the pop song, radio airplay and the fact that no-one likes to see a musician disappear completely up his or her own arse (and there have been many). Nevertheless, 'the deep end, out there' material recorded in Miraval seemed almost indicative of the band's state of mind after nearly two months of intensifying seclusion.

"We lost our minds to an extent in Miraval," says Matt. "It got a point where we had all this stuff and none of it fitted together but it was an exciting process and a good thing to do. It's weird how much being away from everything affected us. This weird paranoia about the future and the world in general began to creep up on me."

Paranoia at the state of the world was, of course, also nothing new to Muse, but as they spent many hours discussing the planet, the ever-worsening situation in Iraq and disillusionment with the mechanics of humanity, their sense of detachment and unease was heightened to new levels – and would provide plenty of input for the new material.

At the time, Matt's preferred reading material was 'Dare To Prepare', a manual that schools its readers in how to survive nuclear fallout – the type of tome you would usually find in the backpacks of gun-toting crackpots.

"The isolation took its toll after a while," recalls Dom. "There was too much fear hanging around us. Sitting around a dinner table, all our talk about how we would survive a nuclear bomb or the impending crisis or all these things that suggest that the world is going to end seemed to be inspired by this isolation. Even though you feel safe in that environment, the fear seemed to increase. It got too intense. We had to go to a city and breath some real life."

"I think it's only when you take a break from the influence of the media, technology and the internet – all these things we surround ourselves with – that you genuinely begin to develop your own ideas," reflected Matt. "It's amazing how much that stuff can control you, maybe not purposely, but they do start to influence your opinions and ideas. But what with the insects and the rockets, the wine and the fireworks and the sense of isolation, things were getting out there. Beards were staring to grow. Things started going a bit mental..."

It was time to move on.

After their extended session of self-enforced solitude, the band relocated to refine their ideas into something more tangible – a complete album, rather than a series of increasingly complicated experiments. At this point, the band could quite easily gone down the non-commercial creative route that so many established artists – David Bowie, Lou Reed, John Lennon being but three examples – had done before, often out of boredom, disillusionment or in an attempt to surprise their own fans. But Muse reigned in these tendencies, packed their bags, left Miraval in September and flew to producer Costey's hometown of New York; a place far removed from the sleepy French countryside, a city buzzing with energy, chaos, ideas and inspiration of a different kind.

"Going to New York was an unbelievable contrast to being in the south of France," said Matt. "I don't know what happened but we suddenly became much more decisive. Maybe it's because we sunk ourselves straight back into that world of influence – where the things around you help you understand how and where to make your weird ideas fit in." "We all love that city and it seemed like the right place to go," adds Dom. "All of a sudden it was full-on, twenty-four hours, non-stop intensity."

Holing up in a hotel, the move to complete the album in New York proved to be an inspired one. Muse, after all, was a rock band. They were young men. They needed entertainment beyond the many things you can do with indigenous insects. And New York provided entertainment in abundance, not least the night life that Matt, Chris and Dom had been denied in France.

When not in the studio, after-hours were often spent at a handful of clubs in downtown Manhattan, soaking up the newer sounds. Matt, for one, picked up on the ever-increasing grey area between dance and rock music; how rock bands like Franz Ferdinand or The Rapture filled dance floors when played in clubs, and how guitars (or samples of rock songs) were featuring ever-more frequently in dance tunes. The climate in many of the hipper NY clubs was akin to that of the UK and US post-punk scenes of the early 1980s, when the likes of funk, disco and dub were incorporated into the music of (for the most part) white boy, punk-inspired bands. Mash-up's – two quite different records mixed together to create a third new alternative – were also increasingly popular. In this sense, the alternative music scene was arguably at its least élitist, its least segregated. Naturally as modern men, Muse picked up on this.

"I've got a friend out there who is a DJ and she does a couple of nights a week in a bar on the Lower East Side that we used to go to," Matt said. "I has hanging out with her quite a lot and she was trying to teach me how to DJ. I didn't quite master the whole scratching and cross-fading thing, but I did go from 'World In My Eyes' by Depeche Mode into something by the Eurythmics, then a Beck song and that seemed to go down quite well. When I played Depeche Mode, a couple of rather nice ladies came over to talk to me and tell me how much they loved it, and I was just going [nonchalantly], 'Yeah, yeah...' It was then that I got the DJ vibe.

I understood that it's all about picking good songs and taking all the glory for it, as if it were your song. Suddenly, some of the new songs like 'Supermassive Black Hole' and 'Map Of The Problematique' which were only really on the fringe of the album, were exciting us the most. Being out in a more fun musical environment – as opposed to being lost in your subconscious as we were in France – definitely swung the album."

"It felt like it all kicked off in New York," smiles Dom. "Where we were staying was near the bars and clubs and that really impacted on the music we were recording, in a positive way. The more positive songs like 'Invincible' or Starlight' were definitely inspired by the mood-change, as were the groovier songs which came out of us dancing around in R&B clubs."

The band recorded in two different studios, Electric Lady and Avatar on West 8th Street and West 53rd Street respectively. Many of the piano-based songs were set aside for possible use on future albums ("Maybe we'll do a whole album of piano songs at some point," says Matt), while those songs written on and for the guitar became the priority. Ironically despite – or perhaps because of – the insight gained from hanging out in clubs, Muse's fourth album was clearly becoming very-much a guitar record. A big, dirty, complex rock album, the bulk of which was recorded in five busy weeks in New York. By the time the trees of Central Park were turning from green to orange to brown, the record was done.

"If there is a theme to the songs on *Black Holes & Revelations* as a whole, then there's definitely a bit of conspiracy theory in there, and ideas about the global élite who control everything around us," says Matt. "Whether or not that is even true, there are definitely characters that I adopt within the songs where I'm saying that that is very much the case. It was very much a process of dismantling ourselves, an important thing to do if you want to move forward. The new album reminds me of *Origin Of Symmetry* in as much as it's a collection of experiments and concepts, whereas as the first and third albums [*Showbiz* and *Absolution*] were more a collection of the best songs we had at the time. This new record is more like the best of our experimentations – at the time."

You can kind of tell, but maybe Matt was doing himself a disservice by describing *Black Holes & Revelations* as mere experimentation. When the album was previewed to members of the press in May, it was clearly a cohesive and tangible, self-contained work. It was the sound of a trio pulling together and playing to all their strengths. And it just so happened that Muse's multitude of trump cards were far more interesting than those of their contemporaries. Here was a modern rock album that once again delved into prog, classical and classic rock but also mariachi, spaghetti western, electro, funk, stoner rock and the fringes of dance music, without them ever once appearing to be dabbling tourists – always a risk for bands out to expand their horizons. Muse had broken into new areas by way of their now-virtuoso playing and Matt's refined and imaginative composition skills alone.

Despite the crossover between genres as heard in the clubs, in the three years since the release of *Absolution* the musical climate in the UK had nevertheless shifted ever-further towards a clutch of traditional last-gang-in-town bands, drawing heavily from US and UK punk of the 1970s, the inventive post-punk period of the early 1980s and, in some cases, the postured Britpop of the 1990s. Guitar music that you could dance to was back in and bands such as the aforementioned Razorlight, Franz Ferdinand, Arctic Monkeys, Bloc Party, Futureheads and Dirty Pretty Things were grabbing headlines and flourishing commercially, all achieving Top 5 albums. Some were brilliant in their own refreshing way, others such as Kaiser Chiefs, appeared to be merely filling a void left by forefathers that they closely resembled, namely Blur. All well and good, but these new wave bands were doing it by rehashing or refining old ideas, or relying on regional dialects and an occasional sense of parochialism or caricatured British identity; the same traits that had, for many, tainted Britpop.

By comparison Muse were so far ahead of their radio airwave rivals that they were now, at least sound-wise, existing in their own universe. Released in July 2006, the new album *Black Holes & Revelations* was nothing like the output of their contemporaries. While the other bands were lording it up as much as they could before their labels pulled their rugs from beneath their winkle-pickered feet and their dealers stopped returning their calls, *Black Holes...* was the sound of a band hitting warp speed, surpassing even the pomposity and stellar production of bands such as Queen and Pink Floyd. It was the sound of a band claiming a crown of their own, once again bursting with ideas and opinions.

"Welcome back Muse, we've missed your widdly bits and the way your drums make John Bonham sound effeminate and the fact that though your lyrics initially sound innocuous, they're actually some of the most politicized and anti-establishment we've heard in recent years," I noted in a piece I wrote for *Kerrang!* following the initial album playbacks. "You must pay for your crimes gains the earth!" scream a bank of falsetto vocals on opener 'Take A Bow', like you've just nuked their motherland. It's all here in this foreboding opener that suggests that Matt Bellamy might not be on the Christmas card lists of many world leaders by the close of the year. Which somehow makes it all the more special."

The album opener was certainly barbed and critical, a lushly-layered, throbbing electro rock sound, deceptively disguising feelings of despair and disillusionment for mankind that had merely increased since the equally pessimistic (but yet joyous-sounding) *Absolution*. Matt sang with convincing conviction about the power of a demonic despot, all filtered through a digital sequencer. "The theme is me being the small man or the ordinary man in society who is trying to comprehend who is in control of the world, and the realisation that he – or us, the people – is so far away from the source of control," he explained. 'Starlight' was the song whose lyrics provided the album with its title and seemed a definite contender for a future single. It was Muse at their melodic, emotive best, complete with handclaps driving it along, futuristic keyboards fluttering in and out and an unwinding melody sure to stick in your head for weeks. "It's not like it's a dance song but that song was much more slow and more mellow when we first recorded it in France. But when we got to New York, we re-recorded it with a glam rock drum beat and made it more … groovy."

The album's lead single, 'Supermassive Black Hole', was the first song on the record to sound like it was influenced in some oblique way by the noise of certain New York clubs and the spiky danceability of Franz Ferdinand. But what listeners probably didn't expect was a song that mixed the clenched-butt strut of Prince and the groove of – eek – Justin Timberlake (or, as some pointed out, a notable similarity to Britney Spears' 'Do Something') and gave them a big, old filthy bass-heavy rock makeover. Remember when everyone used to say Muse sounded just like Radiohead? Well, Thom Yorke had never recorded anything remotely as immediate as this. Suddenly Muse had da fonk. The chorus alone was enough to send the slickest of America's booty-shaking pop diva's back to the drawing board.

'Map Of The Problematique' was a swirling, ethereal vortex of sound. With its pulsing electro intro, it recalled a darker version of both The Bloodhound Gang's 'The Bad Touch' and The Bravery's 'An Honest Mistake'; it was the sound of a rock band making something approaching 1980s-tinged dance music, back when early dance music was about sniffing poppers in dark corners and not necessarily being loved-up. If New Order could sing and dared to totally rock, they might have created something as effecting as this somewhere along the way.

The flipside to Muse's rock beast tendencies, 'Soldier's Poem', was a gently swooning lullaby. Much like System Of A Down's recent two-part song 'Soldier Side' from their *Mezmerize/Hypnotize* pairing of albums in 2005, it considered war and conflict from the perspective of the individual fighting it. Bellamy crooned as if singing a baby to sleep rather than ruminating on the inevitable downfall of mankind.

"People will assume that it's an apolitical statement about the Iraq war, but really it can be related to any war," Matt said. "In that song, I'm putting myself in the perspective of the solider. I always like to sing in the first person, as opposed to tell stories. I've never been a soldier myself and where bands such as Rage Against The Machine have dealt with overtly political, specific subjects, I prefer to put myself in the emotional position of the person who is being affected by it."

Picking up where *Absolution*'s 'Falling Away From You' left off, with a similarly shadowy sound but an uplifting and inspirational sentiment, 'Invincible' was elegiac. After a tempered introduction laid over a military marching band drum beat, a freak-out naturally followed – as Chris Wolstenholme's familiar vast, voluminous and amorphous bass sound kicked in, Matt squeezed out a guitar solo that sounded like a Dalek having an orgasm, while the song built to the type of God-cursing climactic crescendo that Muse are so good at. Like porn legend Ron Jeremy, they could clearly deliver on demand ...

Arguably one of Muse's heaviest moments both musically and thematically, 'Assassin' was a song that, according to Matt, was about the mindset of someone driven to extreme measures for what they believe. "I won't use the obvious buzz words," he says, alluding to terrorism. "But it is about the extremities of beliefs. It's from the point of view of a person who is becoming so psychotically jaded with society to such an extent that they are prepared to shoot the president."

The early influence of the Deftones was there in the heavy riffing and underlying feelings of tension, or maybe if you painted Queen's 'Don't Stop Me Now' black and put it through a mincer, it might turn out like this song, which sees all the Muse components present and correct. Let's run down the check-list. Precision riffing? Yep. Vocals that start out as a murmur but grow into a frenzy? Most definitely. Bass-heavy high-speed skronk rock outro? And how.

"It's the only metal song on the album," says Dom. "At first we were unsure whether it was going to fit, but we realised the album needed some bad-ass rock. It was definitely inspired by a band like Lightning Bolt, or certainly the bass and drums were. It was us trying to find new ways to be heavy. It has an insanity to it at the start that makes you want to lose your mind and smash up the room."

A strident song that began with a guitar riff that was – once again – a close relative of Mr. Funk before laying on the harmonies and the classic rock guitar histrionics, 'Exo-Politics' was perhaps one of the less immediate moments of the album, yet it still posed the type of rhetorical questions that Matt raised throughout the album.

The final quarter of the album offered three of Muse's most interesting and bonkers songs of their recording career. With dramatic flamenco guitars and another swooning vocal delivery, 'City Of Delusion' was a slice of epic rock with Eastern-tinged orchestral strings swooping down from above. Unlike most bands who rope in an orchestra to show they're 'like, proper musicians and shit,' Muse's – and especially Matt's – innate appreciation and understanding of classical music meant their use of strings and orchestral arrangements was delivered with a sense of style and dignity. And that's before we even got to the Ennio Morricone-inspired, mariachi-ish trumpet solo that appeared out of the desert like some sort of mad tequila vision.

'Hoodoo' had more flamenco guitars, this time accompanied by the kind of hushed-up vocals and sombre rockabilly guitar twang last heard on Muse's debut – back when someone said they were an indie rock version of a Tarantino or Lynch movie soundtrack.

The best moment was saved for last though. Album closer 'Knights Of Cydonia' – along with opener 'Take A Bow', one of the tracks actually recorded at Miraval – was perhaps Muse's most over-the-top, technically slick and powerful pieces yet. Utterly ridiculous, of course, but a gripping ride too. Where to begin? The beginning, I suppose, where horses whinnied, Matt Bellamy unveiled a prog guitar sound that was more akin to a light sabre and the band even squeezed in a stirring trumpet solo before the vocals had appeared. While the dramatic chimes of the backing vocals recalled Led Zeppelin at their demonic, wailing best, 'Knights of Cydonia' – named after an area of the moon – was, however, very much a Muse song, a jaw-dropping combination of hyper-speed space rock, tobacco-spitting spaghetti western drama, Queen's propensity for slapping on a thousand demonic backing vocal tracks and a whiplash-inducing conclusion that was pure Queen's Of The Stone Age stoner rock fury. If ever a song could make listeners ride naked on their trusty steed across the Sea of Tranquility while parping on a toy trumpet – and who doesn't from time to time? – then this was surely it.

"I suppose the theme of the album is the small guy – I don't mean miniature ..." Matt laughed during our 2006 catch-up.

"...[but] the man at the bottom of the pile trying to comprehend the bigger picture, and getting jaded by it. I can't say that every song is about that – some are more relationship-type songs. The good old girlfriend-vibe. But there are song such as 'Exo-Politics' [that are] about taking ideas too far by getting in the realm of alien politics and the politics of interaction with who our creators could be – things like the old David Icke lizard blood-line theory. All sorts of weirdness."

Despite their record label's best efforts, Muse's lead single, 'Supermassive Black Hole', leaked onto the internet causing the release date of the single to be hastily brought forward into May, when it was officially made available as a download. A full 'proper' released followed in late June.

The band filmed a video for the new single during a whistle-stop visit to LA in late April (though ever the jet-setter, Dom did find time to nip to the Virgin Islands, where his girlfriend comes from, for a couple of days). The video was odd and nightmarish – the band's faces obscured by hoods and replaced by other images while surrounded by owls and some decidedly shadowy figures. Who knows what it all meant. The band was the first to admit that they didn't.

At the time of writing, Muse's new album is their biggest hit to date. The critics were all highly enthusiastic, the public bought it in droves and all the signs suggest that *Black Holes & Revelations* is the pivotal album that will turn Muse into a trio of genuine rock gods.

As a strange aside, while writing this updated chapter, I had a completely unrelated conversation with an acquaintance at a major record label. When I told him I'd been writing about Muse again, he casually replied 'Muse? Oh, I'm on the cover of their new album..." before going on to explain that he had just spent the weekend in Spain being photographed at very short notice by a friend of his, graphic designer Storm Thorgerson.

Perhaps for the first time, the band were feeling relaxed about an album, one which had been written and recorded at their own pace, in the environments that they demanded – whatever it took to make it right.

"We've been able to live with the songs for a while, which is a luxury we've never had before with a new record," said Chris. "Every album takes several months, but in the past, that last week always seems really rushed because you've got to go straight on tour, straight into that life of chaos. I mean, *Origin...* was essentially recorded in a gap between tours and two days after we finished mixing it, we were touring it. So this time around, it's a little different. With your first and second albums, you want to keep momentum going, but with *Black Holes & Revelations*, we just wanted to get it right, the idea being we could tour it when we're ready. I mean, sometimes it's nice to just stop and unpack once in a while. Put your clothes in a wardrobe. It's a novel concept to us."

This wasn't a luxury the band were going to enjoy any time soon. To do the new material justice live, Muse broke from tradition and enlisted the services of a fourth musician for the first time. Fittingly the band came full circle with their friend Morgan Nicholls, sometime live bassist with The Streets, one-time lo-fi solo artist (as M.Organ) and the man who stepped into the breach when Chris broke his wrist playing football. And, before all that, Morgan was also bassist with grebo band and young Muse favourites Senseless Things. The very same band that provided them with some early live musical epiphanies and mosh-pit experiences.

"Every time we've finished an album, we've always thought we might need to get someone else in to do a few bits and piece live, but we've always found a way to get round that," Matt explained. "But with this album, we've cracked and realised we probably have to get someone in to do some Kraftwerk-style knob-twiddlings to bring in some of the electronic elements. Then it turned out Morgan is a really good keyboard player and knows his electro-stuff. It'll be an interesting development for us."

After a well-received five-song set Radio 1's One Big Weekend in Dundee in May, Muse's tour schedule was filling out again. The summer of 2006 stretched off into the distance, a series of different stages as signposts guiding Muse to more vertigo-inducing heights. June and July would see their passports taking a further battering with festival shows in Germany, France, Belgium, Sweden and Norway, the new material being received with levels of near-hysteria. UK tour dates inevitably beckoned and included a headlining slot at the Reading and Leeds festival at the close of August. Alongside fellow headliners Pearl Jam and Franz Ferdinand, it was another potential career-defining moment – another notch on their bed-post, another scalp claimed. Boldly opening with 'Knights Of Cydonia', the band would play one of their strongest sets yet at the very same festival they'd attended as wide-eyed, cider-drinking teenagers.

If the European festivals formed the heartland of Muse's fanbase, then it was to there they returned as heroes for the summer season. Unlike many of their contemporaries, Muse are still breaking in new countries all the time – just check the internet for the amount of fan sites that keep appearing in unexpected languages.

In the time-span of this final chapter, Muse have already expanded their following in more far-flung territories such as the US and Japan and countries such as Russia, where performances may have been limited but their reputation has continued to grow steadily; the cult of Muse is swelling. And if all goes according to plan, the band's status as a truly internationally successful group will become unquestionable.

In early 2007, they announced their biggest show to date by far – a historic performance at the new Wembley Stadium in June. It was a tenacious move that surprised many who'd not seen the band live and had written them off as just another rock group. But those in the know ... *knew*. Muse would have no problem playing such a place – but could they fill *so many* seats? Easy.

The 90,000 tickets sold out within a few hours on the first day of sale. Amazingly, a second date was added, undeniable evidence that Muse had officially stepped up a final gear, from arena band to stadium rock gods – after all, they were the first UK rock act to play the new national stadium. Many would agree that they are the only stadium band in Britain actually worth watching. Muse also announced that they would likely be appearing at one of the Live Earth concerts in July – truly the domain of the jet-setting rock star.

So then….

From Teignmouth to Texas, Tasmania and Tokyo, it's been a strange and exhilarating journey, one fuelled by a growing sense of invincibility.

And there, once again, just beyond the horizon, sit more chapters in the on-going story of Muse, just waiting to be lived, waiting to be written down and then, in turn, to be lived again and again.

And wherever it takes the band and fans alike, the soundtrack is sure to be brilliant.

UK DISCOGRAPHY

The output of Muse, perhaps more than any other current band, is very difficult to track – largely due to the various record deals they have for different territories. It is for that reason that I cannot claim this to be the definitive discography, more of a comprehensive starting point.

Three years after first compiling and refining this discography, Muse haven't made it any easier tracking and cataloguing their many multi-formats in various countries. Clearly this no bad thing. But for the sake of accuracy, I have concentrated on output in the UK the band's home country, the first in which this book was published. I have also removed the original list of unauthorised Muse bootlegs available, largely because they are of varying degrees of quality and neither the band nor this author could vouch for the quality.

The change in record labels listed for Muse is down to the usual behind-the-scenes buy-outs and takeovers.

Finally, credit should also be given to the Muse's online discography-in-progress that is consistently maintained and updated by the people with the best understanding of the band: the fans. This can be found at www.musewiki.org/Discography

SINGLES
MUSE EP (Dangerous Records) CD
Escape / Coma / Cave / Overdue
Released: May 11, 1998
Note: the release of this EP was limited to 999 copies

MUSCLE MUSEUM EP (Dangerous Records) CD
Muscle Museum / Sober / Uno / Unintended / Instant Messenger / Muscle Museum (Version # 2)
Released: January 11, 1999
Note: the release of this EP was limited to 999 copies.

UNO (Mushroom / Taste Media) CD, UK No 73
Uno (album version) / Jimmy Kane / Forced In
Released: June 14, 1999

UNO (Mushroom / Taste Media) seven-inch vinyl
Uno (alternative version) / Agitated
Released: June 14, 1999

CAVE (Mushroom / Taste Media) CD1, UK No 52
Cave (remix) / Twin / Cave
Released: September 6, 1999

CAVE (Mushroom / Taste Media) CD2
Coma / Host / Cave
Release: September 6, 1999

CAVE (Mushroom / Taste Media) seven-inch vinyl
Cave / Cave (instrumental)
Released: September 6, 1999

MUSCLE MUSEUM (Mushroom / Taste Media) CD1, UK No 43
Muscle Museum (album version) / Do We Need This / Muscle Museum (live
acoustic)
Released: November 22, 1999

MUSCLE MUSEUM (Mushroom / Taste Media) CD2
Muscle Museum / Pink Ego Box / Con-science
Released: November 22, 1999

MUSCLE MUSEUM (Mushroom / Taste Media) seven-inch vinyl
Muscle Museum (album version) / Minimum
Released: November 22, 1999

SUNBURN (Mushroom / Taste Media) CD1, UK No 22
Sunburn (album version) / Ashamed / Sunburn (Live)
Released: February 21, 2000

SUNBURN (Mushroom / Taste Media) CD2
Sunburn (album version) / Yes Please / Uno (Live)
Released: Feb 21, 2000

SUNBURN (Mushroom / Taste Media) seven-inch clear vinyl
Sunburn / Sunburn (live acoustic)
Released: February 21, 2000

SUNBURN (Mushroom / Taste Media) twelve-inch vinyl promo only
Timo Maas Sunstroke Remix / Breakz Again Remix / Steven McCreery
Remix
Released: March 2000

UNINTENDED (Mushroom / Taste Media) CD1, UK No 20
Unintended / Recess / Falling Down (Live) / Unintended (Video)
Released: June 5, 2000

UNINTENDED (Mushroom / Taste Media) CD2
Unintended / Nishe / Hate This & I'll Love You
Released: June 5, 2000

UNINTENDED (Mushroom / Taste Media) seven-inch vinyl
Unintended / Sober (Live)
Released: June 5, 2000

UNINTENDED (Mushroom / Taste Media) cassette
Unintended / Sober (Live)
Released: June 5, 2000

PLUG IN BABY (Mushroom / Taste Media) CD1, UK No 11
Plug In Baby / Nature_1 / Execution Commentary / Plug In Baby (video)
Release Date: March 5, 2001

PLUG IN BABY (Mushroom / Taste Media) CD2
Plug In Baby / Spiral Static / Bedroom Acoustics
Release Date: March 5 2001

PLUG IN BABY (Mushroom / Taste Media) seven-inch vinyl
Plug In Baby / Nature_1
Released: March 18, 2001

NEW BORN (Mushroom /Taste Media) CD1, UK No 12
New Born / Shrinking Universe / Piano Thing / New Born (video)
Released: June 4, 2001

NEW BORN (Mushroom /Taste Media) CD2
New Born / Map Of Your head / Plug In Baby (Live)
Released: June 4, 2001

NEW BORN (Mushroom /Taste Media) seven-inch vinyl
New Born / Shrinking Universe
Released: June 4, 2001

NEW BORN (Mushroom /Taste Media) twelve-inch vinyl promo only
New Born Oakenfold Perfecto remix / Sunburn Timo Maas' Sunstroke remix
/ Sunburn Timo Maas' Breakz Again Mix
Released: June 2001

BLISS (Mushroom /Taste Media) CD1, UK No 22
Bliss / The Gallery / Screenager (live) / Bliss (video)
Released: August 20, 2001

BLISS (Mushroom /Taste Media) CD2
Bliss / Hyper Chondriac Music / New Born (live)
Released: August 20, 2001

BLISS (Mushroom /Taste Media) seven-inch vinyl
Bliss / Hyper Chondriac Music
Released: August 20, 2001

BLISS (Mushroom /Taste Media) DVD
Bliss (DVD audio) / The Making Of Bliss
Release Date: August 2000

BLISS (Mushroom /Taste Media) UK combined double CD and DVD set
Disc 1: Bliss / The Gallery / Screenager (live) / Bliss (video)
Disc 2: Bliss / Hyper Chondriac Music / New Born (live) /
DVD – Bliss (DVD Audio) / The Making Of Bliss
This release combined the above CD and DVD releases/ CD1 features the

Bliss video (enhanced CD), CD2 is both a normal CD and DVD, containing Bliss (audio) and The Making Of Bliss.
Released: August 20, 2001

FEELING GOOD / HYPER MUSIC (Mushroom /Taste Media) CD1, UK No 22
Feeling Good / Hyper Music (live) / Shine / Feeling Good (Video)
Release Date: November 19, 2001

HYPER MUSIC / FEELING GOOD (Mushroom /Taste Media) CD2
Hyper Music / Feeling Good (live) / Please Please Please Let Me Get What I Want /
Hyper Music (video)
Release Date: November 19, 2001

HYPER MUSIC / FEELING GOOD (Mushroom /Taste Media) seven-inch vinyl
Hyper Music / Feeling Good
Release Date: November 19, 2001

DEAD STAR / IN YOUR WORLD (Mushroom / Taste Media) CD1, UK No 13
Dead Star / In Your World / Futurism / Dead Star (Video)
Release Date: June 17, 2002

IN YOUR WORLD / DEAD STAR (Mushroom / Taste Media) CD2
In Your World / Dead Star / Can't Take My Eyes Off You / In Your World (video)

DEAD STAR / IN YOUR WORLD (Mushroom / Taste Media) seven-inch vinyl
Dead Star / In Your World
Release Date: June 17, 2002

DEAD STAR EP (Mushroom / Taste Media) CD
Dead Star / In Your World / Futurism / Can't Take My Eyes Off You
Dead Star (instrumental) / Dead Star (Video) / In Your World (Video)
Release: June 17, 2002
Note: this EP merely collects together the songs from the two single releases.

STOCKHOLM SYNDROME (East West) download single
Stockholm Syndrome
Download-only (and therefore non-chart eligible) single from the band's official website.
Released: July 17, 2003

TIME IS RUNNING OUT (East West) CD, UK No 8
Time Is Running Out / The Groove / Stockholm Syndrome (video)
Released: September 8, 2003

TIME IS RUNNING OUT (East West) seven-inch vinyl
Time Is Running Out / The Groove
Released: September 8, 2003

TIME IS RUNNING OUT (East West) DVD
Includes: Time Is Running Out (video), the making of the video, Time Is Running Out (audio version), photo gallery
Released: September 8, 2003

HYSTERIA (East West) CD1, UK No 17
Hysteria / Eternally Missed
Released: December 1, 2003

HYSTERIA (East West) seven-inch vinyl
Hysteria / Eternally Missed
Released: December 1, 2003
Note: Cover artwork designed by an MTV competition winner.

HYSTERIA (East West) DVD
Hysteria video (Director's Cut) / Hysteria audio version / Hysteria live at MTV2 / Hysteria: the making of the video.
Released: December 1, 2003
Note: also contains a picture Gallery of the ten MTV seven-inch artwork competition runners-up.

SING FOR ABSOLUTION (East West) CD, UK No 16
Sing for Absolution (Full Length US Remix) / Fury
Released: May 17, 2004

SING FOR ABSOLUTION (East West) seven inch vinyl
Sing for Absolution (Full Length US Remix) / Fury
Released: May 17, 2004

SING FOR ABSOLUTION (East West) DVD
Sing For Absolution Video / Sing For Absolution Audio / Sing For
Absolution – 'Making Of The Video' / Big Day Off [Behind the scenes from
the big day out tour] / Photo Gallery

APOCALYPSE PLEASE (East West) download
Apocalypse Please (live from Glastonbury)
Download-only release with all proceeds going to Oxfam. It reached No 10 in
UK download chart.
Released: August 23, 2004

BUTTERFLIES & HURRICANES (WEA / Atlantic) CD, UK No 14
Butterflies & Hurricanes (Remix Full length) / Sing for Absolution (Acoustic
Radio 2)
U-myx technology
Released: September 20 2004

BUTTERFLIES & HURRICANES (WEA / Atlantic) seven inch vinyl
Butterflies & Hurricanes / Butterflies & Hurricanes (Live at Glastonbury)
Released: September 20 2004

BUTTERFLIES & HURRICANES (WEA / Atlantic) DVD
Butterflies & Hurricanes audio / Butterflies & Hurricanes video / The Groove
in the States (ten minute doc of the band in the US) / Raw video edit
Released: September 20 2004

SUPERMASSIVE BLACK HOLE (Warner Brothers) download
Advance download-only track
Released: May 11, 2006

SUPERMASSIVE BLACK HOLE ((Warner Brother) CD, UK No 4
Supermassive Black Hole / Crying Shame
Released: June 27, 2006

SUPERMASSIVE BLACK HOLE ((Warner Brothers)) seven inch vinyl
Supermassive Black Hole / Crying Shame
Released: June 27, 2006

SUPERMASSIVE BLACK HOLE ((Warner Brothers)) DVD
Supermassive Black Hole (Video) / Making of the video / Bonus video /
Photo gallery
Released: June 27, 2006

STARLIGHT (Warner Brothers) CD, UK No 12
Starlight / Easily
Released: September 4, 2006

STARLIGHT (Warner Brothers) seven inch vinyl
Starlight / Supermassive Black Hole (Paul Epworth Phone Control Voltage
Mix
Released: September 4, 2006

STARLIGHT (Warner Brothers) DVD
Starlight (video) / Starlight / Starlight (the making of)
Also includes a hidden track and photo gallery
Released: September 4, 2006

STARLIGHT (Warner Brothers) maxi-CD
Starlight / Easily / Starlight (video) / Starlight
Released: September 4, 2006

KNIGHTS OF CYDONIA (Warner Brothers) CD, UK No 10
Knights Of Cydonia / Supermassive Black Hole
Released: November 23, 2006

KNIGHTS OF CYDONIA (Warner Brothers) seven inch vinyl
Knights Of Cydonia / Assassin (Grand Omega Bosses edit)
Released: November 23, 2006

KNIGHTS OF CYDONIA (Warner Brothers) DVD
Knights Of Cydonia (video) / Knights Of Cydonia (the making of) / Knights
Of Cydonia
Released: November 23, 2006

INVINCIBLE (Warner Brothers) CD, UK No 21
Invincible / Knights Of Cydonia (Simian Mobile Disco Remix)
Released: April 2007

INVINCIBLE (Warner Brothers) seven inch vinyl
Invincible / Glorious
Released: April 9, 2007

INVINCIBLE (Warner Brothers) DVD
Invincible / Invincible (video) / Invincible (live in Milan)
Released: April 9, 2007

ALBUMS
SHOWBIZ (Mushroom / Taste Media) CD and cassette, UK No 29
Sunburn / Muscle Museum / Fillip / Falling Down / Cave / Showbiz /
Unintended /
Uno / Sober / Escape / Overdue / Hate This And I'll Love You
Released : October 4, 1999

SHOWBIZ (Mushroom / Taste Media) Double twelve-inch vinyl (limited to
1500)
Sunburn / Muscle Museum / Fillip / Falling Down / Cave / Showbiz /
Unintended /
Uno / Sober / Escape / Overdue / Hate This And I'll Love You
Released : October 4, 1999

ORIGIN OF SYMMETRY (Mushroom / Taste Media) CD, UK No 3.
New Born / Bliss / Space Dementia / Hyper Music / Plug In Baby / Citizen
Erased /.
Micro Cuts / Screenager / Darkshines / Feeling Good / Megalomania
Released : June 18, 2001

ORIGIN OF SYMMETRY (Mushroom / Taste Media) Double twelve-inch
vinyl (limited to 1500)
New Born / Bliss / Space Dementia / Hyper Music / Plug In Baby / Citizen
Erased /.

Micro Cuts / Screenager / Darkshines / Feeling Good / Megalomania
Released : June 18, 2001

ORIGIN OF SYMMETRY (Mushroom/Taste Media) Japanese CD
New Born / Bliss / Space Dementia / Hyper Music / Plug In Baby / Citizen
Erased /.
Micro Cuts / Screenager / Darkshines / Feeling Good / Megalomania
Released: June 22, 2001

HULLABALOO (Mushroom / Taste Media) CD, UK No. 10
Disc 1 (B-sides): Forced In / Shrinking Universe / Recess / Yes Please / Map
of Your Head / Nature_1 / Shine (acoustic) / Ashamed / The Gallery /Hyper
Chondriac Music
Disc 2 (live at Le Zenith, Paris): Dead Star / Micro Cuts / Citizen Erased /
Showbiz / Megalomania / Dark Shines / Screenager / Space Dementia / In
Your World / Muscle Museum / Agitated
Note: the soundtrack to the DVD, Hullabaloo is comprised of a collection of B-
sides on disc 1 and Muse live at Le Zenith, Paris on October 28/29 2001 on
disc 2. It also contains a secret track of Tom Wait's 'What's He Building In
There?', which the band used as intro music for their live show. You can get it
by rewinding the first track ('Dead Star') of CD2. The live recording of Dark
Shines is the only live song here not included on DVD release.
Released: July 1, 2002

ABSOLUTION (East West) UK CD, UK No. 1
Intro / Time Is Running Out / Sing For Absolution / Stockholm Syndrome /
Falling Away With You / Interlude / Hysteria / Blackout / Butterflies and
Hurricanes / The Small Print / Endlessly / Thoughts Of A Dying Atheist /
Ruled By Secrecy
Released: September 22, 2003

ABSOLUTION (East West) limited UK double twelve-inch vinyl
Intro / Time Is Running Out / Sing For Absolution / Stockholm Syndrome /
Falling Away With You / Interlude / Hysteria / Blackout / Butterflies and
Hurricanes / The Small Print / Endlessly / Thoughts Of A Dying Atheist /
Ruled By Secrecy
Released: September 22, 2003

BLACK HOLES & REVELATIONS (Warner Brothers) CD, CD/DVD package,

cassette, UK No. 1
Take A Bow / Starlight / Supermassive Black Hole / Map Of The
Problematique / Soldier's Poem / Invincible / Assassin / Exo-Politics / City
Of Delusion / Hoodoo / Knights Of Cydonia
Released: July 2006

BLACK HOLES & REVELATIONS (Warner Brothers), twelve inch vinyl
Take A Bow / Starlight / Supermassive Black Hole / Map Of The
Problematique / Soldier's Poem / Invincible / Assassin / Exo-Politics / City
Of Delusion / Hoodoo / Knights Of Cydonia
Note though the vinyl release is catalogued no copies have yet appeared on
the market
Released: July 2006

DVD
HULLABALOO (Mushroom / Taste Media)
Introduction / Dead Star / Microcuts / Citizen Erased / Sunburn /
Megalomania / Screenager / Feeling Good / Space Dementia / In Your
World / Muscle Museum / Cave / New Born / Hypermusic / Agitated /
Unintended / Plug In Baby / Bliss
Notes: Disc 1 captures the band live at Le Zenith, Paris, disc 2 features a 40
minute film shot throughout 2001 featuring unseen off-stage footage from
around the world including b-sides taken from the 'Hullabaloo Soundtrack'
album, plus photo gallery and interactive discography
Released: July 1, 2002

ABSOLUTION TOUR
Hysteria / New Born / Sing For Absolution / Muscle Museum / Apocalypse
Please /
Ruled By Secrecy / Sunburn / Butterflies and Hurricanes / Bliss / Time Is
Running Out /
Plug In Baby / Blackout.
This also features the bonus tracks: Fury / The Small Print / Stockholm
Syndrome / The Groove In The States. Hidden extras: Endlessly / Thoughts
Of A Dying Atheist
Released: December 12, 2005

VARIOUS / COMPILATIONS / MISC.
All releases are on CD, unless otherwise stated.

VARIOUS - HELPING YOU BACK TO WORK VOLUME 1
Compilation from UK punk label Lockjaw. The Muse track featured is Balloonatic, an old demo version of a song later re-recorded as 'Twin'.
Released: 1997

VARIOUS - IN THE CITY 1999
Rare 21-track promo CD of unsigned bands given to In The City delegates.
Features Muscle Museum (pre-Dangerous Records version).
Released: September 1998

VARIOUS - STEVE LAMACQ'S BOOTLEG SESSION VOL 2 ON TOUR
Free CD with Melody Maker. Features Cave
Released: May 1999 (CD free with Melody Maker)

VARIOUS – THE BANDS WHO...
Free CD with NME. Features Sober
Released: February 2000

VARIOUS: LITTLE NICKY SOUNDTRACK
Features Cave
Released October 31, 2000
Note: this song does not actually feature in the film

CROSSING ALL OVER VOL 14
Features Bliss (live keyboard version)
Released 2001

RANDOM 8
Japanese-only mini album CD that features: Host / Coma / Pink Ego Box / Forced In / Agitated / Yes Please / Fillip (Live) / Do We Need This (Live). It also includes the three Timo Maas remixes of 'Sunburn' as hidden bonus tracks.
Released: 2001

PAUL OAKENFOLD – SWORDFISH SOUNDTRACK
Features Paul Oakenfold's remix of New Born
Release: June 5, 2001

VARIOUS: NOT ANOTHER TEEN MOVIE SOUNDTRACK
Features Muse's version of Please Please Please Let Me Get What I Want by
The Smiths.
Released: December 4, 2001

VARIOUS: THE NME CARLING AWARDS 2002
Features Hyper Music.
Released: January 2002

MARILYN MANSON 'TAINTED LOVE'
UK single release From the 'Not Another Teen Movie' soundtrack that
features Muse's version of The Smiths' Please Please Please, Let Me Get What
I Want on the B-side.
March 12, 2002

VARIOUS - 1 LOVE
Charity album for Warchild. Features Muse's version of House Of The Rising
Sun by The Animals
Released: October 28, 2002

VARIOUS – PARIS DERNIERE VOL 3
Features 'Can't Take My Eyes Of You'
Released: November 19 2003

VARIOUS - TEEN SPIRIT VOLUME 2
Features Feeling Good.
Released: Jan 14, 2003

VARIOUS - BRIT AWARDS 2004
Features Time Is Running Out
Released: February 2004

VARIOUS - 3 PETITIES FILLES SOUNDTRACK
Features New Born
Released: September 28, 2004

VARIOUS - BRIT AWARDS 2005
Features Sing for Absolution
Released: February 2005

VARIOUS – MILLIONS SOUNDTRACK
Features Blackout.
Released: April 4, 2005

VARIOUS – LIVE 8 PARIS (DVD)
Features Time Is Running Out, Hysteria, Bliss and Plug In Baby
November 7, 2005

LINKS / FANSITES

This book could not have happened without Muse's fanbase – an obsessively, wonderfully, scarily dedicated bunch of people stretched across the globe and united by one common passion. Nowhere but on the worldwide web is this more apparent.

I'd recommend the following websites as interesting sources of information for any Muse fans and hope that this account does their work justice:

English language sites
www.muse.mu (official site)
www.muse.net
www.inmuseworld.net
www.rocketbabydolls.com
www.microcuts.net
www.musenet.co.uk
www.muse.now.nu
www.netdementia.tk
www.musclemuse.com
www.deadstar.fsnet.co.uk
www.dead-star.net
www.museandamuse.com
www.invictus.softmeg.com

Other languages
www.naïve.fr *(French)*
www.museandamuse.com (French)
www.magalomuse.free.fr (French)
www.musemania.com (French)
www.darkshine.free.fr (French)
www.feelinggood.fr.fm (French)
www.muse-in-belgium.be.tf (French)
www.muse-poetry.fr.fm (French)
www.iespana.es (Spanish)
www.musefan.de (German)
www.dead-star.net (Icelandic)
www.musefansite.moonfruit.com (Dutch)
www.musemuseum.cjb.net Italian)
www.museit.it (Italian)

www.musemania.de.vu (German)
www.museager.de.vu (German)
www.blissworld.de.vu (German)
www.hyperspace.net.tc (German)
www.muse.nl.nu (Dutch)
www.mjuz.rock.it (Norwegian)
www.koti.mbnet.fi/musepw (Finnish)
www.musefan.tk (Dutch)
www.clik.to/darkmuse (Italian)
www.sunburn.tk (Icelandic)
www.musezone.interia.pl (Polish)
www.members.lycos.nl/musenet (Dutch)
www.iespana.es/muse-mjb (Spanish)
www.overdue.ru (Russian)
www.geocities.com/hullabaloo (Hebrew)

INDEX OF ARTICLES REFERENCED

Unless otherwise referenced all interviews done by Ben Myers between September 1999 and December 2006. Some chapters feature unpublished quotes from an interview by Catherine Yates (June 2003) and extracts from 'Sex, Guys And Videotape' by Paul Brannigan, *Kerrang!*, June 23, 2001.

The following publications have proved to be valuable in the writing of this book and have been quoted as referenced: *Kerrang!*, *NME*, *Melody Maker*, *Select*, *X-Ray*, *The Fly*, *Q*, *Mojo*, *Uncut*, *Top Of The Pops*, *Guitarist*, *Guitar World*, *The South Devon Herald*, *The Independent*, *The Guardian*, *The Observer*, *The Times*, *The Daily Telegraph*, *Record Collector*, *Rolling Stone*, *CMJ Update*, *Billboard*, *The Phoenix*,

The following websites were also useful sources of information: *www.drownedinsound.com*, *www.playlouder.com*, *www.music365.com*, *www.mtv.com*, *www.allmusic.com*, *www.rollingstone.com*

CHAPTER 1:1. The Tornados biographical information taken from www.allmusic.com; 2. 'We Have Come For Your Children' by Dave Everley, Kerrang!, *March 2001; 3. ibid; 4. 'I See Dead People' by Ian Winwood,* Kerrang!, *June 2002; 5. They Want You As A New Recruit' by John Mullen,* Select, *May 2000*

CHAPTER 2: 1. Extract taken from 'Where Be Ye Going, You Devon Maid?' by John Keats (1795-1821); 2. From www.bbc.co.uk; 3. from www.knowhere.co.uk; 4. Band biography taken from www.inmuseworld.net; 5. 'We Have Come For Your Children' by Dave Everley, Kerrang!, *March 2001; 6. Interview in* Guitarist *by Ben Bartlett, November 2003; interview by Simon Netherwood,* Soundculture, *February 2003; 8.* NME *news story, October 1999; 9. From interview by Simon Netherwood,* Soundculture, *February 2003; 10. from interview in* Flipside, *November 1999; 11. From interview 'We Have Come For Your Children' by Dave Everley,* Kerrang!, *March 2001; 12. Ibid; 13. Muse interview by Stephen Dalton,* Times Metro, *May 27, 2000; 14. Matt Bellamy interview,* Total Guitar *by Helen Dalley, July 2000; 15. from* www.microcuts.com; *16. from www.inmuseworld.net ; 17. 'They Want You As A New Recruit' by John Mullen,* Select, *May 2000; 18. From CD Now, 1999*

CHAPTER 3: 1. From www.inmuseworld.net; *2. From interview by Tim Cashmere,* www.undercover.net.au; *3. Ibid; 4. from 'They Want You As A New Recruit' by John Mullen,* Select, *May 2000; 5. from www.fmrecords.co.nz; 6. interview by Paul Connelly,* The Times, *October 6 2003; 7. 'On The Couch' interview,* NME, *January 2000*

CHAPTER 4: 1. *From 'I See Dead People' by Ian Winwood,* Kerrang!, *June 22 2002; 2. from www.tastemedia.com; 3. from* Billboard, *August 1999; 4. 'Time Is Running Out' by Ronnie Kerswell,* Rock Sound, *September 2003*

CHAPTER 5: 1: *from www.geocities.com/showbiznet; 2. from interview by Stephen Dalton,* Uncut, *January 2000; 3. Matt Bellamy interview in* Guitarist *by Ben Bartlett, November 2003; 4. from interview in* Melody Maker *by Sean Price, June 1999; 5. from www.unbarred.co.uk; 6. from live review in* NME, *March 1999; 7. From 'They Want You As A New Recruit' by John Mullen,* Select, *May 2000*

CHAPTER 6: 1. *From interview in* Melody Maker *by Sean Price, June 1999*

CHAPTER 7: 1. *From 'They Want You As A New Recruit' by John Mullen,* Select, *May 2000; 2. From interview in* Record Collector, *December 1999; 3. From 'We Have Come For Your Children' by Dave Everley,* Kerrang!, *March 2001*

CHAPTER 8: 1. *news story in* Melody Maker, *May 10 2000; 2. ibid; 3. from interview by Simon Young in* Kerrang!, *2001; 4. From* Australian Juice, *June 2000; 5. From 'I Don't Care If I Fuck It Up Any More' by Sarah Bee in* Melody Maker, *June 28 2000; 6. From interview by Simon Young in* Kerrang!, *2000; 7. From 'Do Not Feed The Band',* Q, *November 2000; 8. from www.microcuts.net, August 14, 2000; 9. From 'Welcome Matt' by Siobhan Grogan,* X-Ray, *October 2003 ; 10 'I See Dead People' by Ian Winwood,* Kerrang!, *2002; 11. from interview in* NME, *October 19 2000; 12. From 'We Have Come For Your Children' by Dave Everley,* Kerrang!, *March 2001.*

CHAPTER 9: 1. *From interview by Mark Beaumont in* NME, *March 10 2001; 2. from interview on www.dotmusic.com, March 2001; 3. from www.microcuts.net; 4. From www.inmuseworld.net.*

CHAPTER 10: 1. *From www.btinternet.com/mrgnet/muse/webchat.html; 2. from* Kerrang! *news story, May 2001.*

CHAPTER 11: 1. *'Roll Over Beethoven' by Catherine Yates,* Kerrang! *July 2003; 2. ibid; 3. interview in* The Fly *by Niall Doherty, September 2003.*

CHAPTER 12: 1. *From 'Blood On Our Hands' by Niall Doherty,* The Fly, *September 2003; 2. from interview in* NME *by Mark Beaumont, September 13, 2003;*

3. *ibid;* 4. *ibid;* 5. *from interview by Alexia Loundras in* The Independent, *November 28 2003.*

CHAPTER 13: *1. from interview in* Guitarist *by Ben Bartlett, November 2003; 2. from interview in* Kerrang! *by Dom Lawson, September 2003; 3. Ibid; 4. From unpublished interview with Catherine Yates, June 2003; 5. from interview in* Kerrang! *by Dom Lawson, September 2003; 6. From interview in* Guitarist *by Ben Bartlett, November 2003.*

While every attempt has been made to credit all references to author and publication, the occasional quote has been taken from the internet where the exact origin – ie. where the quote first appeared – is unknown. If you are the author of any uncredited quotes please contact the publisher so that future versions of the book can be altered.

ALSO
AVAILABLE
FROM INDEPENDENT MUSIC PRESS

Also available from Independent Music Press

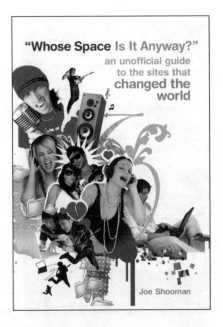

"WHOSE SPACE IS IT ANYWAY?"
AN UNOFFICIAL GUIDE TO
THE SITES THAT CHANGED THE WORLD
by Joe Shooman

On social network sites, everyone can hear you squirm. Artists, film-makers, musicians, lonely kids looking for love ... all twists on life can be found here in their dubious glory. These sites are the most powerful social force since the formation of the internet itself. For example, since Myspace's launch as an online social community in July 2003 by Santa Monica-based Tom Anderson, its easy-to-use interface has allowed users to upload and share music, videos, online diaries and search for users with similar interests in a way that has revolutionised not only the internet, but an entire generation's social lives. On these sites, bloggers have found love, unwise liaisons have been discovered and careers have been launched. Contains dozens of interviews with bands, music industry professionals, and a host of weird and wonderful characters whose lives have been changed forever by social networking sites – such as Bebo, Friendster, Friends Reunited and MySpace. The history and development of these unique sites and their social impact is told for the first time in a suitably easy-to-read style and presented in this user-friendly format with scores of irreverent hand-drawn illustrations.

ISBN: 0-9552822-1-7 & 978-0-9552822-1-8
224 Pages Paperback £5.99 World Rights

Also available from Independent Music Press

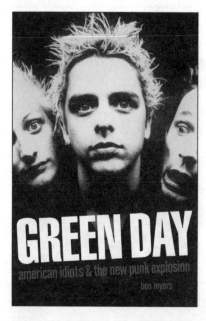

GREEN DAY: AMERICAN IDIOTS AND THE NEW PUNK EXPLOSION
by Ben Myers

The world's first and only full biography of Green Day. Self-confessed latch-key kids from small blue-collar Californian towns, Green Day have gone on to sell 50 million albums and single-handedly redefine the punk and rock genre for an entire generation. Inspired by both the energy of British punk bands as well as cult American groups, Green Day gigged relentlessly across the US underground before eventually signing to Warners and releasing their 1994 major label debut *Dookie*, which was a 10-million-selling worldwide hit album. With the arrival of Green Day, suddenly music was dumb, fun, upbeat and colourful again. Many now credit the band with saving rock from the hands of a hundred grunge-lite acts. In 2004 Green Day reached a career pinnacle with the concept album *American Idiot*, a sophisticated commentary on modern life - not least their dissatisfaction with their president. Myers is an authority on punk and hardcore and in this unauthorised book charts the band members' difficult childhoods and their rise to success, speaking to key members of the punk underground and music industry figures along the way.

ISBN 0-9539942-9-5 Paperback, 208 Pages 8pp b/w pics £12.99 World Rights

Visit our website at *www.impbooks.com*
or *www.myspace.com/independentmusicpress*
for more information on our full list of titles,
including books on:

My Chemical Romance, MC5,
Dave Grohl, Slash, The Streets,
Green Day, Ian Hunter, Mick Ronson,
David Bowie, Robert Smith, The Killers,
System of a Down, The Prodigy and many more.